Developmental Social Work
Dialogue with Social Innovation

Editor in Chief:

Julian Chow

Pei-Shan Yang

Eden Social Welfare Foundation

Published by Eden Social Welfare Foundation

Developmental Social Work
Dialogue with Social Innovation

First published: January 2021

Editor in Chief	Julian Chow, Pei-Shan Yang, Eden Social Welfare Foundation
Reviewer	Yeun-Wen Ku, Julian Chow, Yung-Hsing Kao, Pei-shan Yang
Managing Editor	Shu-Tzu Wu, Ying Lien, Wen-Yi Huang
Publisher	Eden Social Welfare Foundation
Co-Publisher	Chuliu Book Company
Address	10F.-12, No. 57, Sec. 1, Chongqing S. Rd., Zhongzheng Dist., Taipei City 100, Taiwan (R.O.C.)
TEL	02-2922-2396
FAX	02-2922-0464
E-mail	chuliu@liwen.com.tw
WEB	http://www.liwen.com.tw

ISBN 978-957-8819-40-5（paperback）

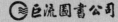

財團法人 EDEN SOCIAL WELFARE FOUNDATION 伊甸社會福利基金會　巨流圖書公司

Price: NT$1,650

Contents

Part III: Dialogue

Foreword I

Developmental social work is rooted in the profession's historic commitment to fostering progressive social change. This commitment can be traced back to the nineteenth century when social workers first advocated for improvements in local conditions, increased community participation and greater political engagement. The settlement houses, community centers and local organizations were identified as the major practice methods by which social workers could achieve this goal. These practice methods contrasted sharply with social casework which was primarily concerned with treating the personal troubles facing individuals and their families. Focusing on pathologies rather than strengths, this approach drew an analogy between social workers and physicians who would use their knowledge and therapeutic skills to remedy social problems by helping individuals address their problems. Advocates of the alternative, social change approach believed that collective action primarily at the community level was the best means of bringing about social improvements. In time, they joined with progressive political parties, trade unions and activists to urge the adoption of national social policies and programs which could utilize the authority and resources of governments to improve the welfare of citizens. Subsequently, many governments enacted progressive legislation, created social service administrations and adopted budgets which addressed pressing social needs. Often referred to as welfare states, these governments were believed to be ushering in a new era of widespread prosperity.

The expansion of the social services and rising social expenditure was opposed by many who believed that individuals rather than government should be responsible for social welfare. They claimed that societies would prosper if people worked hard, prudently saved for the future and cared for themselves and their families instead of relying on state-sponsored social welfare programs. These programs, they insisted, created disincentives to work, dependency and other social problems. Some criticized the expansion of government by alleging that welfare services are prohibitively costly and would undermine the economy. If the economy is to grow and create prosperity, government spending on social welfare should be curtailed. This argument was countered by many others who argued that governments have a moral responsibility to care for those in need. In addition, some suggested that social welfare spending actually contributes to economic development. Instead of draining the economy of its vitality, social spending increases demand and consumption resulting in increased production. It also invests in human capital, creates jobs and fosters economic and social stability. Social workers were at the forefront of this argument proposing that conventional social work with its emphasis on treating pathologies should be refocused to draw on people's strengths and capabilities. Known as developmental social work, this approach identified practice strategies which would promote both social and economic development.

Developmental social work first emerged in the developing countries of the Global South where social work was initially introduced to respond to urban problems such as juvenile delinquency, family breakup, substance abuse and homelessness which had become critical as the cities attracted large numbers of rural migrants in search of work and grew rapidly. At the time, it was generally accepted that social work was the best means of dealing with these problems and a variety of organizations including governments, international agencies, nonprofits and faith-based organizations helped create professional social work training schools as well as practice agencies in which social workers would deal with these problems. Extensive use was made of residential and counseling services and in some cases, social assistance payments were made to particularly needy families. However, it soon became clear that these interventions were expensive and reached only a small proportion of those in need. In addition, the wider social problems of rural poverty, ill-health, malnutrition and deprivation were largely ignored. It was in this context that social work academics and practitioners began critically to assess social work's conventional role and to offer alternatives which, as mentioned earlier, evolved into what is now known as developmental social work. Since then, it has informed social work education and practice in several Western countries as well. This is compatible with the changing emphasis in the profession on strengths and capabilities rather than pathologies and personal deficits. It also addresses the claim that welfare services have negative social and economic effects.

Developmental social work operates primarily at the community level but it is also relevant to the formulation and implementation of social policies at the national level. In addition, it informs development practitioners who seek to link community practice with wider economic initiatives. As an ongoing, evolving process in which new interventions emerge and are tested, developmental social work is a form of social innovation which does not only bring about significant changes in conventional social work practice but is contributing to improvements in people's livelihoods around the world. Many of these innovations have come about through the creativity and commitment of individuals, nonprofit organizations and community groups. Indeed, entrepreneurship is a distinctive characteristic of developmental social work and many examples can be given of how novel forms of practice have been shaped by their dedicated leadership.

In addition, developmental social work has distinctive features. It seeks to enhance client capabilities and draws on their strengths rather than emphasizing pathologies and deficits. However, it does not reject the need for clinical practice but requires that it be used sparingly and be implemented in community settings. It rejects the use of residential care and office counselling except in exceptional circumstances. Also, it prioritizes interventions that improve the livelihoods of clients by fostering their participation in the productive economy. Many families that social workers seek to help have low-incomes and struggle to make ends meet. Developmental social workers believe that the problems facing these families are directly associated with poverty and that addressing these problems requires interventions that increase their incomes, and assets. Developmental social work is also committed to social investment by accessing government resources as well as those of nonprofits. These enhance capabilities in ways that contribute positively to social well-being. It is also committed to prevention which is unfortunately not given high priority in professional social work today.

Developmental social work can be illustrated with reference to child welfare which is a major field of social work practice. In most countries, child welfare focuses on abused and neglected children and uses professional social workers, employed by child protection agencies, to respond by undertaking home visits and investigations and removing the child from the home. Subject to a court hearing, the child may be placed in residential homes or foster care. Developmental social workers use an alternative approach in which community-run childcare centers are the focal point for social work intervention. The centers provide preschool education, nutritional supplements and health checkups in order to address the most pressing problems facing children from poor families. They rely extensively on paraprofessional childcare workers, teachers and healthcare workers as well as local volunteers who work under the supervision of professionally qualified staff. In addition to improving the education, health and nutrition of children, the centers also facilitate clinical interventions. Staff and volunteers are trained to identify children who are neglected or abused or who have special needs or are frequently absent and this prompts an investigation by a professionally qualified social worker who assesses and seeks to remedy the causes of the problem.

A similar community-based approach is used by developmental social workers to serve people with mental health issues. While conventional remedial practice with these clients often involves institutionalization and extensive counselling, developmental social workers utilize community centers and the creation of support groups as well as cooperative enterprises among mental health consumers so that clinical treatment is provided within a community setting. Strong networks are created among mental health consumers and by participating in productive economic activities, such as catering, operating coffee shops and restaurants, and engaging in small-scaled crafts and manufacture, they create mutual interdependence and gain confidence which fosters positive living experiences. Together, these activities have a preventive as well as welfare and developmental dimension. By working in group settings and gaining support from peers, fewer mental health consumers experienced debilitating clinical episodes. In addition, those who become ill have a positive support network to rely on.

These are just two fields of practice in which developmental social work has been adopted but other examples can be given. Together with other colleagues, I have been very fortunate to have contributed to the developmental social work. I have learned a great deal from colleagues who questioned social work's conventional methods and who proposed viable alternatives before I began to write on the subject. I am grateful to them for helping me to articulate developmental social work's basic principles and practice methods. I also drew on my own experience of practicing as a professional social worker in the urban informal settlements in Cape Town, South Africa many years ago where I realized that the problems facing my clients could not be resolved through direct social work practice unless wider policies and programs that address the underlying problems of poverty and deprivation were adopted. Although this required government intervention in the form of progressive development policies, I realized that social workers could play a more effective role if they helped clients engage in activities that improved their livelihoods. I also recognized that social workers should focus on strengths rather than pathologies, utilize community-based interventions and facilitate the participation of local people addressing community needs.

Over the years, I have shared my views on developmental social work with colleagues in different parts of the world and I have benefited enormously from their experiences and ideas. I was also fortunate to promote the developmental perspective in several publications, most notably in the book Social Work and Social Development (published by Oxford University Press in 2010), which I edited with Amy Conley Wright, a former doctoral student at the University of California, Berkeley. The book shows that the developmental approach can be applied in well-established fields of social work practice such as child welfare, mental health, aging, social work with people with disabilities and corrections among others. Several colleagues who contributed to this book were students at Berkeley and their enthusiasm for the developmental perspective in social work has been inspiring. I am grateful to colleagues in Taiwan and especially to Professor Rosa Luo for translating the book into Chinese and making it available to a wider audience. Thanks also to the Eden Social Welfare Foundation which took an interest in developmental social work and sponsored several conferences and publications on the subject. Professor Julian Chun-Chung Chow has played a leading role in promoting developmental social work ideas in Taiwan and more broadly in China and other East Asian countries and I am very grateful to him for all he has done not only for the profession but for me personally.

It is an honor to write a brief foreword to this important book on *Developmental Social Work: Dialogue with Social Innovation* which raises numerous important issues. In addition to its theoretical chapters dealing with developmental social work, social innovation and social entrepreneurship, it contains several interesting and helpful case studies dealing with different aspects of developmental social work practice. These include chapters on the role of local investment in revitalizing community industry, long-term care transportation, co-living community care, empowerment and employment of people facing financial disadvantage, independent living and playful activities, child development, employment opportunity in catering for people with disabilities and the promotion of psychiatric wellness. In addition, the book concludes with a summary of a panel discussion on empowerment and capacity building in developmental social work. Written by experienced practitioners as well as educators and professional leaders, the book comprises a collection of chapters that contributed significantly to the field. The editor and authors are to be congratulated on producing a wide-ranging and useful book that should be widely consulted by everyone interested in developmental social work today. Many thanks to them and the Eden Social Welfare Foundation for providing an opportunity to examine developmental social work and the issues it raises from many different perspectives.

James Midgley
Professor United States
Dean Emeritus, School of Social Welfare
University of California, Berkeley, USA

Foreword II

The 2019 International Conference on Developmental Social Work: Dialogue with Social Innovation co – convened by Eden Social Welfare Foundation and the National Taiwan University held in Taipei in November 2019, brought an unprecedented opportunity to showcase the most recent thinking, research and developments in developmental social work. The conference provided true dialogue between developmental social work and social innovation with presenters from around the globe sharing a common platform. The resulting papers, presented here, represent the breadth and depth of developmental social work practice and social enterprise, spanning diverse applications including: community transport; local investment in community industry; social design of co-living housing for the elderly; community catering; independent living, mental health and community employment projects, to mention only some areas of practice explored here.

Developmental social work is an important area of practice for social work which aims to both understand and act on underlying causes of societal dysfunction. Its emergence reflects the resurgent emphasis within the profession of a focus on the socio-political- economic dimensions of practice. Through developmental social work, service providers are helped to look at clients strength and potential, and equips service providers with tools and skills to facilitate clients fully integration into the social and economic life of the community.

The Social Work group at the University Of Wollongong has been privileged to participate in this knowledge exchange, through partnering with

Eden and the National Taiwan University. Highlights include presentations at earlier conferences by Prof Lynne Keevers, Prof Peter Camilleri, and Dr Amy Conley Wright. More important has been the generous support provided to the University of Wollongong's social work students to establish our international exchange program and then host visiting students to visit Taiwan and experience developmental social work first hand, including through visits to rural communities. This connection is emblematic of a goal of social development to bring about new international relationships jointly looking to bring about increased social justice, and the satisfaction of basic human needs at the global level.

The papers contained in this volume provide evidence of the power this approach has to make a difference to the lives of the most vulnerable, through approaches where empowerment and collaboration are held firmly at the forefront.

Jo Spangaro
Social Work Chairperson
University of Wollongong, Australia

Foreword III

The endeavours of Eden Social Welfare Foundation on the promotion of developmental social work in recent years, has made it one of the major milestones in the field of social work. The outstanding performance such as organize international conference, has brought renowned international scholars and leading non-profit organizations to Taiwan. Their engagement with local counterparts further provided a comprehensive interpretation regarding the concept and practice of developmental social work. While in general a conference often adjourned like a passing boat which leaves no trace upon the water, Eden Social Welfare Foundation has mobilized scholars and non-profit organizations who participated this conference to further edit and compile the papers for publication. As a result, the respective wisdom can be inherited for further promotion. This contribution is especially valuable and touched the hearts.

After careful calculation, this is the third collection of developmental social work articles published by Eden Social Welfare Foundation! Different from the previous two collections which mainly focused on the promotion of developmental social work concepts, this collection is named "Developmental Social Work: Dialogue with Social Innovation". The goal is to identify innovative experience and measurements for developmental social work.

"Social Innovation" is a major shift recently in the field of social sciences. On the one hand, at the beginning of the 21st century, when the problem of poverty from the previous century has not reached a satisfactory solution, yet the new poverty issues still are emerging in the society. On the other hand, the social work and welfare system that we have established in the past has declined effectiveness in solving new poverty issues. In recent years, the issues of youth poverty, work poverty, social safety nets, pension reforms and long-term care etc. have been unceasingly emerged in Taiwan. It means that we must have new policy ideas and operation measurements in order to meet the social needs of the new century.

This collection gathers new social innovation concepts, experience from local cases and overseas innovation programs, which can be applied as an important reference for the promotion of developmental social work. Hence I would like to highly recommend this book, and I foresee that this book will play a very important role as a major momentum in promoting social work education here in Taiwan and abroad.

Yeun-wen Ku
Professor
Department of Social Work
National Taiwan University, Taiwan

President
Taiwan Association of Social Work Eduction, Taiwan

Foreword IV

The transportation subsidy of Long-term Care 2.0 in Taichung city is based on "trips" per reimbursement. Citizens have a quota of eight trips per month with government subsidy of 300 dollars for each trip. However, when people coming down from Lishan mountain to downtown, it is a 100-kilometer distance for one-way trip. As a result, no vender is interested in this program since it left contractor no profit at all. On the other hand, the situation became a social innovation mission for "Donkey Move", who provides shuttle matching services.

In the conference, Professor Sheng-Tsung Hou shared the experience of social innovation from "Donkey Move". It is a mobile approach to drive regional innovation which matched more than 22,000 shuttle services in 2019. Professor Hou has repeatedly emphasized that " value co-creation" is a prerequisite for public-private partnerships to implement regional innovation. In fact, many of the speakers in this 2019 International Symposium on Developmental Social Work have highlighted the importance of value co-creation. With that, we ponder how come " value co-creation " is so important, and what will happen to partners participating in public-private partnership if they lack the knowledge and practice of value co-creation? If we want to promote value co-creation, what kind of design philosophy is needed? How to establish a cross-sectoral collaboration system of value co-creation in different themes and fields? If these issues inspire your curiosity, the articles in this book can definitely satisfy your appetite for knowledge.

The subtitle of this International Symposium on Developmental Social

Work is "Dialogue with Social Innovation". In his keynote speech, Professor Jer-San Hu pointed out the social implications of social innovation, and guided us to think critically about the economically dominant logic and the emphasis of GDP as our development goals. Instead, we should focus on social development from a more balanced perspective that emphasizes socio-economically oriented logic and quality of life. From this perception, "Donkey Move" or "Homie Puli" (transliteration of the Taiwanese (Hokkien) term for "taking care of one another") are successful cases of social innovation.

The million-dollar question behind the daycare system of Homie Puli in Puli Township shared by Professor Kailin Liang, is "How to break away from the capitalist market concept, and to develop an "age-friendly social economy model". It is a concern shared among National Chi-Nan University, Quixotic Implement Foundation, Puli Christian Hospital and local social networks. It is the only way where lives of the elders can be averted from being "commodified." Otherwise, when all services are denominated in currency, for the elders with highly uneven distribution of resources in remote villages, how can they have a good quality of life without sufficient wealth? The answer to this million-dollar question is from "Homie Puli" and "Donkey Move", who provided a sounding solution to it. As this book collected the social innovation models and experience reflections shown in different fields of developmental social work in Taiwan, Hong Kong, Philippines, and Australia, we cordially invite you to read and taste this book.

Leemen Lee
Associate Professor
Department of Business Administration,
Fu Jen Catholic University, Taiwan

Preface

Eden Social Welfare Foundation first held the International Symposium on "Developmental Social Work: Theory and Practices" in 2014. Back then the concept of "Developmental Social Work" was a groundbreaking initiative which has drawn immense attentions. In 2016, it was held once again with the theme of "Global Application, Dialogue Development ", followed by the third international conference when it proposed the theme of "Social Innovation" in 2019. These three international conferences have gradually accumulated a broader scope of concepts and practical fields. Nevertheless, the core spirit of developmental social work has always been focused around "dialogue", "symbiosis and integration", "in-depth localization " and "transformation of perpetual innovation".

What's more commendable is that the presentations of these three conferences were all officially published in the form of a collection of theses with the highly professional assistance of colleagues from the foundation. As a result, this album can be referred and quoted while the insightful speeches in the conference were not in vain. This is really a very immense project, and can even be claimed to be the only major production in the social work community at Taiwan in recent years. Hence I would like to take this opportunity to give all colleagues in Eden Social Welfare Foundation a big applause and a warm hug, you are awesome! For many years, Department of Social Work of National Taiwan University is very honored to be a loyal partner of Eden Social Welfare Foundation. Professor Yunwen Gu and Professor Lizhen Zheng from this department, and my long-time friend Professor Julian Chow from School of Social Welfare, University of California, Berkeley, who have worked on the theme of "Developmental Social Work" and accompanied colleagues in the foundation as a mentor and friend for a long time. In 2019, I was very privileged to take over the baton from my fellow senior professors and chairmen to host the international conference at Tsai Lecture Hall, College of Law, National Taiwan University. In the meantime, I am also very honored to serve as Editor-in-chief of the 2019 Symposium Proceedings. I will continue to carry over the endeavors to fulfill this meaningful task and further enrich the literature and database of Taiwan's developmental social work.

We have invited experts and scholars on developmental social work at home and abroad to participate in the 2019 conference. The contents were brilliant. I participated in the whole process and witnessed the warm atmosphere at the conference in addition to the visions and goals shared by social workers of different generations, namely: changing the social structural poverty, the promotion of personal development and well-being, and the continuous application of social innovation to respond to the changing economic and social challenges in Asian countries as well as globally. These excellent reports not only propelled social workers to sprint forward, but also inspired each of us to return back to the original passion of social work. No matter for children, the elderly, the mentally challenged, the intellectually disabled, the empowerment of the disadvantaged, work in remote communities under insufficient resources, and emerging social enterprises, etc., people can always apply the pivotal spirit of this conference to continuously improve and adjust service content and service delivery under the standards of sustainability and appropriateness.

This collection of essays is consisted of three main sections of concept, local and overseas practice, and integrated dialogue. Conference speakers have meticulously compiled their respective deliveries into papers. With a total of 12 articles, it not only explains core concepts of developmental social work once again, but also shares practical cases at home and abroad in recent years. It is indeed a paradigm of dialogue between theory and actual practice. Such dialogues are very worthwhile for deep reading and reflection. In the meantime, it can also be regarded as a reference for agencies to share with each other, so that it can inspire more sparks of innovation and effective approaches for implementation.

The sharing of developmental social work practice and the narratives by the colleagues are the highlights of the 2019 conference. In this album, we can have a deeper understanding of the achievements of long-term investment by Eden Social Welfare Foundation in developmental social work. It covers the empowerment and poverty alleviation for the economically disadvantaged, and the independent living of the intellectually disabled. Furtheremore, the Hong Kong delegations have also shared their works with regard to social development plans for the autistic friends, the social inclusive restaurant, and the splendid work model transforming mental rehabilitation to mental health, all of which are de facto marvelous social innovations. These projects have demonstrated the "partnership" and "resource network" accentuated in developmental social work. In other words, social workers must cooperate with each other in the journey to implement developmental social work. At the same time, we must break through our comfort zone and hold the hands of partners with various resources from enterprises, governments, and communities to create a better new world. But the challenge is that while holding hands, social workers must uphold our independence and initiative, so as not to be constrained by the hierarchical management from the government and the mud of capitalism.

Last but not least, I would like to reiterate that the nature of social work is always "progressive" and radical. We are committed to challenge the existing frameworks and components of inequality, injustice, and restrictions on human development and liberation. According to the interpretation of Merriam-Webster dictionary, "progressive" must be advanced. Therefore, social workers must always preserve keen agility and vigilance. We are not supposed to spend time in daily repetitive work as long as the claimed reimbursement for the project can be written-off smoothly. As one of the speakers Marie Lisa M. Dacanay, founding President of Institute for Social Entrepreneurship in Asia, emphasized: "Social innovation should be obliged to actualize revolution or transformation in the society." The said revolution or transformation refers directly to the mainstream society, not just within the social worker's own unit or circle.

Moreover, "progressive" must mean to apply new concepts, new knowledge, and new opportunities. Social workers are always responding to the needs and dreams of the underprivileged, scanty, and concealed groups in the society. Consequently, it is very critical that we should focus on how to keep learning, to challenge ourselves and our profession, so as to facilitate superior service performances. If not, we will end up chasing the ever-changing social issues in vain and never be free from the cycle of poverty, discrimination, trauma, and loneliness. As Professor Ping-Der Huang, member of Board of Directors of Eden Social Welfare Foundation, has observed, the current investment scale in social innovation is far behind enough. Professor Sheng-Tsun Hou from the Institute of Public Affairs and Social Innovation of Feng Chia University, has experienced the scarcity of momentum in the process of transition from old to innovative paradigms, plus the difficulty of cooperation between different agencies. All of these critiques have challenged us to verify whether we have achieved an authentic successful conversion regarding the consequences of structural oppression in the mainstream society, namely "the underprivileged population" and "social problems", at this moment and in the coming years.

As the keynote speaker at the conference, Manohar Pawar who is the President of the International Consortium for Social Development, advocated: "Developmental social work is the social innovation of our time; when the breeze of social innovation emerged, please grasp the opportunity to soar with the wind. " My dear fellow social workers and partners, I hope this album can become the wind under your wings when you soar into the sky!

Pei-Shan Yang
Chair (2017-2020)
Department of Social Work
National Taiwan University, Taiwan

Acknowledgements

The advent of the term "developmental social work" emerged from the relevant theory, application and technology formally proposed by Professor James Midgley in 2010, which highlighted the need for cross-disciplinary integration. It believes that social development and economic development should be harmonized as two sides to the same coin. It emphasizes the perspectives of strengths and empowerment, utilizes social investment to enhance the abilities of the stakeholders and promotes their engagement in community living and economic activities. Based on the experiences from long term commissions on various social services in the past, Eden Social Welfare Foundation also shares similar appreciation to such concepts. Meanwhile, from the accumulated experiences in daily practice, we have also witnessed the structural challenges and professional restrictions among community practitioners in applying developmental social work.

It seems to be a norm for non-profit organizations to have unstable resources. People can always feel the pinch of such structural challenge when implementing social investment. The cultivation of social service practitioners in Taiwan is mostly focused on the society aspect and overlooked the economy, hence the priority is always on taking care of the subjects before rebuilding them. Since they are not familiar with social investment, it further limited the professionalism of social workers. Nevertheless, we believe that investing in developmental social work would be beneficial to a more accurate respond to the clents' needs, while creating a comprehensive impact on stakeholders and society. Therefore, the immediate difficulties and restrictions have specifically depicted the direction that the social welfare sector needs to pursue further improvement.

This is the tenth anniversary since Eden Social Welfare Foundation inaugurated developmental social work, during which it has organized numerous international seminars, published specific books, and conducted internal trainings. The objective is to promote the theories, methods and sharing cases of developmental social work, while explore the changing demand and trend of social work with all other sectors, in order to review and cast a professional core competency in line with contemporary values. Following the events in 2013 and 2015, Eden has organized the "The Third International Conference on Developmental Social Work - Dialogue with Social Innovation" in November 2019. It initiated a dialogue with social innovation from the perspective of social work, symbolizing that we have examined and profoundly recognized that in order to identify solutions for social issues, cross-sector and cross-disciplinary connections and collaborations are extremely pivotal.

This book is a collection of seminar articles, speeches, and panel discussions from the conference. The articles are categorized on four themes namely "Community Participation and Independent living", "Community Industry", "Employment and Poverty Alleviation", and "Social Enterprise". It furnished the readers with a glimpse of the status of developmental social work in four countries, including Australia, Philippines, Hong Kong, and Taiwan. It may not only help us establish practical knowledge base, but even transform into a guideline to implement developmental social work. Lectures and panel discussions are divided into "concepts" and "dialogues". Through such authentic interactions, it allows us to hear about the interpretations of relevant social service issues from the perspectives of academics and practical field, as well as the voices from practitioners, care-givers, and all the concerned parties. Either their statements are consensus or assorted, eventually this book reveals the true color of genuine issues among social services.

The publication of this book documents a remarkable journey of exploration and practice of developmental social work. On behalf of Eden Social Welfare Foundation, I would like to extend my sincere gratitude to all the leaders and partners for their relentless contributions. First of all, I would like to thank the members of the editing team of this book, Professor Julian Chow from School of Social Welfare, University of California, Berkeley; Professor Pei-Shan Yang and Professor Yuen-Wen Ku from Department of Social Work at National Taiwan University, as well as Eden consultant Yong-Xing Gao. From the days we organized the international seminar in 2019, they have rendered Eden immense encouragement and patronage, while sparing no efforts to provide valuable guidance for the editing and compiling of the articles. Meanwhile, I would like to thank all the authors who contributed the articles. Their experience and knowledge of developmental social work have created the opportunity for more extensive communications. Special thanks to Professor James Midgley, School of Social Welfare, University of California, Berkeley; Professor Jo Spangaro, Department of Social Work, University of Wollongong, Australia; Professor Yuen-Wen Ku, Department of Social Work, National Taiwan University; and Associate Professor Leemen Lee, Department of Business Administration, Fu Jen Catholic University; who composed the preambles to augment the glory of learning and cultivation. Furthermore, I would like to thank the team from Chu Liu Book Company for assisting in professional editing and design, so that the book can be published smoothly.

Madam Liu Hsia, the Founder of Eden Social Welfare Foundation once wrote an article:

"In my vision, the fruit farm, orchid garden, deer ranch, and all the factories should be consolidated in one venue and organized as a community format. There are dormitories, canteens, sports fields, recreation rooms and all other facilities. As for the daily life, among other things from being supervised by dedicated staffs, they must be educated to be amenable and be able to manage

themselves such as procurement, cooking, cleaning, decorating and organizing the environment, etc. Here, no one is a spoiled child, no one serves anyone else, and no one depends on others.

Let the children apply the best of their imagination to design their homes and making the whole community as a magnificent garden. One day, it can be opened to the outside world and become a place for the public to enjoy their leisure time."

This is "Dream Eden" by Madam Liu Hsia, a person with disability who depicted the equal and integrated society in her mind. From another perspective, it is also a practical blueprint for developmental social work: by developing local characteristics, forming a "community industry", planning "employment" opportunities, recruiting persons with disabilities and under-privileged groups, support "poverty alleviation". On top of it, through a comprehensive design to exert the sustainable impact of "social enterprise", it can further benefit every member to implement "independent living". The ultimate goal of all tasks and approaches is to establish a de facto equal and integrated society.

Developmental social work is not simply a working method; it also touches on the value of a paradigm. The publication of this book manifested the status quo of application and stretch of developmental social work, of which the journey will sustain perpetually. I wish all well who set the pace on the journey of developmental social work, even if you are in different corners of the world and in different positions in society respectively, you can finally ring the bell of hope to shatter poverty, deprivation and despair.

Wen-Ben Lin
Chief Executive Officer
Eden Social Welfare Foundation, Taiwan

Part I:

Theoretical Perspectives

Developmental Social Work and Social Innovation

Manohar Pawar[*]

Developmental social work is a social innovation of our times; when the wind of social innovation blows, fly with it.   Manohar Pawar (2019)

Abstract

The contemporary socio-economic, political, and environmental conditions that we face suggest the need for developmental social work and social innovation. Together, these two concepts have the potential to improve and sustain the quality of life of people, their communities, and of the natural environment within which they live. By offering the conceptual clarity of developmental social work and social development, and of social innovation, in the historical and the current context, this article brings to light the increasing relevance of the application of social development ideas in developmental social work. It points out the significance of the context and certain conditions for innovation. Further, it critically discusses some of the bottlenecks and opportunities for developmental social work and social innovation. Finally, it argues that developmental social work is an innovation, and professional bodies and other relevant agencies need to play more proactive and active roles in adopting and adapting developmental social work so as to contribute to the well-being of the whole population and the sustainability of that population's environment.

[*] Professor of Social Work, Charles Sturt University, Australia; President, International Consortium for Social Development.

At the outset, I would like to thank Professor Julian Chow for generously introducing me and chairing this keynote address session. It is a real honor and privilege to deliver a keynote address at this third conference on Developmental Social Work: Dialogue with Social Innovation. I feel very happy to be here; it is my first visit to Taiwan, Taipei. When I stepped out from the airport, after seeing the volunteer who was displaying my name on a piece of paper, I did not feel like I was in another country. I felt as if I were at home, since there was someone to greet and receive me, and accompany me to the hotel to ensure that I arrived safely at my destination. Thank you for the kind and generous hospitality. Warmly looking after guests with respect is so embedded in our culture—something which we should learn from and cherish. There is also an element of innovation in this practice.

Before I start my presentation, I would like to thank Mr. Chen Liang, the president of the Eden Social Welfare Foundation (ESWF), as well as Ms. Ivy Chen, Ms. Emma Lee, and Ms. Eileen Lu, who have been looking after me and spending a lot of time communicating with me. I would like to express my appreciation for their efforts and commitment. I would also like to acknowledge all of the dignitaries here, the international organizing committee, local governmental and non-governmental organizations, and universities. Although I am not able to mention everybody by name, I would like to convey my appreciation for their presence at the August gathering this morning.

After looking at the work of the ESWF, I feel that the work foundation is doing is very close to my heart. When I graduated in 1983–1984, one of my first jobs was that of Rehabilitation and Placement Officer, and I was working for the NSD Industrial Home for the Blind, Mumbai, India. My main task was to find employment for visually disabled people. The above-mentioned institute was a residential care facility for the visually disabled, and I worked there for approximately one and half years. During that time, I visited a number of industries, asking them to provide jobs for the visually disabled people. They did not require residential care, but employment. They are capable of carrying out a lot of work, which they do. However, over a period of one year, I was able to arrange a job for just one visually disabled person. This shows societal, industrial, and employers' attitude toward disabled people. When I left that job, I always felt that, despite working for the organization for one and a half years, I did not produce enough results. Every day I visited many organizations, but there was no outcome in terms of providing employment to the disabled people. This is something I feel very strongly about—having worked for one and a half years at an organization, drawing one and a half years' salary, but organizing only one job, as only one employer came forward. It must therefore be said that the ESWF is doing a great job in this area and it needs to be well acknowledged and supported.

Similarly, I have personal experience of disability within my home. My grandmother, due to her old age, had an unfortunate fall onto her bed, fracturing her hip. She was bedridden for more than a decade, and we grand children were not able to provide and organize enough support for her, since we were all working far away from home, as most people do in this modern life. Although some elderly people may not be able to directly contribute to the productive economy, may not be employed, and may not generate income, it is crucial to care for them, particularly when they experience disability. This realization comes from my own life experience in terms of disabled people and taking care of the elderly (see Pawar, 2017a; https://www.youtube.com/watch?v=dH_IBqMpfuk). As such, the ESWF has a special place in my heart. It has been doing an outstanding job, employing more than 3,000 people to serve the disabled community and so many vulnerable and disadvantaged groups.

"Developmental social work is a social innovation of our times; when the wind of social innovation blows, fly with it" (Pawar, 2019). I have coined this catchphrase specially for my keynote address and would like to dedicate it to this conference and to the ESWF. I would like to congratulate the organization on embracing the social development idea and developmental social work, and on practicing both to a great extent in the field. I have not come across any non-governmental organization that is explicitly following a developmental social work approach. The ESWF has embraced developmental social work in such a significant way, showing in practice how it is possible to carry out developmental social work and how one can achieve this. In fact, the ESWF is a good model for many social work schools and similar government and non-governmental organizations which are keen to make a change in the world and in the people who are greatly disadvantaged.

The topic of my keynote address is developmental social work and social innovation. I am very fond of the theme of this conference, namely Developmental Social Work: Dialogue with Social Innovation. The term "dialogue" suggests that the topic/issue is open for discussion, its meaning is evolving through a dialogical process, and nothing is concluded or judged. It also suggests that it is open for interpretation, and we can all contribute to its meaning. It is an excellent and critical way of putting the topic together. We are discussing, discovering the meaning, and trying to find out what it is. It is not a conclusive judgment, and so we are all partners in its meaning making. From this perspective, in light of the current socio-economic, political, and ecological context, the present paper discusses developmental social work and social development, social innovation, and social enterprise. Further, it looks at the conditions needed for innovation and how innovation is context specific. It also analyses some of the bottlenecks for adopting and adapting developmental social work, following which it explores opportunities for developmental social work and social innovation. It argues that developmental social work in itself is an innovation, but, unfortunately, its adoption and adaptation is taking a long time, and so it is fitting to pursue it vigorously by following the paths of the ESWF.

I. Socio-political, economic, and environmental context

Practicing of developmental social work and innovations and their applications occurs in the prevailing socio-political, economic, and environmental context. Understanding this context is important because it can cause or curb developmental practice and innovation. Although the above-mentioned context can be delineated in terms of socio-political, economic, and environmental for heuristic purposes, these purposes are all connected and impact each other in both positive and negative ways. The socio-political context can be discussed in terms of two broad social forces of local/national identity and globalization. Globalization facilitated by trade liberalization and increasing use of digital technology has made the world a small village, as the time required to produce goods and services along with socio-cultural exchanges and deliver them in different parts of the world has significantly reduced. This globalization process over a period of approximately three or four decades, through outsourcing processes, has moved the means of production—land, labor, and capital—around the world. Importantly, due to the search for cheap labor in the southern world and digital innovations, auto mechanizations, and artificial intelligence, this process has diminished the significance of one of the crucial means of production, namely labor. Consequently, it has increased the production, consumption, profits, and accumulation of wealth by a few. It has also increased cultural imperialism, generally from northern to southern countries and/or western to eastern countries.

A general fallout of this globalization process over a period is the emergence of unemployed and frustrated pockets and communities in some parts of the world, particularly in Europe and the USA; stagnation of or low growth; and some people's disenchantment with major political parties and governments. Globalization has also, to some extent, eroded the sense of locality, nationality, and identity, as local language, religion, and social cultural practices have been weakening to varied degrees in different parts of the world. These socio-economic processes have altered the perceptions of the affected people and their attitude towards "insiders" and "outsiders" of their community, globalization, liberalization, and free trade. The above processes also appear to have increased their discontent with political parties and the governance systems. Often, certain political leaders and governments have been accused of being "out of touch".

In my analysis, this process over a period has led to nationalism and populism trends to counter the forces of globalization and its consequences. Recognizing these and similar issues in certain constituencies, some shrewd politicians seem to have capitalized on this growing discontent and appeased people's traumatic sentiments by promising employment, recreation of local industry and trade, and the protection of local and national interest by promoting certain policies (Fenger, 2018; Ketola & Nordensvard, 2018); such policies cover, for example, building international border fences, treating boat people differently or detaining them, restricting free trade, increasing tariffs, excluding people from state-provided social security benefits, and increasing the rights of the natives over outsiders, as well as causing blatant discrimination. Such nationalistic populist trends have given rise to conservative political parties, which seem to have some implicit and/or explicit sympathy for right wing ideas, which have increased racism, bigotry anti-Semitism, and Islamophobia. In essence, these trends have led to, or have the potential to lead to, discrimination based on caste, religion, color, place of origin, language, rural–urban base, and other social cultural practices. These processes are creating significant insecurity for certain vulnerable groups such as migrants, refugees and asylum seekers, as well as other minority groups. Although civilized and/or civilizing society has achieved a great deal over the last 150 years in terms of human rights, social justice, and equality, it appears that these conservative processes have begun undoing those values and achievements.

Along with these concerning socio-political processes, economic inequality has increased despite the rise in income, production, and consumption. The world's richest 1%, specifically those with more than $1 million, own 44% of the world's wealth (Credit Suisse, 1019). While the share of national income going to the richest 1% has increased in the USA, Canada, China, India, and Russia, and moderately in Europe, the Middle East, sub-Saharan Africa, and Brazil, high levels of inequality continue (World Inequality Lab, 2017). The bottom half of wealth holders collectively accounted for less than 1% of the total global wealth in 2019 (Credit Suisse, 1019). The average poverty rate in Africa is 41%, and of the world's 28 poorest countries, 27 are in sub-Saharan Africa (World Bank, 2018; United Nations, 2019). More than half of the world's population (55%) does not have access to social protection (United Nations, 2019). Although agricultural production provides enough food for everyone in the world, of the total 7.3 billion population, 820 million people were suffering from hunger in 2018 (FAO et al., 2019). The highest prevalence of undernourishment was found in sub-Saharan Africa (20%), followed by Asia and Western Asia (12%) and Latin America and the Caribbean (7%). FAO et al. (2019) estimated that over 2 billion people do not have regular access to safe, nutritious, and sufficient food. Equally shocking is the fact that this figure includes 8% of the population in Northern America and Europe, which is home to developed countries. More than 20 million children suffered from low birth weight in 2015. In contrast, approximately one-third of overweight adolescents and adults and 44% of children aged between 5 and 9 years were obese (see FAO et al., 2019). These data, as an example, suggest that people experience inequality beyond income and wealth, although they may contribute to gender, race, education, and health inequalities.

Sustaining a range of inequalities, including income and wealth, economic growth has occurred at the cost of a healthy environment and healthy ecosystems. Therefore, environmental context has become increasingly important as global warming and climate change are manifesting through devastating disasters such as fires, floods, and droughts, while some have gone to the extent of including pandemics, as we have been insensitively and recklessly playing with the natural systems. The Intergovernmental Panel on Climate Change (IPCC, 2018) has argued that the world is headed for painful problems sooner than expected, as emissions continue to rise, and has sought a major solution to reduce emissions (Leahy, 2018). These problems are likely to have more impact on the poor and the most vulnerable groups, unless climate change mitigation and adaptation strategies are globally implemented. Of the 17 sustainable development goals (SDGs), over one-third of them directly or indirectly address the environmental issues. The SDGs, among others, emphasize sustainability, gender equality, inclusiveness, and innovation (see SDGs 5, 8, 9, 11 and 16; Pawar, 2017).

It is crucial to be aware of this socio-political, economic, and environmental issue, as developmental social work practice and social innovation need to occur within this context to address a range of inequalities and discrimination, and environmental concerns. Toward that end, the next section discusses a perspective of developmental social work and social development and social innovation.

II. Developmental social work and social development

Understanding developmental social work requires the understanding of social development. In my view, the application of social development ideas in terms of social development theory, knowledge and skills to social work education, training and practice is generally known as developmental social work. Since the publication, in 1924, of the first relevant book, entitled Social Development by Leonard Hobhouse (Midgley, 1995, p. 29), social development thoughts have been developed by many scholars (e.g. Gore, 1973, 2003; Paiva, 1977; Jones & Pandey, 1981; Sanders, 1982; Midgley, 1995, 2014; Pawar, 2014; Mohan, 2015; Patel, 2016; Midgley & Pawar, 2017). Attempts have been made to relate social development ideas to different fields or disciplines such as social work (Midgley & Conley, 2010; Hugman, 2015; Drolet, 2016), health (Bell & Aggelton, 2016), and sustainability (Lintsen, Veraart, Smits, & Grin, 2018). Social development ideas, policies, and programs were followed and supported by the British colony administrates, the World Bank, and the Department for International Development, while they were also popularized by the United Nations, eventually culminating in the Copenhagen Social Development Summit in 1995, the Millennium Development Goals, 2-1-2015, and the Sustainable Development Goals, 2016 to 2030 (Midgley, 1995, 2014; Pawar, 2014; Midgley & Pawar, 2017). Conceptual understanding of social development in the literature and the practice of social development by a range of agencies vary, and both together have led to some confusion and misunderstanding as to what exactly social development is. These misunderstandings and misperceptions include an unattainable ideal (idealizing) social development, excluding certain countries and regions from social development, neglecting and/or favoring some sectors or dimensions from social development, and segregating social and economic development, while unduly focusing on one rather than the other.

To address these misunderstandings and misperceptions and to develop a better clarity of social development, it is critical to underscore four basic features of social development (Pawar, 2014, 2017) before delving into its meaning. First, social development is not an ideal; it is a practical idea, and social development thoughts can be effectively practiced to enhance individual, community, and societal well-being. Second, social development universally applies to all, both developed and developing countries, small islands and landlocked countries, all regions, and the whole planet. Third, economic development is one part or one dimension of social development. Many have segregated and often excluded economic development from social development and juxtaposed one against the other as if they are enemies or competitors. These are not two sides of the same coin, both are both sides of the same coin; economic development is well embedded as an integral part of social development, not separate from or opposite to it. Fourth, the purview of social development is a comprehensive and sustainable development of individuals, families and communities, and their environment. This comprehensiveness of social development will be explained later. Understanding and recognizing these four critical features of social development will aid in understanding the concept of social development.

Drawing on the analysis of social development definitions in my earlier writing (Pawar, 2014), the concept of social development has been delineated and discussed from three interrelated and overlapping perspectives. The first perspective suggests that many scholars have attempted to describe the concept of social development in terms of purposeful planning, planned social change, and comprehensive economic and social development (see, e.g., Gore, 1973; Midgley, 1995, 2014; Barker, 2003). The second perspective of social development includes realizing human potential, meeting human needs, distributing resources, developing institutions, and achieving participation and quality of life/well-being (Pandey, 1981; Paiva, 1982; Hollister, 1982; Meinert & Kohn, 1987; Billups, 1994; Cox et al., 1997). The third perspective emphasizes planned structural change and transformation to see universal equality and social justice (Pathak, 1987; Todaro, 1997; Mohan, 2010), which has a little radical and/or social action element, and sometimes that element is necessary to achieve social development.

To implement these perspectives in developmental social work, it is necessary to further elaborate on, and understand, one of the basic features of social development, namely comprehensiveness. Comprehensiveness refers to the well-being of the whole population and the sustainability of their environment. Further, it includes practicing social development at multiple levels and in multiple dimensions. These multiple levels (Figure 1) range from local level to international level. In Figure 1, I emphasize that developmental social work needs to focus on the local level, which includes local governance systems, villages, and grassroots-level communities. This is because they have been neglected for a long time, and there is a dire need for comprehensive development at that level; although all other levels are equally important, they have not been neglected to the extent that the local level has.

As presented in Figure 2, multiple dimensional practice calls for focusing on each dimension at all of the multiple levels, particularly at the local level, as the need is greater there, relative to the other levels. Developmental social work practice calls for the development of each one of these dimensions at the local level, that is, grassroots-level villages and communities. This suggests that social work practitioners need to focus on the development of culture, political economy, education, health, housing, sanitation, institution-building, and so on at the local level, and not just in one or two dimensions. Contrary to this comprehensive nature of social development, what we generally observe is that often there is a focus on only one or a few dimensions, e.g. economy, health, education, or politics, at the neglect of, or the assignment of low importance to, the other dimensions, which are crucial for the comprehensive and sustainable development of individuals, families and communities and their environment.

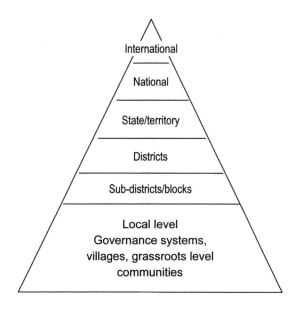

Figure 1: Multiple levels of developmental social work practice

Source: Pawar (2014, p. 37; 2017b)

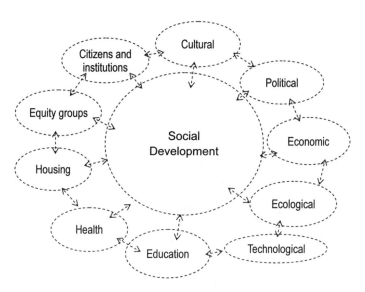

Figure 2: Multiple dimensions for developmental social work practice

Source: Pawar (2014, p. 60; 2017b)

To facilitate the practice of this social development perspective, developmental practitioners can raise the following practice questions with a view to understanding and addressing them.

Table 1: Developmental social work practice questions

> ➡ What are the current conditions at the local level and why do they exist?
>
> ➡ What are the clear goals to bring change in those conditions?
>
> ➡ What are the values and ideologies in which goals are located?
>
> ➡ What processes need to be followed?
>
> ➡ What are the appropriate strategies for practice?
>
> ➡ What are the appropriate levels and dimensions for the application of strategies?

Source: Pawar (2014; 2017b)

To ascertain answers to these questions, practitioners may need to undertake research and interact with local individuals, institutions, and communities by applying their research, community organization, and communication knowledge and skills. These questions can be translated into a developmental social work practice model, as presented in Figure 3. The model suggests that, first, developmental social work practitioners need to understand the current conditions of local communities in all dimensions, with a view to bringing about change in those dimensions by following clear values and processes, and plans and strategies to achieve the set goals at each dimension level by engaging people and their communities. For example, values may include respect, humanity, diversity, connecting human existence in environment, rights and responsibilities, and equal opportunities. Moreover, goals may include achieving quality of life and freedom, and realizing the human potential. To achieve such goals, values need to be translated by following participatory, people-centered, and empowering processes and by following plans and strategies such as participatory planning, awareness-raising, enabling, capacity-building, self-reliance, and resourcing.

Please note that this is not the universal model for developmental social work practice, but is one of the approaches used to achieve social development, as conceptualized here. Having clarified the concept of social development for developmental social work practice, now let us look at social innovation and its relevance for developmental social work.

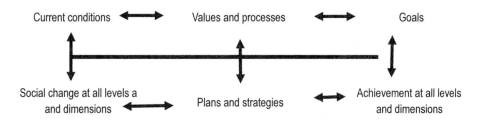

Figure 3: Developmental social work practice model

Source: Pawar (2014: 23; 2017b)

III. Social Innovation

Social innovation has received, and is still receiving, a great deal of attention from governments, non-governmental organizations such as the ESWF, and practitioners and intelligentsia generally. There has been an increasing emphasis on innovation and social innovation, while recently these two terms have been popularly in vogue. The theme of many conferences, such as that organized by the ESWF in 2019, is innovation, while numerous other organizations also focus on this topic. For example, our own International Consortium for Social Development will organize its 22nd Biennial International Conference in South Africa, hosted by the University of Johannesburg, in July 13-16, 2021, and one of the proposed themes of the conference is social innovation. Many books and articles on social innovation have been published (see, e.g., Moulaert & MacCallum, 2019; Pawar et al., 2018; Phillips & Shaw, 2011), and I am certainly curious as to why there has been a sudden surge in the search for social innovation. Although innovation and social innovation are good, depending upon how we use them, the question must still be asked: Why is the increasing need for social innovation felt now? As the saying goes, necessity is the mother of innovation. What is the necessity now? Has there been created any fear or pressure that something is not working now, and something is not going to work in the future or might be inadequate? Existing systems are lacking in many respects, and therefore we need to be innovative and to ascertain new ways of doing things and doing better.

Figure 4: Developmental social work and the focus of innovation

Source: Pawar (2019)

The term "innovation" often conjures an association with science, technology, industry, business, creativity, research, management, organization, growth, and profits. However, developmental social work's thinking of innovation is quite distinct from the latter's traditional locations. We need to shift the mindset of science and technology-based innovation to innovation that is related to welfare, inequality, non-profit, aging/disability and mental health, poverty, unemployment, and social welfare (see Figure 4). That is, in developmental social work, we need to think about how we can be innovative in addressing a range of issues and needs, which are presented in Figure 4. According to Phillips and

Shaw (2011, p. 611), "The call for innovations has been a public call by academics, service users, agencies and most definitively by funding bodies requiring articulated information about innovatory contributions".

Although there is no consensus on explaining the concept of social innovation, it is useful to consider a few authoritative definitions which could facilitate our understanding. The term can mean "to make changes in something established", to alter and renew, and has even been used in the context of revolution (Shorter Oxford English Dictionary, cited in Phillips & Shaw, 2011, p. 611). It involves making changes or introducing new things in order to develop, make progress, or improve social conditions. Thus, some originality, new things, and improvement are essential elements of innovation (Grisolia & Ferragina, 2015). According to Phills et al. (2008, p. 39), social innovation is:

> ... a novel solution to a social problem that is more effective, efficient, sustainable
> . . . and for which the value created accrues primarily to society as a whole rather
> than private individuals. A social innovation can be a product, production
> process, or technology . . . but it can also be a principle, an idea, a piece of
> legislation, a social movement, an intervention, or some combination of them.

In Flynn's (2017, pp. 124-125) view, social innovation is usually proposed either explicitly or implicitly as an alternative to traditional government processes or programs that are perceived as unsuccessful, and it is often characterized by disruption to customary relationships, problem-solving processes, structures, or some combination (Flynn, 2017, pp. 124-125). The Canadian Policy Research Networks conceives several models of social innovation, which:

> . . . reflect a variety of strategies for collaboration and working with others, and
> for tapping into different kinds and sources of financial and other resources. The
> confluence of sectors in society involved in social innovation offers opportunities
> for exploring new ventures, sharing models, and enhancing knowledge transfer.
> (Goldenberg et al., 2009, p. 5)

Although strategies for collaboration, mobilizing resources, and new ventures are critical, unlike the focus on innovation in business, industry, and the corporate sector, the Bureau of European Policy Advisers (2011) contended that as social innovation seeks social good, no private value should be accrued and innovators must employ justifiable means, which clearly suggests that both the means and the end are important in social innovation.

From this perspective, it is important to ask: Where does social entrepreneurship sit with social innovation, as people often relate social entrepreneurship to social innovation? Social entrepreneurship essentially involves the application of business solutions to social problems, but it has to maintain social good without accruing private value. According to Barraket, Mason, and Blain (2016), "Social entrepreneurship ventures are organisations that: are led by an economic, social, cultural, or environmental mission consistent with a public or community benefit; trade to fulfil their mission; derive a substantial portion of their income from trade; and reinvest the majority of their profit/surplus in the fulfilment of their mission" (p. 3). A range of agencies are engaged in social entrepreneurship, among which are for-profit firms; dual-mission organizations; hybrid models including benefit corporations, low-profit limited liability companies (L3C) and flexible Purpose Corporations in the USA (Battilana et al., 2012); NGOs; and charities. Thus, it is not clear how many of these agencies maintain public good and public value. In addition, Social Enterprise UK's (2015) research showed that nearly two-thirds of social enterprises are actively engaged in some form of innovation, having introduced a new or improved product or service in the preceding year. This means that over one-third of social enterprises are not engaged in social innovation. Thus, it may be inferred that not all social enterprises can be equated with social innovation.

IV. Innovation is context specific

Another important factor in comprehending innovation is the

understanding of the context in which it occurs. An innovation in one place, time, and need/problem context, may not be considered as innovation in another place, time, cultural, and societal context, because such innovation, practices, or resources are taken for granted in those contexts. However, it is important to recognize and appreciate innovation in whatever context and to whatever extent it occurs. An example would be installing telephone booths near houses in remote communities so that women can easily access them to report domestic violence and abuse incidents; indeed, this is an innovative project in the context of those women. Similarly, installing door bells that can be used by police at night instead of hitting doors with sticks, which may wake people up, is an innovative practice in remote communities or similar contexts. In place of kerosene, the use of solar lamps is an innovation in rural and remote areas, but not in urban areas. Different methods for raising awareness of the need to adopt sanitation infrastructure, which is known as community-led total sanitation, in Bangladesh constitute an innovation in that context (see Kar, 2005; Pawar, 2010). Watershed development, various rain harvesting methods, and using water for different purposes, both in developed and developing countries, are additional innovations. Similarly, various ways of organizing self-help groups and micro-credit in different communities are innovations in those respective contexts. Of note here is "Thankyou"—a social enterprise organization in Australia that innovatively generates income through business and trade and distributes profits for welfare and development activities in several developing countries (see Flynn, 2016; Pawar, 2019a); indeed, this is an innovation in the Australian context.

V. Conditions conducive to social innovation

Although in all cultures, regions, and rural–urban contexts, innovations occur and can be found, certain conditions are more conducive to social innovation. Some of these conditions are as follows: first, it is important to create conditions where people experience a sense of freedom; families, groups, communities, organizations, societies, and cultures are open for ideas, and they recognize and appreciate peoples' efforts. Second, different ways of addressing basic needs and complex collective problems are encouraged, at least for some time. Third, due to whatever reason, whether it is limited resources, life/survival or value, people's experience of pressure, tension or urgency may lead to innovation. Fourth, to facilitate innovation, it is crucial to cultivate a network of committed organizations and creative individuals from groups, communities, and organizations. Fifth, it is vital to maintain constant critical intellectual engagement about needs/problems and solutions. Regarding this, Phillips and Shaw (2011, p. 616) observed that (research) innovation may be more likely to occur when there is a deep and collective, though coincidental, sense of a problem, a network of able and creative researchers, and a degree of intellectual and experimental tension. Finally, the role of enabling leadership, including the political variety, cannot be underestimated in creating conditions for innovation.

VI. Bottlenecks for adopting/adapting developmental social work

While discussing the bottlenecks encountered when adopting/adapting developmental social work, it is apt to refer to a Chinese proverb: "When the winds of change blow, some people build walls and others build windmills". The idea of social development and developmental social work has existed for a long time—at least 50 years, if we consider the beginning of the International Consortium for Social Development as a starting point. But this concept has not been fully embraced in the social work profession or in education and practice. Some of the reasons for this may be professional imperialism (Midgely, 1981; Pawar, 1999), and the western dominance of clinical social work throughout the world (although at the time it might have been perceived as new and innovative). The social work profession may have built rigid professional boundaries, which have not entertained new thoughts. Many organizations also have rigid bureaucratic structures that tend to maintain the status quo and remain risk averse. There may also be general resistance to new ideas and new ways of doing things and expanding the scope of work/practice/discipline. As stated earlier, there is confusion and lack of clarity as to what developmental social work is. Even if one is willing to adopt/adapt developmental social work, necessary educational and training resources are not well prepared, and whatever is there is not readily available. Thus, it appears that many have built walls to combat developmental social work, rather than building windmills.

VII. Opportunities for developmental social work and social innovation

These and similar bottlenecks notwithstanding, in my view, there are great opportunities for developmental social work practice and social innovation. First, the current demographic changes are creating new demands and new challenges, and developmental social work provides a comprehensive framework with which to proactively plan to meet those demands and challenges. Within the overall increasing global population, it has been suggested that a large proportion of the aged and young people offer both challenges and resources to society. Ascertaining how to productively engage them is a meaningful task for developmental social work. It is also estimated that approximately half of the world population will live in urban areas. This implies huge population movements from rural to urban areas and undue stress on the urban infrastructure. Significant proactive planning and need-based policies and programs must be designed and implemented before the problems occur both in rural and urban areas.

The second source of opportunities stems from technological changes and a rapidly-digitizing world. Technological applications, whether it is the use of social media, artificial intelligence, or telehealth, are going to change our lifestyles, as some human activities will be replaced by machines, with both positive and negative consequences. Developmental social work in a proactive and innovative way adopts and adapts these technologies by reducing negative consequences and increasing positive consequences, yet without losing the human element or dimension, as there is a threat that the aforementioned human element may be lost in this process, posing significant challenges to human relationships.

Third, as discussed in the introduction, ecological issues and needs offer huge opportunities for developmental social work practice and innovation. Reducing the carbon footprint, preparing for and coping with the consequences of disasters, combating desertification, and ensuring food security all require action from the local to global levels. There is increasing urgency to live in harmony with nature, and opportunities seem endless. Fourth, and as also referred to in the introduction, growing inequality and new forms of poverty show that redistribution policies are not transforming the world the way they should. Thus, the question must be asked: What can be done to reduce inequality and poverty?

Finally, the most neglected element of developmental social work is cultural development in a broad sense. There is a lot of emphasis on material or infrastructure development at the neglect of cultural development, which may include values, principles, virtues, language, music, and art. This is an important dimension of developmental social work, and we need to innovatively think about ways of strengthening it, particularly at local levels. These five opportunities, as an example, suggest that there is tremendous scope and potential for developmental social work and innovation.

VIII. Was developmental social work a social innovation?

Before concluding this article, a critical question must be raised: Was developmental social work a social innovation? If so, then why did it not spread or why was it not adapted or adopted? Still, clinical and often pathologically-oriented social work dominates; although relevant at certain levels, the above-mentioned kind of social work requires desperate expansion to embrace developmental social work. It appears that such expansion is occurring at a slow pace, but it needs to be globally accelerated, given the magnitude of global needs and issues, as discussed in the introduction and under opportunities for developmental social work (see also Figure 4), and advancement of digital technology available to facilitate it. As discussed earlier, developmental social work provides an apt framework incorporating multiple levels and multiple dimensions with clear values, goals, and strategies to respond to challenges and opportunities at all levels. More than a decade ago, all of the three professional bodies—the International Association of Schools of Social Work (IASSW), the International Federation of Social Workers (IFSW), and the International Council on Social Welfare (ICSW)—embraced the phrase social development along with social work, but that phrase seems to be moving only around conferences without entering the classroom curriculum and field practice. A small number of voluntary organizations, such as the ESWF, the ICSD, and many others, including some educational and research institutions, are good examples of creating and spreading the knowledge and skills of social development. I am strongly of the view that the current social innovation climate is favorable and can, or has the potential to, offer a renewed opportunity for developmental social work. Social work schools and professional bodies, as well as other organizations, need to be proactive and make concerted efforts to practice developmental social work, just as the ESWF is doing in collaboration with the Department of Social Work, National Taiwan University. I would like to reassert that developmental social work is a social innovation of our times; when the wind of social innovation blows, we must fly with it (Pawar, 2019).

IX. Conclusion

In concluding, I would like to again thank the ESWF and the organizers of this conference for providing me with an opportunity to further think on developmental social work and social innovation, and to share my thoughts with practitioners, policy-makers, and intellectuals. In this paper, by introducing the socio-economic, political, and environmental conditions, I have discussed the concept and the model of developmental social work that can be practiced to improve current conditions and thus enhance the quality and well-being of individuals, families, and communities at all levels. Further, by clarifying the concept of innovation and social innovation, I have pointed out the relevance of context and creating certain conditions for innovation to occur. I have also discussed, in brief, some of the constraints and opportunities for developmental social work practice and innovation. Kindly note that I have drawn some particulars from several sources to develop these ideas, which are limited by my own subjectivity, which fully favors developmental social work and innovation. Finally, I have argued that developmental social work is a social innovation of our time, and we need to work more to facilitate its adoption and adaption so as to improve the quality of life and well-being of the whole population and their environment.

References

Barker, R. L. (2003). *The Social Work Dictionary*. Washington: NASW Press DC.

Barraket, J., Mason, C., & Blain, B. (2016). Finding Australia's Social Enterprise Sector 2016: Final Report. Social Traders and the Centre for Social Impact Swinburne. Melbourne: Swinburne University of Technology. Retrieved from http://apo.org.au/system/files/64444/apo-nid64444-48516.pdf

Battilana, J., Lee, M., Walker, J., & Dorsey, C. (2012). In Search of the Hybrid Ideal. *Stanford Social Innovation Review*, 12, 51-55.

Billups, J. (1994). The social development model as an organising framework for social work practice. In R. G. Meinert, T. Pardeck, & P. Sullivan (eds.), *Issues in social work: A critical analysis* (pp. 21-37).Westport CT: Auburn House.

Bureau of European Policy Advisers (2011). *Empowering people, driving change: Social innovation in the European Union*. Luxembourg City, Luxembourg: Publications Office of the European Union.

Cox, D., Pawar, M., & Picton, C. (1997). *Introducing a social development perspective into social work curricula at all levels*. Melbourne: RSDC, La Trobe University.

Credit Suisse. (2019). Global wealth report 2019. Credit Suisse Research Institute: Zurich. Retrieved on 20 April 2020 from file:///D:/Users/mpawar/Downloads/global-wealth-report-2019-en.pdf

Bell, S. & Aggelton, P. (2016). *Monitoring and Evaluation in Health and Social Development: Interpretive and Ethnographic Perspectives*. Oxon: Routledge.

Drolet, J. L. (2016). *Social Development and social work: Perspectives on social protection*. New York: Routledge.

FAO, IFAD, UNICEF, WFP, and WHO (2019). *The State of Food Security and Nutrition in the World 2019. Safeguarding against economic slowdowns and downturns*. Rome: FAO.

Fenger, M. (2018). The social policy agendas of populist radical right parties in comparative perspective. *Journal of International and Comparative Social Policy*, 34(3), 188-209.

Flynn, D. (2016). *Chapter one: You have the power to change stuff*. Sydney: The Messenger Group.

Flynn, M. L. (2017). Science, Innovation, and Social Work: Clash or Convergence? *Research on Social Work Practice*, 27(2), 123-128.

Goldenberg, M., Kamoji, W., Orton, L., & Williamson, M. (2009). *Social Innovation in Canada: An Update*. Ottawa, Canadian Policy Research Networks.

Gore, M. (1973). *Some aspects of social development*. Hong Kong: Dept. of Social Work, University of Hong Kong.

Gore, M. (2003). *Social Development: Challenges faced in an unequal and plural society*. Jaipur: Rawat.

Grisolia, F. & Ferragina, E. (2015). Social innovation on the rise: Yet another buzzword in a time of austerity? *Salute e Società* 1, 169-179. doi:10.3280/SES2015-001013p

Hollister, D. (1982). The knowledge and skills bases of social development. In D. S. Saunders (ed.), *The developmental perspective in social work* (pp. 31-42). Manoa: University of Hawaii Press.

Hugman, R. (2015). *Understanding international social work: A critical analysis*. Basingstoke: Palgrave Macmillan.

IPCC (Intergovernmental Panel on Climate Change) (2018). Summary for policy makers of IPCC special report on global warming of 1.5.c. Retrieved on 9 March 2020 from https://www.ipcc.ch/2018/10/08/summary-for-policymakers-of-ipcc-special-report-on-global-warming-of-1-5c-approved-by-governments/

Jones, J. F. & Pandey, R. S. (Eds.) (1981). *Social development: Conceptual, methodological and policy issues*. Delhi: Macmillan.

Kar, K. (2005). Practical guide to triggering community-led total sanitation. Retrieved on 28 June 2007 from http://www.ids.ac.uk/ids/bookshop/wp/Wp257%20pg.pdf

Ketola, M. & Nordensvard, J. (2018). Reviewing the relationship between social policy and the contemporary populist radical right: welfare chauvinism, welfare nation state and social citizenship. *Journal of International and Comparative Social Policy*, 34(3), 172-187.

Leahy, S. (2018). Climate change impacts worse than expected, global report warns. *National Geographic*. Retrieved on 9 March 2020 from https://www.nationalgeographic.com/environment/2018/10/ipcc-report-climate-change-impacts-forests-emissions/

Lintsen, H., Veraart, F., Smits, J. P., & Grin, J. (2018). *Well-being, Sustainability and Social Development: The Netherlands 1850-2050*. Cham: Springer.

Meinert, R. G. & Kohn, E. (1987). Towards operationalization of social development concepts. *Social Development Issues*, 10(3), 4-18.

Midgley, J. (1981). *Professional Imperialism: Social Work in the Third World*. London: Heinemann.

Midgley, J. (1995). *Social Development: The developmental perspective in social welfare*. London: Sage.

Midgley, J. (2014). *Social Development: Theory and practice*. London: Sage.

Midgley, J. & Conley, A. (2010). *Social Work and Social development: Theories and skills for developmental social work*. New York: Oxford University Press.

Midgley, J. & Pawar, M. (2017). *Future Directions in Social Development*. New York: Palgrave Macmillan.

Mohan, B. (2010). Toward a new social development. In M. Pawar & D. Cox (eds.), *Social Development: Critical themes and perspectives* (pp. 205-223). New York: Routledge.

Mohan, B. (2015). *Global frontiers of social development in theory and practice*. New York: Palgrave Macmillan.

Moulaert, F. & MacCallum, D. (2019). *Advanced introduction to social innovation*. Cheltenham: Edward Elgar.

Pandey, R. (1981). Strategies for social development: An international approach. In J. Jones & R. Pandey (eds.), *Social development: Conceptual, methodological and policy issues* (pp. 33-49). New York: St. Martin's Press.

Paiva, F. J. X. (1977). A conception of social development. *Social Service review*, 51(2), 327-36.

Paiva, J. F. X. (1982). The dynamics of social development and social work. In D. S. Saunders (ed.), *The developmental perspective in social work* (pp. 1-11). Manoa: University of Hawaii Press.

Patel, L. (2016). *Social welfare and social development*. Johannesburg: Oxford University Press.

Pathak, S. (1997). Social Welfare, Social Work and Development: Review of Literature. *The Indian Journal of Social Work*, 58 (2), 161-184.

Pawar, M. (1999). Professional Social Work in India: Some Issues and Strategies. *Indian Journal of Social Work*, 60(4), 566-586.

Pawar, M. (2010). *Community Development in Asia and the Pacific*. New York: Routledge.

Pawar, M. (2014). *Social and community development practice*. New Delhi: SAGE.

Pawar, M. (2017). Social Development: Progress So Far. In J. Midgley & M. Pawar (eds.), *Future Directions in Social Development* (pp. 41-57). New York: Palgrave Macmillan.

Pawar, M. (2017a). Kant, Bentham, Aristotle and my Grandmother: Developing the 'caring being' by social workers. The 11th M.C. "Terry" Hokenstad International Lecture 2017 delivered at the 63rd Council of Social Work Education, Annual Program Meeting, theme, Educating for the Social work Grand Challenges, 19-22 October 2017, Dallas, USA. https://www.youtube.com/watch?v=dH_IBqMpfuk

Pawar, M. (2017b). 社会与社区发展实践 (Chinese translated). *Social and Community Development Practice*. Chongqing: 西南师范大学出版社 /Southwest normal university press.

Pawar, M. (2019). Developmental Social Work and Social Innovation. Keynote address (Power points) presented at the third annual international conference on Developmental social work: Dialogue with social innovation, organised by the Eden Social Welfare Foundation and Department of Social Work, National Taiwan University, 28-29 November 2019, Taipei, Taiwan.

Pawar, M. (2019). Community development, empowerment and social entrepreneurship by "Thankyou". In Monica Nandan, Tricia B. Bent-Goodley and Gokul Mandayam (eds.), *Social entrepreneurship and intrapreneurship and social value creation: Relevance for contemporary social work practice*. Washington DC: NASW Press.

Pawar, M., Bowles, W., & Bell, K. (2018). *Social work: Innovations and insights*. Melbourne: Australian Scholarly Publishing.

Phills, J. A., Deiglmeier, K., & Miller, D. T. (2008). Rediscovering social innovation. *Stanford Social Innovation Review*, 6(4), 34-43.

Phillips, C. & Shaw, I. (2011). Editorial. *The British Journal of Social Work*, 41, 609-624.

Sanders, D. S. (1982). *The developmental perspective in social work*. Manoa, HI: University of Hawaii Press.

Social Enterprise UK (2015). *The state of social enterprise survey 2015*. London: Social Enterprise UK.

Todaro, M. P. (1997). *Economic development*, 6th Edn. London: Longman.

United Nations (2019). *The sustainable development goals report 2019*. New York: United Nations.

World Bank (2018). *Poverty and shared prosperity 2018: Piecing together the poverty puzzle*. Washington DC: World Bank.

World Inequality Lab (2017). World Inequality report 2018. World Inequality Lab: Berlin. Retrieved on 20 April 2020 from https://wir2018.wid.world/files/download/wir2018-summary-english.pdf

Q&A

Q1: During your talk, it was mentioned that the practice of developmental social work involves traditional social work. At the same time, it is necessary to break through traditional boundaries and social innovation limitations are mainly related to economic development. I would like to ask, why is it that you think that social development and economic development are unable to resolve social issues alone or to eliminate poverty?

A1: This is a very important question. However, I do not believe there is a clear or precise answer. In terms of economic and social development, usually people focus on economic development, and social development is seen as something completely different. Therefore, we need to seek a goal, that is "the building of a bridge to balance social and economic development".

By resolving unemployment, we can help them to develop their livestock or breeding industries to increase their income. However, when we do this, we need to consider whether the nutritional needs of children of farming families in those communities can be met if all the products of their livestock and breeding industries are sold elsewhere. This is what I want to emphasize—the balance between economic and social development.

Q2: In terms of social work training, what do you think is missing from conventional training? During social work training, which aspects should be emphasized?

A2: I believe that for professional social workers, in addition to professional training, what is even more important is cultivation of "character" and "values". Social workers should have an attitude of commitment, courage, and enthusiasm. These are the basic characteristics that social workers need to possess. This means that they are not only able to complete their work, but also gain a sense of achievement from it.

Q3: When you talked about social innovation, you mentioned the importance of "leadership". Do you think that we should encourage political leaders or non-profit organizations to develop social innovation leadership abilities?

A3: I think that no matter if we are talking about government or non-government social workers, if they value doctrine and slogans over social innovation, then social innovation cannot be achieved. Leaders must identify with and affirm social innovation, and there must be a suitable organizational environment for implementing it. Even if it is a small innovation or idea, it should be valued. Only in this way can organizations experience better development.

Co-evolution of Economic Development and Social Improvement—Social Economy

Jer-San Hu[*]

Abstract

Long-term social challenges require urgent solutions. However, it has been shown that the government, enterprises, and social organizations within the conventional social system design are unable to effectively handle such challenges. Social enterprises are organizations that are willing to proactively face challenges while receiving proper financial return. Social entrepreneurship involves innovative thoughts on how to handle specific social issues and a willingness to bear organizational risk during the implementation of resolutions. Only then can there be a social economy, a supplemental system for social improvement, in addition to the mainstream capitalist economy.

Social entrepreneurship is not an alternative economic system; it serves to increase quality of life and create a more sustainable environment, making up for the oversight and harm from past economic development while simultaneously creating social innovation to produce new economic domains. Only when the mainstream economy enters the new social economic system can more comprehensive social improvement be achieved.

Keywords: Social economy, social entrepreneurship, social enterprise, social innovation, capitalist economy

[*] President of Taiwan Social Enterprise Innovation and Entrepreneurship Society; Honorary Professor of National Yunlin University of Science & Technology; Professor Emeritus of Fu Jen Catholic University.

It is reasonable for people to want to live in a society in which material goods are abundant, work and income are stable, the living environment is clean, and social order and education are of a high level. Other ideal conditions include no pollution or destruction of the natural environment and people being free and having equal opportunities; but how can such a society be achieved?

During the long-term pursuit of a modern industrial economy, people have become accustomed to industrial and economic development that is accompanied by pollution and environmental destruction, resource consumption and consumer waste, disproportionate accumulation of wealth, imbalances in rural and urban development, and crowding and high cost of living in cities.

In terms of this topic, are we facing economic or social development? Are economy and society mutually exclusive or compatible? Can they go hand in hand? If the answer is yes, then how can we coordinate the simultaneous development of the economic and social sectors? Or, is the fundamental question, under current capitalist economic thinking, is it possible for us to have a new economic system that can offset the after-effects and complications of economic development?

This is the social economy, which is the focus of the present article.

I. Introduction: What Is Expected Social Improvement?

What is your holistic view of society? Figure 1 presents three different social improvement concepts. Which concept do you find most acceptable? Based on your reasoning, conduct a comparison with the other two concepts and infer the outcomes of each type of social improvement situation.

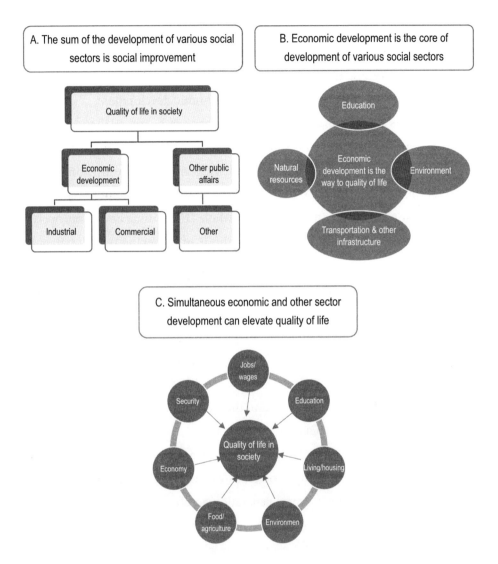

Figure1: Three social improvement concepts

Source: Produced by the author

A: It is thought that the various sectors of society develop on their own using resources distributed by the government or society for maximum resources usage efficiency. The various sectors resolve social problems for which they are responsible, in order to create maximum social well-being.

B: This is the commonly held belief of "fighting for the economy", with no resources for social welfare. The economy plays the pivotal role. Other social affairs and services are forgone or sacrificed. This concept is common in countries that are completely focused on economic development.

C: The belief is that different sectors of society are partners that assist one another and jointly pursue improvement in the overall quality of life, including the economy, environment, resources, consumption, labor, sanitation, and education. When there is excess or inadequate development in any sector, this affects the society as a whole. There must be an appropriate slowing or elevation of efficiency in the hope of achieving overall balanced development of society.

In societies, due to differences in social mainstream consciousness, there is different thinking, usually in regard to the life pressures or cultural values of society. Not all poor countries possess B-type thinking. In actuality, most nations with high happiness indexes are those that lag behind economically.

The author agrees with concept C. Added to that are the social entrepreneurship concepts emphasized in this paper. More specifically, the aim of this paper is to put forth "social economy" thinking.

In the social structure of the current mainstream economy, there are certain characteristics and competencies, as well as blind spots, after-effects, or social costs (harm). How can a new generation enterprise or social organization transform the harm brought about by the mainstream economy into new business opportunities and, at the same time, resolve social issues and create new economic output? This is the basis of the social economy.

II. Current Mainstream Economic and Social Systems and Characteristics

Current economic and social systems refer to the focal points of social improvement placed on the first sector (government), the second sector (private enterprise), and the third sector (non-profit organizations, NPOs). It is not necessary to explain in detail these systems' competencies and existing goals/operating resources. Based on the establishment goals of these three sectors, social motivation or economic motivation, and the macro-view or micro-view of the level of services, the classification of social structures is shown in Table 1.

Table1: Current Social System Service Organizations

Level Sector-determined goals	Macro-view	Micro-view
Social motivation	Public policy, budget, welfare	NPO, NGO, charity
Economic motivation	State-owned company, subsidy	Business and free market

Source: Produced by the author

i. Current social system design—effective or not?

As shown in Table 1, the government sector carries out social welfare services based on policies and budget. However, the service level emphasizes the society's macro-view. There is relatively little interaction with the basic micro-view. Thus, there will be discrepancies in the intention of a policy and its outcomes. At the same time, due to the restrictions imposed by policy and budget, it is impossible to implement resolutions for society's pressing problems.

The government commissions NPOs and charities to implement policies and provide real-time and frontline services to those in need. However, NPOs must rely on government funding or donations from individuals and enterprises for their operating resources, meaning that they may not be able to provide services permanently.

Enterprises seek profits from investment in private property (maximization). They make every effort, in terms of customer service, to achieve customer satisfaction and loyalty. As part of their operating strategy, they naturally seek cost minimization (sacrificing the environment and worker value) and revenue maximization (encouraging excess buying), while neglecting consumer groups that do not offer immediate returns and issues. Blind spots are created through the operation of self-interest-oriented enterprises and neglect of social needs.

This is the current state of so-called government failure, enterprise blind spots, and unstable operations of social organizations. Added to these are government agencies, each with its own specific area or duties, and lack of channels for mutual assistance between government and private/social organizations. Behind the economic prosperity (due to the strength of technology and enterprises) created in this system may be hidden and neglected needs, damage to the environment and natural resources, consumer waste, and replacement of low-level or obsolete labor forces, all of which become service items for other social sectors.

Even if tax revenue from enterprises is used to supplement services to offset the above-mentioned problems, this is a process of "causing injury first, then providing medical care", meaning providing relief after the fact. Can we reduce these problems during the process of economic development? Moreover, even if we do offset problems after the fact, it might not be possible to completely reverse the situation. Can a complementary system design eliminate these problems in a timely manner?

ii. Capitalist economic trends and their "after-effects"

It is difficult to talk about social improvement without discussing economic development. Economic development stresses the effective use of resources to create goods and services for mass consumption. In addition, during the process of supply and demand transactions, job opportunities and wealth are created, thus stimulating production activities in which private resources and knowledge are applied in order to serve society.

The capitalist economic system is the key to social productivity. Capital-based entrepreneurs or investors are indeed effective promoters. Due to their self-interest and operations and management push, the capacity and social influence of private capital enterprises cannot be ignored.

1. Centralization, mass production, artificial intelligence, and automation mean that even high-level or specialized workers may face replacement.

2. nd to encourage excess consumption with profits used to invest in continuing research and development. This even becomes a weapon against the competition, while consuming natural resources and creating waste.

3. Development of synthetic materials and work procedures elevates production efficiency, leaving behind artificial substances in the environment, and thus increasing the risks to the health and adaptability of organisms.

4. Mutual conversions of funds and assets (capital, real estate, commodities) encourages the amassing of capital and even the creation of monopolies.

5. When social resource capital transactions and self-interest motives are combined, profitable behavior flourishes. However, unprofitable social services or responsible behaviors are neglected.

In a capitalist-based social system, the profits from commercial production and transactions go to the capitalists. Enterprise operators must provide the maximum return on investment to the capitalists who commissioned them. As such, they will not proactively consider socially-responsible activities that are not of direct benefit. If this continues, capitalists will control more resources. Through their control of new and old enterprises, they control research and development of new technologies. Priority for use of technologies is given to businesses, which obtain environmental resources for commercial benefit. Based on financial analyses, hiring and salary decisions are made and industrial upstream and downstream clusters are formed, thus providing leverage in negotiations with government or social organizations. This leads to the formation of a society focused on the economy.

Under the social concepts of working for the economy or economic priority, social harm and unhealthy development are ignored or temporarily endured. This leads to many "after-effects" of economic development, such as those related to the environment and resources, urban and rural development, and social injustices, etc.

iii. Neglected social costs

Due to the above-mentioned after-effects of economic development, social resources and knowledge are eventually required to restore society. The debt incurred by previous generations must be paid. However, if we inquire as to whom should repay the debt, this is controversial. The undisputed fact is that this is an intangible or purposely neglected social cost.

Based on profit and loss statements, it is possible to see such neglected or hidden costs/expenses. They are also shown in Table 2.

To maximize profits, enterprises need to achieve maximum revenue and minimum costs. To maximize revenue, it is necessary to develop a variety of goods and services, encourage excessive purchases, and create a material culture of waste. Behind that is overproduction and overconsumption of resources, excessive amounts of waste, and reliance on financial investments to increase profits from non-operating income. However, this drives up capital and real estate prices, stimulates speculation, and increases living costs in urban areas.

In terms of minimizing costs, enterprises first deal with labor and material cost pressures. Large multinational companies take advantage of globalized production, with upstream and downstream manufacturers moving to countries where costs are lower, thus creating social pressures from the loss of jobs and enterprises. Moreover, to achieve manufacturing efficiency, enterprises develop new technologies and make use of non-natural additives. However, toxic products and production facilities negatively affect urban and rural areas.

Table 2: Social Costs and Hidden Expenditures Based on Profit and Loss Statement

Accounting statement/item	Financial indicator	Hidden social cost
Revenue: (maximization) Sales revenue Non-operating income (Hidden revenue)	Max $\sum_j^i P_{ij} X Q_{ij}$ (wide variety of goods are produced to encourage overconsumption) Financial manipulation and investment Land and housing transactions	Oversupply leads to competitive consumption. Overconsumption leads to hoarding. Waste produced from consumption. Fluctuating real estate prices. Disparities in basic infrastructure between urban and rural areas. Technology development supports favoritism
Costs: (minimization) Materials Labor (streamlined)	Direct material consumption: Components Consumption of materials and production additives Direct labor and insurance	Natural resources are consumed. Artificial additives and speeded up processes lead to product risks Production moves to other countries/ foreign laborers (elimination or replacement of manpower)
Manufacturing expenses: Manufacturing process and technology Wear and tear Water and electricity consumption	Automated equipment depreciation Handling of contaminants from the production process Energy consumption	(Direct replacement of manpower) Air and water pollution Worsening of the environment and pollution prevention Investment in and consumption of water and electricity
Administrative expenses Marketing expenses	Expenses related to administrative salaries and affairs Channels, logistics, marketing, and services support	Number of strategies for excessive cost decreases Marketing channel control, payment of commissions
Net profit (maximization) Taxes/dividends/retained earnings	ROI; stock price contribution Shareholder owned	Non-laborer owned Unequal distribution of wealth

Source: Produced by the author

These after-effects can perhaps be handled by taxation, the revenues of which are transferred to the environmental sector. However, this is similar to the above-mentioned saying: "causing injury, then providing medical care". Is this the best method? The inefficient policies and administration of the public sector have resulted in social organizations drawing attention to social issues, as well as taking action and creating improvement.

III. Expectations of the Socially-Traumatized—the Social Improvement Movement

Under the current system design and social theories, before it is possible to provide a comprehensive new social concept, we must face these after-effects or hidden social costs and develop innovative concepts and ideas in order to solve them. Moreover, such solutions should be implemented within the existing economic system; that is, by solving existing problems brought about by the economy, we can create new economic output.

i. Innovative ideas are needed to solve problems

In addition to Adam Smith's views on the capitalist economy, another branch of thought emerged in Europe which emphasized developmental economy concepts based on innovative entrepreneurship (Schumpeter, 1912). Such concepts held that economic development involves searching for "new needs" that have not yet been discovered or satisfied. Based on these needs or demands, it is necessary to think about "new products", "new production methods", "new materials", and "new operating structures". These are the five elements of innovation.

In addition to new needs related to commercial consumption, there may be the needs of the poor who have no purchasing power. Factories have been unwilling to provide goods or invest in technologies to satisfy these needs (Hu, 2009), such that there is a non-market with an incomplete supply and demand structure. In the past, the unserved needs of certain groups due to particular social factors were referred to as "social issues". As such, they were the responsibility of government or charity organizations. However, after a long period of time, the government and the social sector have done what they can. The remaining problems have not been resolved and new problems have emerged. Therefore, we must consider new ways of thinking, new technologies, new investment of resources, or new concept organizations in the development of problem-solving strategies (Seelos & Mair, 2005).

In Europe (especially during the time that Margaret Thatcher served as the UK Prime Minister), there was advocacy for the social innovation and social entrepreneurship movements, which cited the work of Schumpeter.

Henley (2008) proposed that social innovation means enabling community residents to create better services for the community and to resolve cross-sector social issues using new ideas or methods. George et al. (2012) added commercial operating concepts, suggesting that those in the lower echelons of society have new ideas for development and practices, creating opportunities to increase their own social and economic benefits. OECD (2003) defined social innovation as "seeking new answers to social problems by identifying and delivering new services that improve the quality of life of individuals and communities". These definitions possess two common points: (1) Resolution of public or community issues and improvement of quality of life; (2) New ideas and methods.

However, can innovative concepts and methods, resolving issues, and bringing about new needs or opportunities become a long-term continuous resolution system? There must be people who can set up formal organizations for long-term operation, especially self-supporting commercial organizations. Therefore, it is necessary to welcome new concepts of social entrepreneurship.

ii. Social entrepreneurship

The term entrepreneur can be traced back to 17th-century France. At that time, it referred to a person able to shoulder risk and responsibility, to search for market opportunities, and to dispatch resources, creating value by shifting goods from a low-price to a high-price area (Stevenson, 1983). In the term social entrepreneurship, "social" refers to the entrepreneurship objective—underserved groups in society (Martin & Osberg, 2007). It is the same meaning as that of social innovation, which is the setting up of organizations to serve vulnerable and marginalized groups and the integration of care for society and commercial operations by entrepreneurs with a mission to serve society (Dees, 1998).

As an academic term, social entrepreneurship has been around for nearly 30 years. It is associated with enterprises whose mission is to resolve social issues (Dees, 1998). The earliest relevant literature was a study on publicly-operated enterprises by King and Roberts (1987). However, at that time, there was no clear discussion of concepts. Rather, the emphasis was on innovation and leadership qualities of social entrepreneurs. In 1991, Waddock and Post began defining social entrepreneurship as being comprised of the public sector and social domain and including economy, education, research, social welfare, society, and spirituality (Leadbeater, 1997). In 1998, Dees proposed a definition that met with widespread approval (Weerwardena, 2005).

Commercial entrepreneurs see opportunities to earn profits based on market demand. Through business design and market transactions they create value for shareholders, with incentives and achievements based on financial rewards (Zadek & Thake, 1997). Therefore, they will not enter markets without the potential for financial profit or in which financial profit is inadequate. Social entrepreneurs emphasize social value. Starting with a concern for society, their objective is to resolve social needs that have not been satisfied by the commercial market. At the same time, they must produce a reasonable profit to be self-supporting. Therefore, there is a higher level of operating difficulty in social entrepreneurship. Social entrepreneurs must use enterprise operating methods, including new concepts, ideas, skills and systems. At the same time, they must possess a detailed understanding of society and methods for raising funds to resolve social issues or overcome new challenges.

iii. Social enterprises with a new mindset

Social entrepreneurship upholds concern for a specific social issue or group and designs services and commercial systems to satisfy those needs. Such systems must be long-term formal organizations. Therefore, enterprises or other social organizations include a commercial component. The Taiwan Social Enterprise Innovation and Entrepreneurship Society (2009) has defined social enterprise as "organizations that give consideration to social value and profitability". They are organizations with dual operating objectives.

The term "organizations" reflects the many existing organizations with dual objectives. In England, these include: (1) employee-owned businesses; (2) credit unions; (3) consumer cooperatives; (4) joint development organizations; (5) shelter workshops; (6) adjusted labor market companies; (7) charity organization-attached industries; and (8) community enterprises (Social Enterprise Charter, 2001; Social Enterprise London, 2001). In Taiwan, these organizations include: (1) socially transformed enterprises; (2) NPOs investing in business; (3) cooperatives; (4) start-ups; (5) fair trade ventures; (6) community economy organizations; (7) residential self-help organizations; (8) platform-integrated organizations; and (9) shelter workshops (Hu, 2013; Hu, Lo, & Prasetyo, 2017).

As there are needs that have not yet been met in society, this has challenged entrepreneurs to pay attention to social issues. When someone produces a feasible and innovative resolution, the next step is to prepare financial and social resources and to design a continuously running social enterprise. The operational outcomes include social service benefits and financial self-sufficiency. In simple terms, the establishment and operation of social enterprises are based on specific social issues. If these social issues are effectively resolved, they can be incorporated into national development goals, leading to the simultaneous evolution of economic development and social development.

IV. National-Level Social Improvement Goals

In 2017, due to disproportionate development among nations and global unfairness and injustice, as well as the worsening of the environment, the United Nations put forth 17 sustainable development goals (SDGs). These SDGs can assist government organizations, enterprises, and social organizations in jointly identifying the most urgent needs in the drafting of goals for social improvement. They also remind various organizations that, in addition to existing goals, they should exert effort in their own society and in the international society.

i. Descriptions and meanings of sustainable development goals

These 17 SDGs, listed below, cover social justice, environmental, and economic issues. It is expected that within the next 15 years the practices of enterprises and social organizations in respective countries will bring about restoration of, and improvements in, living environments.

1. End poverty in all its forms everywhere.
2. End hunger, achieve food security and improved nutrition, and promote sustainable agriculture.
3. Ensure healthy lives and promote well-being for everyone at all ages.
4. Ensure inclusive and equitable quality education and promote lifelong learning opportunities for all.
5. Achieve gender equality and empower all women and girls.
6. Ensure availability and sustainable management of water and sanitation for all.
7. Ensure access to affordable, reliable, sustainable, and modern energy for all.
8. Promote sustained, inclusive, and sustainable economic growth, full and productive employment, and decent work for all.
9. Build resilient infrastructure, promote inclusive and sustainable industrialization and foster innovation.
10. Reduce inequality in and among countries.

11. Make cities and human settlements inclusive, safe, resilient, and sustainable.

12. Ensure sustainable consumption and production patterns.

13. Take urgent action to combat climate change and its impacts.

14. Conserve and sustainably use the oceans, seas, and marine resources for sustainable development.

15. Protect, restore, and promote sustainable use of terrestrial ecosystems, sustainably manage forests, combat desertification, stop and reverse land degradation, and halt biodiversity loss.

16. Promote peaceful and inclusive societies for sustainable development, provide access to justice for all, and build effective, accountable, and inclusive institutions at all levels.

17. Strengthen the means of implementation and revitalize the global partnership for sustainable development.

Florian (2017) suggested that even ordinary businesses can search for ways to contribute to sustainable value. However, businesses mainly emphasize employment, revenue, and poverty, as well goals related to the economy, such as the first, second, eighth, ninth, 12th, and 14th goals. The remaining goals stress fairness, justice, and human rights. They are not suited to inclusion in (ordinary) commercial organization goals. However, economic revenues are an important tool for creating income and material freedom.

ii. Achieving sustainable development goals requires action. Who are the actors?

These SDGs are not merely slogans. They reflect fundamental crises of current social development. If not properly faced and resolved, these crises can cause serious damage to the global environment and world peace. Under the limitations of the present system framework, social entrepreneurial action and establishment of social enterprises are urgently needed. Only through local action by social enterprises can there be basic-level local resolution of problems and expanding effects.

Based on the experience of the author in promoting domestic and international social entrepreneurship, exchanges, and learning over the past nearly 10 years, specific organizations carry out social entrepreneurship to implement social improvement. They possess resources and action plans, are especially adapted for implementing innovation, come in many forms and sizes, and handle various problems.

iii. Social improvement action organizations

Although the 21st century has been fraught with natural and man-made disasters, no matter in terms of civic organizations, businesses, or even government agencies, all impart or implement entrepreneurial actions to encourage a basic level of autonomy. The driving force of entrepreneurship is social sensitivity and responsibility, with social surplus that transcends profit (Fowler, 2000). Subsidies from the government or large foundations guide basic-level action (NPOs) and grassroots organizations with the ability to be autonomous (start-ups). These organizations with a new mindset not only present the vitality of organizational reform but also the loosening of conventional systems and opportunities for merging. Such opportunities include:

1. Government and private sector collaboration—Governments break away from management and control, or only subsidize, NPOs. They collaborate with organizations that are professional, knowledgeable, and skilled on particular issues and jointly take action to resolve social issues, even planning relevant polices.

2. Mutual assistance between businesses and public welfare organizations—In the same way, under the guidance of corporate social responsibility (CSR), an increasing number of businesses are going beyond providing financial contributions to establish their own foundations. Through these foundations, they take social action that they agree with, and encourage employees and members of society to create new action organizations.

3. Urban and rural interactions—As urban residents better understand rural

areas, they stop seeing them just as recreational destinations. Instead, they invest funds and expertise into running farms or improving the quality of their lives in rural areas. This leads to close interactive and mutually beneficial relationships between urban and rural areas.

4. Complementary crossover (employment, rural areas, agriculture, farmland)—As more professionals invest in actions related to specific social issues, they understand that agriculture is not just ecologically friendly or related to organic growing methods, but that it also involves marketing, elevation of second- and third-tier agriculture, manpower, misuse of farmland, and farm village environment and culture, etc. There are many aspects or relevant issues for which there are cross-disciplinary collaborative challenges.

5. Cross-industry (technological, traditional, artisanal, and cultural creative industries) merging and innovation—Due to urban and rural interactions, there have been collaborations between vulnerable groups and technical professionals. More and more, the simplicity and dependability of traditional technologies and the applications of new technologies are leading to exchanges. Rural area artisanal techniques are stimulating the cultural aspects of industrial technologies, thus leading to positive and mutually beneficial learning.

6. Integration of multiple facets, roles, and value of business entities and flexible organizational integration—Interactions among enterprises and NPOs or rural area organizations spark new thinking, as well as resource coordination and team structure options beyond enterprise-type organizations and commercial resources.

To sum up, government agencies, NPOs, enterprises (particularly small and medium enterprises and start-ups), communities, and foundations stimulate and create new mindsets and structural organizational innovation among themselves.

(1) Social entrepreneurship model of government and NPOs or enterprise collaboration

Based on government policy guidance, action organizations, no matter if NPOs or commercial organizations, are mostly of a public services or community development nature.

a. Multiple employment program—The Ministry of Labor subsidizes community service organizations.

b. Career training programs—The Ministry of Labor subsidizes social (community) services. However, they must be commercial and self-supporting organizations.

c. NPO-invested businesses—NPOs invest in businesses. However, such businesses must be related to the service aims of the NPO or extend its existing service activities.

d. Community-based entrepreneurships, community invest companies (CICs) —Local entrepreneurship activities target communities. In England, CICs are legally defined organizations.

e. Cooperative organizations—These include cooperatives, credit unions, and resource sharing organizations.

f. Works integration social enterprise (WISE)—European countries, such as Germany and France, have established service manpower under a new government policy of connecting the unemployed and providing group training and employment assistance.

g. Solidarity social enterprise—In Northern Europe, within a community, public sector subsidies, social organizations, and existing enterprises are integrated under a newly-created operations and management system.

h. Social entrepreneurship incubation—Incubation of innovative entrepreneurial organizations is backed by the government.

i. Empowering social enterprises in financing, selling, facilitated location—Organizations that are backed by the government provide financial guidance and marketing support to start-ups, NPOs, and even vulnerable families.

(2) Social enterprises or organizations with commercial characteristics

From commercial organization-led social action, commercial organization concern for society is gradually revealed.

a. CSR—CSR-based procurement (purchasing of social organization or community products), enterprise volunteer services, and enterprise collective donations.

b. Social connection—An enterprise adopts or supports a specific social activity or organization.

c. Inclusive business—A designated social group or social organization is merged with an enterprise's operating and management system.

d. Social entrepreneurship—An enterprise actively promotes or supports entrepreneurial activities that benefit communities or social issues.

e. Cooperative economy organization—People of a like mind establish an organization for mutual assistance in collective production, marketing, consumption, and purchasing.

f. Community economy organization—Members of a community or existing service organization establish a commercial organization to benefit the community.

g. Fair trade organization—Connecting the producers in poor countries around the world; these producers' products are purchased at a fair price to enable them to earn the proper amount of profit.

h. Communal economy—People who share the same religious beliefs or ideas establish a mutually beneficial communal living area to share the benefits of their work.

(3) Characteristics of start-ups

Due to a community need or a need derived from a specific social issue, people at the grassroots level, as a result of their observation and experience, have the confidence to resolve this need and establish a start-up. Such people fall into the following categories:

a. Multiple jobber—Simultaneously works several jobs to earn an adequate income.

b. Multiple functions service—This kind of person, in addition to having a full-time job, carries out interesting work in a self-employed manner.

c. Studio house—Accepts work of an irregular amount on an irregular basis on top of a basic living.

d. Team entrepreneurship—Core members guide entrepreneurship activities. Other members have a job to earn entrepreneurship funds and support entrepreneurship on a part-time basis.

e. Venture explorations—This kind of person is attached to an organization or works as a volunteer to gain experience and search for entrepreneurship opportunities.

f. Empowerment training—Such an individual rents a rundown residence or farm at a low price, to establish a base for gradual growth.

g. Reverse takeover—Borrows from an organization with shared interests to apply to other organizations for purchasing or services to build entrepreneurial strength.

h. Small-scale ventures—Carries out small-scale community entrepreneurship for consumer targets or as a production base until resources are adequate to start formal operations.

i. Progressive ventures—Students put into practice what they have learned in the classroom and continue after winning the social venture contest, building up a network and understanding the feasibility of their idea.

From flourishing start-ups in various places adapting to the local economic situation and social structure have come action and power. They resolve local social issues and create economic output from the social sector. How should this source of economic output be described? Perhaps we should earnestly consider "social economy" concepts.

V. Significance and Meaning of the Social Economy

The term social economy can be traced back to 19th-century France (Defourny & Develtere, 2009). However, to this very day, the social economy is a contested concept. There is no consistent definition or a definition agreed upon by everyone (OECD, 2003), although European countries have reached a relatively higher level of consensus. It is believed that the social economy includes cooperatives, associations, mutuals, and foundations (OECD, 2003; Quarter, Mook, & Armstrong, 2009). Therefore, in the definition of the social economy, from the scope of organizational types, organizations can all be termed social economy organizations (SEOs) (OECD, 2003).

Europeans have seen social organizations working to resolve social issues. The economic value that they bring should be termed the social economy. However, this concept ignores the roles and contributions of enterprises and start-ups in resolving social issues.

According to the Social Business Initiative published by the European Commission (2011), "In order to promote a 'highly competitive social market economy', the Commission has placed the social economy and social innovation at the heart of its concerns". This advocacy for social enterprise has already been set out in a series of comprehensive action plans by the European Commission that are expected to support social innovation and create an advantageous environment for social enterprises.

Defourny and Delveterre (1999) defined the social economy from the perspective of economic activities of cooperatives, associations and mutuals. Moreover, the economic activities of these associations comply with the following principles: (1) placing services for its members or the community ahead of profit; (2) autonomous management; (3) democratic decision-making process; and (4) the primacy of people and work over capital in the distribution of revenues.

Compared to the emphasis on various types of enterprise organizations and the nature of social affairs, the social economy is based on the substance of organizational aims and objectives and possesses economic entities with social objectives.

In this paper, the economic point of view is carefully defended. Based on the marketing notion of supply and demand, social economy concepts are analyzed. Moreover, adopting Schumpeter's development economy theory is a must. Based on the nature of its five elements of innovation, we can differentiate two directions which are representative of market supply and demand, as follows:

Demand aspect—Unearth new demands/new service targets.

Supply aspect—New products and concepts, new production techniques, new materials, and new types of operating organizations that satisfy new demands.

When unserved demands encounter corresponding new supply systems, there is a new and effective market, as shown by the formula below:

New (demand) = New (product concept, production techniques, materials, operating organization)

Social entrepreneurship and social enterprises independent of the conventional capital and free market economic systems, no matter if output is calculated in terms of financial profit or social value or impact, can be considered outside the capitalist economy and part of the broader social economy.

From social issues of joint concern among countries and economic development processes in each country come many challenges, such as poverty gap, environmental destruction, unemployment and re-employment, and waste and pollution. It is expected that the public sector will develop effective new policies, the capacity of the social sector will be elevated, and new types of social and commercial organizations making use of commercial methods will resolve social issues while providing economic output.

Table 3: Comparisons of the Capitalist Economy and the Social Economy

Item	Capitalist economy	Social economy
Focuses	GNP, NI, employment, investment, consumption, taxes, national finance, currency	Unserved needs in society, social value, financial returns
Social wealth	GNP=C+I+G +(X-M)	Social GNP={GNP, social outcomes}
Action organizations	Capitalist enterprises (companies)	Enterprises, NPOs, cooperatives, community organizations, fair trade organizations
Transaction mechanisms	Free market (interaction of supply and demand)	Poorly structured market (non-market, weak demand)
Operating logic	Profit=(PxQ-C)-Exp., maximized revenue, minimized expenses	{(Social issue – social service); (commercial demand – commercial product/service): social and commercial activities are complementary}
Benefits/After effects	Production and sales benefits, overall wealth/resources consumption, production and consumption-induced pollution, shareholder-owned companies, shareholder gains (maximization), production scale (minimization of costs), substitution of labor (decreased labor value), decline in traditional artisanal industries	Recovery from the harm caused by the capitalist economy, supplementation of deficiencies in welfare policies, market system blind spots/attachment to mainstream economy, operating difficulties and major challenges.

Source: Produced by the author

VI. Social Entrepreneurship and Social Economy

Due to the existing economic blind spots and harm to society caused by capitalist industrial and commercial activities and economic development, five new economic domains that urgently require innovative services are becoming increasingly obvious:

i. Green & re-cycle economy (GE)

Owing to the hidden costs of business and the harm to the environment in the form of, for example, pollution (air, water, and land), waste from production and consumption, and exhaustive use of resources, GE is focused on the reduction of waste and consumption:

1. Green economy—low-polluting (air, water, farmland) technologies, low-consumption (water and power) technologies, product miles, emissions trading.
2. (Blue) Re-use economy – Secondhand goods industries, waste recycling and re-use industries, leftover (ugly produce) food kitchens.
3. Frugal economy—Minimalist design industry, bricolage technology industry.
4. Sharing economy—Food banks, equipment-sharing organizations.

ii. Remedial economy

This type of economy is focused on the damage done to natural environments and ecosystems due to industrialization.

1. Trash processing industries—Clearing trash from streams and the sea, purifying water sources and the air.
2. Poison-free farming—Organic farming, natural farming, ecological farming, eco enzyme and other types of farming ecosystem restoration.
3. Industries for ecological restoration—desert greening, reforestation, fishing moratorium, and marine waste, etc.

iii. Caring economy (CE)

This type of economy is focused on providing special care to vulnerable groups, families, and age groups affected by disability or social structure.

1. NPO-provided care to marginalized groups, persons with disabilities, and families in poverty.
2. Cooperation with communities to provide long-term care to senior citizens and young children.
3. Employment training and services for the unemployed and weak-in-employment.

iv. Village economy (VE)

Refers to economic development in communities where there has been an exodus of young people and gaps between urban and rural areas.

1. Village resource development and local entrepreneurship (community entrepreneurship).
2. Village culture, arts and crafts, landscapes, and historical sites (maintenance economy).

v. Humanity economy (HE)

Advocacy for, and implementation of, practices for social fairness and justice, with attention paid to specific social issues.

1. Human rights issues—Guarantees of wages and job safety, employment of children and women, prevention of discrimination based on sex.
2. Social rights issues—Youth entrepreneurship development, small-scale (individual) entrepreneurship support, microfinance.
3. International care and support—Support through resources, medical supplies, skills, and emergency assistance.

VII. Description of the Social Economy

Due to the blind spots and after-effects of capitalist economic development, it is necessary for new commercial organizations with concern for society to provide services that are currently deficient in society, and to resolve specific issues in society or the neglected needs of various groups. Moreover, development of these non-markets and creation of a "new" blue ocean market can increase a country's productivity and output.

Satisfying unmet social needs or resolving social issues, while creating economic output, is the economy external to economic output and system. This becomes the social economy, which is complementary to the capitalist economy.

The definition of social economy put forth in this paper is:

Total economy=Capital economy + Social economy

Capital economy=GNP = C + I + G + (X − M)

Social Economy={GE, RE, CE, VE, HE}

VIII. Conclusion

Social entrepreneurship is not an alternative economic system. It increases quality of life and environmental sustainability, offsets omissions and harm from past economic development, and creates new economic domains from social innovation. We should not judge it based on its output but, rather, its social reparative value.

Economic development is the expectation of a society. It refers to the comprehensive production and consumption systems in which modern technology is used for development of resources through industrial production to create large quantities of products to fulfill the public's material demands and economic benefit. However, it is not perfect. There is post-production and post-consumption environmental destruction. New production technologies replace human labor and there is disproportionate distribution of wealth. Moreover, shifts in population and urban crowding are caused by industrial and commercial activities. The suffering of specific groups and environmental damage have long been challenges, which require the attention of society and, more importantly, methods for urgent resolution. It has been shown that a traditional system design with government, businesses, and NPOs is unable to effectively handle these issues. It is thus necessary for there to be social enterprises willing to face issues and in the process of resolving them obtain proper financial return. With social entrepreneurship, which refers to innovative ideas for handling specific social issues and a willingness to bear organizational risk, can the social economy, a supplementary system for improving society that works outside the capitalist economy, be created.

References

Chinese

胡哲生、張子揚、黃浩然（2013）。社會創業模式與社會企業資源整合的關聯性。**創業管理研究**，7（1），1-26。

胡哲生、陳志遠（2009）。社會企業本質、任務與發展。**創業管理研究**，4（4），1-28。

臺灣社會企業創新創業學會（2009）。「社會企業」定義。學會章程第一條。

English

Defourny, J. & Develtere, P. (2009). Defourny, J. & Develtere, P. (2009). The Social Economy: The Worldwide Making of a Third Sector. In *The worldwide Making of the Social Economy: Innovations and Changes* (pp. 15-40). Leuven & The Hague: Acco.

George, G., McGahan, A. M., & Prabhu, J. (2012). Innovation for inclusive growth: Towards a theoretical framework and a research agenda. *Journal of management studies*, 49(4), 661-683.

Henley, M. (2008). Success in social innovation in South Australia-what has happened? what has worked? Paper presented at The History & Future of Social Innovation Conference, South Australia.

Hu, Jersan, Lo, wei, & Prasetyo, Aries Heru (2017). Explore a Structure for Building a Social Entrepreneurship Promotion System. ISTR, 10th. Jakarta, Indonesia: Asia Pacific Regional Conference.

Leadbeater, C. (1997). *The rise of the social entrepreneur*. London: Demos. Online: http://www.demos.co.uk/publications/socialentrepreneur (accessed February 2012).

Martin, R. L. & Osberg, S. (2007). Social entrepreneurship: the case for definition. *Stanford Social Innovation Review*, 5(2), 28-39.

Quarter, J., Mook, L., & Armstrong, A. (2009). *Understanding the Social Economy: A Canadian Perspective*. Toronto: University of Toronto Press.

Schumpeter, J. A. (1912). *The Theory of Economic Development: An inquiry into profits, capital, credit, interest and the business cycle*. New Jersey: Transaction Publishers.

Seelos, O. & Mair, J. (2005). Social entrepreneurship: Creating new business models to serve the poor. *Business Horizons*, 48(3), 241-246.

Stevenson, H. H. (1983) A perspective on entrepreneurship, Harvard Business School. *Working Paper*, 9-384-131.

Weerawardena, J. & Mort, G. S. (2006). Investigating social entrepreneurship: A multidimensional model. *Journal of World Business*, 41(1), 21-35.

Zadek, S. & Thake, S. (1997). Send in the social entrepreneurs. *New Statesman*, 26, 31.

Online Data

Dees, J. G. (1998). The meaning of social entrepreneurship. Retrieved on 15 January 2018 from http://www.fuqua.duke.edu/centers/case

European Commission (2011). Social business initiative. Retrieved on 13 February 2018 from http://eur-lex.europa.eu/legal-content/EN/TXT/?uri=CELEX:52011DC0682

Fowler, A. (2000). NGDOs as a moment in history: beyond aid to social entrepreneurship or civic innovation?. *Third world quarterly*, 21(4), 637-654. Doi:10.1080/713701063

Nebel, F. (2017). 6 things to keep in mind when applying the SDGs. In Sanford Sustainable Development Report, Sanford Company (Australia). Retrieved from https://www.ait.org.tw/wp-content/uploads/sites/269/un-sdg.pdf

OECD (2003). Job Creation through Social Economy and Social Entrepreneurship. Retrieved on 13 November 2017 from http://www.oecd.org/cfe/leed/130228_Job%20Creation%20throught%20the%20Social%20Economy%20and%20Social%20Entrepreneurship_RC_FINALBIS.pdf

Q&A

Q1： Since 2000, the Organization for Economic Co-operation and Development (OECD) has published many studies on transformation of economic, social, and cultural capital. Moreover, many countries have passed legislation regarding social enterprises driving the transformation of these three types of capital. As Taiwan does not yet have such legislation, how can it go about transforming these three types of capital?

A1： I believe that most entrepreneurs are well skilled in naturally transforming these three types of capital. For example, I implemented a vocational rehabilitation program in Hualien. No money was spent hiring human resources. Through contacts and understanding of the organization's concepts, people were willing to join and become human resources, thus creating cultural capital. Facilities and equipment were obtained through donations by like-minded organizations and companies, which became social capital. When donated items were entered into the unit's accounting records, they became economic capital. These three types of capital should not be relegated to theoretical definitions. We only need to delineate what is economic capital and what is social capital. By observing these kinds of capital at the operational level, programs can be put in place to implement models of operation.

Q2： During your talk, it was mentioned that, from the enterprise point of view, markets of concern to the social economy cover five areas: remedial economy, green & re-cycle economy, caring economy, village economy, and humanity economy. In which area should we start to create close industrial connections between social work and social enterprise?

A2： From the perspective of social enterprise, if it is young people, I will encourage them to participate in the remedial economy and green & re-cycle economy, and to learn how to determine social potential based on commercial considerations. For those who are slightly older, I will suggest that they start from the "elderly". From the enterprise perspective, of course it is hoped that there can be more customers in the service market. Based on commercial potential, the elderly demographic has higher spending and saving power, and is an expanding market.

Social Enterprise Development in Asia: Insights and Lessons for Developmental Social Work

Marie Lisa M. Dacanay[*]

Distinguished guests, stakeholders of the Eden Social Welfare Foundation, and social workers from Taiwan and abroad, good morning! It is my pleasure to take this opportunity to discuss the state of social enterprise development in Asia and to participate in dialogue with stakeholders of developmental social work.

My presentation today will cover five aspects. The first is social entrepreneurship and social enterprise from the global and developing country perspectives. Second, I will provide some cases and models of social enterprises in Asia as a reference. Third, I will explain the hybrid nature of social enterprises and social enterprise stakeholder engagement models. Fourth, I will share some of the challenges faced and the importance of building enabling ecosystems and platforms. Finally, I will provide insights and lessons for stakeholders of developmental social work.

I. Social Entrepreneurship and Social Enterprise: Global and Developing Country Perspectives

In 2006, I came across a definition of social entrepreneurship. As this was a developing field of research, it was somewhat broad. I believe that it can serve as a starting point for the following dialogue. Social entrepreneurship entails innovations designed to resolve social issues. As such, it must possess three

[*] President of Institute for Social Entrepreneurship in Asia.

elements: the first is "innovation", while the second is improvement of societal well-being, and the third is entrepreneurial organizations that initiate, guide, and promote change in society (Perrini, 2006).

i. Global perspective

From the global perspective, social entrepreneurship is a phenomenon that involves multiple models. Due to variations in local conditions, social entrepreneurship movements in different countries have taken on different forms.

In the USA, social entrepreneurship was a response to the economic downturn in the 1970s and 1980s. Due to cutbacks in federal funding to non-profit organizations, these organizations had to turn to the market for their major income source. They made use of business tools to solve social problems. This led to the expansion of social innovation models, which became the American social entrepreneurship phenomenon.

In Europe, social entrepreneurship can be traced back to the 1980s. It was at that time that welfare states retreated from public services. Added to this was the emergence of structural unemployment. For these reasons, government-assisted social cooperatives and community interest companies emerged. In other words, in Europe, with the move away from public services by governments, social enterprises made up for the gap in public welfare.

In my research area of the developing countries of Asia, social entrepreneurship is focused on responding to the "continuing development" crisis and paradox. For example, in my home country of the Philippines, approximately 25% of the population is living in poverty. The situation is similar in other developing countries in Asia. From this, we can see that, while there is rapid economic growth, there is also inequality and unfairness. Neither the government nor the market is able to provide adequate attention or resources to the poor. This has led to the rise of social enterprises with the poor or marginalized as primary stakeholders.

To sum up, observing social enterprises from the global perspective, there is commonality, initiating new ways of sharing responsibility for the common good in today's economies and societies. At the same time, they are moving toward economic and business models driven by a social mission (Defourny, Nyssens, & Brolis; Bidet & Defourny, 2019).

ii. Developing country perspective

From the perspective of developing countries, there has been a rise in social enterprises with the poor or marginalized as primary stakeholders. This phenomenon is a response to poverty and inequality.

Based on my research, it is clear that this type of social enterprise possesses three characteristics. First, it is driven by a social mission. This is similar to what is happening globally. Its primary mission is to reduce or alleviate poverty. Second, it is a wealth-creating organization, but at the same time it is motivated by a social mission. Third, while the aim of mainstream companies is to benefit shareholders, a social enterprise in which the poor are stakeholders operates on the philosophy that the wealth that is produced is distributed among stakeholders (Dacanay, 2012; 2015).

II. Social Enterprises in Asia: Cases and Models

i. Children Are Us Foundation

The first case I want to introduce is that of Taiwan's Children Are Us Foundation. Its mission is to inspire and promote the potential talent of persons with intelligence disabilities (PID) and assist them in returning to the social mainstream to enjoy the dignity and happiness of life. This foundation is comprised of social welfare and business departments. In the past, it served more than 300 PID. Today, that number has reached 800. In its world-class bakery and restaurant, 25% of hires are stakeholders. In addition, 51% of this foundation's income is from its businesses.

ii. Tahanang Walang Hagdanan (House of No Stairs)

The second case is that of Tahanang Walang Hagdanan, or the House of No Stairs. Its mission is to assist in the rehabilitation of persons with physical disabilities (PWD) and provide them with skills which will allow them to lead gainful and productive lives. This organization runs several sheltered workshops that employ 309 PWD. They produce metalcraft, woodcraft, and needlecraft works, in addition to packaging and fish hooks. Moreover, its business center assists PWD with development and marketing of products to enable them to become micro-entrepreneurs.

In the beginning, the board of directors of the House of No Stairs was composed mostly of people from the religious sector, with some from private enterprise, while management was dominated by persons without disabilities. Today, there has been a shift, with the majority of management positions filled by PWD. Moreover, in the past, PWD were worker beneficiaries who took on subcontracted jobs. Today, the focus is on providing rehabilitation and services to PWD and involving them in participatory planning and problem-solving processes.

iii. National Federation of Cooperatives of Persons with Disability (NFCPWD)

The third case that I want to discuss is the National Federation of Cooperatives of Persons with Disability (NFCPWD) of the Philippines. This is a federation of primary cooperatives comprised of PWD working together to develop an enterprise for producing chairs for schools, so as to increase employment opportunities for PWD.

In the beginning, this federation was composed of "one-person shows", meaning that there was one leader. Today, under the federation's guidance, organization value has been cultivated among members to build and elevate core capacities and develop proactive members. In addition, this federation has worked to cultivate collaborative partners, leading to the joint establishment of a foundation that assists in the development of federation members.

iv. Gandang Kalikasan (Human Nature)

The fourth case is an organization in the Philippines with an environmental conservation vision—Gandang Kalikasan. It mainly carries out personal care product manufacturing, marketing, and sales. Among its workers, 74% were once living below the poverty level. (The income of each worker was only 480 Philippine pesos per month, which is equal to approximately NT$285.) It has a no firing policy and has elevated the wages and benefits of workers. It also works to promote empowerment of workers in four dimensions: transformation in the workplace, freedom from usury and soundness of personal financial management, improved quality of family life, and spirituality and involvement in community development. The result is that colleagues are not just colleagues; they are involved in each other's lives.

v. Dragon (DIVC)

The fifth case is that of Dragon (DIVC) of Vietnam. Based on Global Good Agricultural Practice (GAP) standards, this company exports fresh and processed ginger. It provides small producers with assistance, training, and continuing technical support, so as to encourage sustainable agriculture, biological composting, and non-usage of herbicides. It has also enabled more than 2,000 indigenous men and women (H'mong people) to become members of interest groups sustainably cultivating ginger. Moreover, DIVC purchases all of its produce at flexible market rates, but at a minimum price, so as to protect farmers when prices drop. In a society where most farmers are male, DIVC has worked to enable women to enter the agricultural field and become small producers to contribute to their household farm income, earning 5-10 times more compared to producing corn.

vi. Alter Trade Foundation

The final case is that of the Alter Trade Foundation of the Philippines. Its achievements include the Negros Organic & Fair Trade Association (NOFTA) and NOFTA Fair Trade Haus. This foundation has helped more than 700 agricultural workers or beneficiaries of land reform to become entrepreneurial farmer leaders.

In 1986, this foundation mainly assisted members of cooperatives in becoming entrepreneurs. It has supported supplier communities which produce organic muscovado sugar and has become an important channel for a diversity of crops and household income. As a result of community development, planning, and implementation, this federation of producers' cooperatives and associations (NOFTA) now owns 60% of the trading and marketing arm. In addition, support has been provided for improving farm water conservancy and irrigation systems. Currently, this area has achieved food sufficiency and the majority of farmers have moved out of poverty.

Looking at these cases, it is clear that there are three social enterprise models in Asia. The first is the entrepreneurial non-profit model in which non-profit organizations operate as enterprises. They are financially self-sufficient and able to hire people. The Children Are Us Foundation and the House of Stairs are representative examples. The second is the social cooperative model. This model differs from that of traditional cooperatives, emphasizing members' needs and social objectives to elevate members and social welfare. An example is the NFCPWD. The third type is the social business model, which is based on a social mission, such as Gandang Kalilasan and DIVC.

In addition, there is an integrated model that expands on and extends these three models. Examples include the Alter Trade Foundation, NOFTA, and NOFTA Trade Haus. They have been able to empower entire societies and communities and have enabled their members to overcome poverty.

III. Understanding the Hybrid Nature of Social Enterprises and Social Enterprise Stakeholder Engagement Models

i. Hybrid nature of social enterprises

In one aspect, social enterprises are non-profit organizations with different operating models. In another aspect, they are akin to private enterprises, but can easily be mistakenly identified as for-profit organizations. This is characteristic of their "hybrid" nature. Moreover, from my surveys of social enterprises in various countries, I have discovered that social enterprises mainly provide three types of services to their members, especially poor or marginalized stakeholders (ISEA, 2015).

1. Transactional services

The first type is transactional services. These are mainly market-oriented and designed to assist the poor in becoming effective workers. Examples include product development and marketing, savings, credit, and micro-insurance.

2. Social inclusion services

The second type is social inclusion services. These are oriented toward providing access to basic needs and social services for the poor. They can be individual or group directed and are usually non-fee-based. Examples include community-based health and sanitation.

3. Transformational services

The third type is transformational services, which integrate transactional and social inclusion services. They are oriented toward enabling the poor to overcome capability deprivation to become actors in their own development. No matter if individual or group directed, these are non-fee-based services. This model can be used to truly assist the poor in overcoming poverty by organizing them into self-governing associations and building up leadership capacity.

ii. Social enterprise stakeholder engagement models

I have also observed that social enterprise stakeholder engagement models differ from general enterprise models. In social enterprises, participation of the poor and marginalized is at the core and a model is formed through the interactions of suppliers, buyers, and consumers.

For example, I have worked with an organization focused on the needs of persons with physical and mental disabilities. A joint value chain was constructed with customers, suppliers, and social enterprise partners. This enabled the establishment of a cooperative to increase the income of persons with physical and mental disabilities. At the same time, these persons' level of social participation and ability to live independently were elevated, helping them to overcome poverty. Most importantly, they overcame poverty on their own, rather than relying solely on the assistance of others. This empowerment model integrates transactional and transformational services. Different social enterprise stakeholder engagement models impact the poor differently. Empowerment means that stakeholders are able to transition from passive beneficiaries to business partners, leading to a proactive, transformational, and transactional model. Therefore, true empowerment models create different levels of participation and different influences and results.

Table 1: Social Enterprise Stakeholder Engagement Models

Orientation toward the poor	Nature of roles and capabilities among the poor	Impact on the poor
The poor as passive beneficiaries (CONTROL MODEL)	The poor are passive workers, suppliers, or clients	Limited to the negative (mission drift)
The poor as transactional partners (COLLABORATION MODEL)	Proactive workers, suppliers, and clients Partners in social enterprise and value chain management	Increased incomes, access to services (social inclusion)
The poor as transformational and transactional partners (EMPOWERMENT MODEL)	Empowered workers, suppliers, clients, and owners Organized partners in poverty reduction, and community, sector, and societal changes	Significant outcomes in overcoming poverty as capability deprivation

IV. Challenges Faced and the Importance of Building Enabling Ecosystems and Platforms for Social Enterprise Development

The research which I conducted in 2015 indicated that social enterprises face many challenges, including access to appropriate technologies; access to adequate financing; capacity development among leaders, managers, and people; effective and efficient management and operations to meet volume and quality requirements of markets; measurements of social impact and outcomes; extreme weather disturbances; government policies negatively affecting social enterprises; corruption in government regulatory bodies; inadequacy of programs supporting social enterprise development; and industry/market practices negatively affecting social enterprises (ISEA, 2015).

In regard to capacity development among leaders, managers, and people, as social enterprises grow, they not only possess enterprise management and social services management aspects, but also the need to manage multiple bottom lines. Due to their hybrid nature, their management is more complex than that of private enterprises or non-profit organizations. Moreover, in terms of government policies negatively affecting social enterprises, due to government procurement and tender regulations, social enterprises are caught up in bureaucratic models. There is a large investment of resources, but with negative effect. In terms of industry/market practices negatively affecting social enterprises, I would like to give an example. In supermarkets in the Philippines, social enterprise products are sold on consignment. Only after a consumer purchases a product will the supermarket pay for it. If there is flooding due to a typhoon and products are damaged, supermarkets will not provide compensation, as no transaction was involved. There are many situations like this.

Based on these internal and external challenges, I would like to "validate the importance of platforms". With a platform it is not just one social enterprise attempting to solve all problems. It is necessary to build ecosystems to assist social enterprises in their development and growth.

Here, I would like to provide three examples of social enterprise platforms. The first is the Institute for Social Entrepreneurship in Asia (ISEA) in the Philippines. The ISEA was established in 2012. Participants include those working in social enterprises, scholars, and other advocates. Through the Poverty Reduction Through Social Entrepreneurship Platform, policies and regulations are drafted based on the perspectives of stakeholders with advocacy in Congress. However, due to election trends, we have gradually lost our voice. As of 2017, there are relevant bills that have not yet passed. However, through our efforts, the current administration has made these bills a priority and it is hoped that not too long in the future they will become law and the government will assist in the development of social enterprises by jointly creating an environment conducive to social entrepreneurship.

The second example is the multistakeholder initiatives of the Association of Southeast Asian Nations (ASEAN). Through these initiatives, male and female producers are cultivated and undergo transformation. Moreover, a set of benchmarks for transformational partnerships and women's economic empowerment in agricultural value chains are promoted.

The last example is the setting up of social entrepreneurship pathways to accelerate implementation of Sustainable Development Goals (SDGs). According to a survey on global poverty, Asian countries make up two-thirds of the world's poor countries. Although the United Nations asserts that Asia is currently experiencing good economic growth, given current efforts, the region is not expected to achieve the SDGs of ending poverty and hunger by 2030. Therefore, many people are attempting to develop social innovation and social entrepreneurship to accelerate achievement of these SDGs. Moreover, the above-mentioned SDGs are aimed at "leaving no one behind". It is hoped that all people can participate, which complies with the mission of developmental social work. We can dramatically increase the scope of our work through cross-disciplinary collaborations and social enterprise platforms. With social entrepreneurship as an accelerator, we can achieve SDGs of zero poverty, no hunger, reduced inequality, gender equality, decent jobs and inclusive growth, inclusive and sustainable industrialization and innovation, responsible production and consumption, and sustainable communities. Among them, reducing inequality is very important. Social enterprises differ from mainstream enterprises in that the wealth they create is distributed among the poor, which represents a distributive concept. It is not only governments that can distribute wealth, but also social enterprises.

V. Insights and Lessons for Stakeholders of Developmental Social Work

i. Added value created by the development of social entrepreneurship and social enterprise

When discussing the various levels of exclusion, inequality, and sustainability, for which innovative thought can be applied to adjust key directions and resolve challenges, social entrepreneurship and social enterprise development may add value for stakeholders of developmental social work. Below are four aspects:

1. Sustainable livelihood development

Social enterprises cross social and market economies. They must have the desire and ability to establish a good social economy and be based on the concept of distribution of wealth. In addition, the role of social enterprises is to develop inclusive markets based on proper ethics and morals. From these two perspectives, the added value that social enterprises bring is development of sustainable livelihoods, especially for the poor and marginalized who are excluded from markets and the economy.

2. Sustainable provision of quality social services

When marginalized sectors are underserved or not effectively served by market or state institutions, they can obtain sustainable social services through developmental social work. Sometimes the market or state does provide services, but they are of inconsistent quality, especially services for persons with physical or mental disabilities. Through a social enterprise model, the overall quality of services and methods can be improved, providing public agencies with examples to follow.

3. Effective service to the poor and marginalized sectors

Currently, social enterprises are expected to produce their own resource chains and to be self-reliant. Through the continuous elevation of sustainable organizations and programs, social entrepreneurship and social enterprises can effectively serve the poor and marginalized sectors.

4. Scalable solutions to social problems

The final added value is that social entrepreneurship and social enterprises, through social innovation platforms and working together with other shareholders, can advance scalable solutions to social problems to accelerate the achievement of SDGs. I believe that the Eden Social Welfare Foundation and other relevant organizations are doing outstanding work in providing services to persons with physical and mental disabilities. However, only via cross-disciplinary collaboration can we strengthen the effectiveness of our own organizations, so that we "leave no one behind". As we work in our own sectors, it is necessary to remember to develop social enterprises to truly expand benefits.

ii. Social enterprises with multiple bottom lines are in a state of tension

Social enterprise development entails management competencies that include the understanding that social enterprises are hybrid organizations with multiple bottom lines. At face value, these organizations are always in a state of tension in terms of financial versus social objectives. Therefore, social enterprises cannot be managed or led by simply applying business or non-profit management tools. Instead, a hybrid model must be used to achieve management diversity.

In addition, teams of social entrepreneurs need to perfect the art of managing multiple bottom lines, entailing creativity and innovation in crafting management strategies and approaches and solving strategic and operational management issues.

iii. It is necessary to understand different stakeholders and impacts

When we view social enterprises as hybrid organizations, we must understand that there are different stakeholder engagement models, all of which have different impacts, especially on the poor and marginalized. As I mentioned earlier, I believe that only by applying empowerment models of stakeholder engagement in the provision of services can we truly improve the quality of life for the poor and marginalized and assist developmental social work in achieving its ultimate goals.

iv. It is difficult to resolve challenges at the level of individual social enterprises

The multitude of challenges that social enterprises face cannot be resolved by a single social enterprise. Therefore, it is necessary to build enabling ecosystems and put in place government policies and programs that effectively support social enterprise development. Then, social enterprises and social entrepreneurship platforms will have the potential to provide scalable solutions to social problems. As social entrepreneurship is a pathway for accelerating the achievement of SDGs, such as zero poverty, no hunger, reduced inequality, and sustainable and resilient communities, social enterprises must leave no one behind while working together to face challenges.

These insights and lessons are from my own observations. I look forward to sharing them with you and building dialogue. I have conducted social enterprise research in the Asian region for 10 years. Today, I hope that the insights and impressions I have gained through my research can be of help to you in the development of social enterprises. Thank you!

(This is an excerpt from Keynote Speech III of the International Conference on Developmental Social Work: Dialogue with Social Innovation co-organized by the Eden Social Welfare Foundation and the Department of Social Work of National Taiwan University, which was held on 29 November, 2019.)

Q&A

Q1: In accounting, bottom line refers to the profit and loss statement bottom line. It usually has just one meaning, that is to make a profit. What do you mean by multiple types of bottom lines in social enterprises?

A1: Social enterprises have adopted the accounting term "bottom line" to describe the outcomes and effects they should achieve. Social enterprises have many types of bottom lines, which means that in addition to satisfying the basic financial bottom line, i.e. making a profit to ensure their sustainability, they must hold fast to their social bottom line. Moreover, the social bottom line involves many aspects, such as gender issues, environmental issues, and training. No matter in which area, effectively maintaining the social bottom line is the first and foremost goal of social enterprises and is the true driving force for the growth of social enterprises.

Taking the National Federation of Cooperatives of Persons with Disability in the Philippines as an example, they must meet the needs for employment and, thus, help job seekers to cultivate job skills. They can become participants in the organization or develop into leaders.

Q2: Citizen-developed spaces of community service organizations (CSOs) in Asia have begun to come under pressure from enterprises. Since social enterprises possess a complexity of characteristics, can they adapt to shrinking citizen spaces?

A2: This is a global issue, and I feel that only relying on social enterprises is not enough to resolve it. Social enterprises should be looked upon as business partners for civil society (non-governmental organizations, social citizen organizations, community service organizations). Of particular note is the situation whereby social enterprises are set up by young people; indeed, such people may have a talent for business, but they do not know how to carry out community development. Through collaborations with non-governmental organizations, they can gain a better understanding of communities and have a better chance for success.

Part II:
Areas of Practice

Rejuvenate the community industry with local investment

Yung-Hsing Kao[*]

Abstract

Residents in remote areas (tribes) are often restricted by insufficient local employment opportunities, making it difficult for them to secure a livelihood and sustain their families. Since such deficiency has become a long-term issue, community residents have tended to become impoverished. Hence, the promotion of the community industry is not only designed to drive the overall development of the community, but can also benefit impacted families.

Rural communities or tribes are often limited by inconvenient transportation and insufficient local resources. While it is very difficult to promote the community industry, people also have to face many external environmental challenges, including abnormal natural environments. The situation faced by the community industry is not only a challenge but also a new opportunity. If the community can have innovative consideration of the type of industry and development strategy, instead of sticking to traditional crops and farming experience, the community industry can still embrace multiple opportunities and transform into organic farming, eco-tourism, or development of an under-forest economy.

Communities always have their respective geographic characteristics or restrictions. If one simply copies the experience of others without realizing local conditions, the community industry may end up frustrated and with financial losses; people must therefore be prudent and exercise good due diligence. This article recommends that the community adopt the concept of sustainable livelihood to construct the community industry, so that planners and participants can deeply

[*] Executive Consultant of the Eden Social Welfare Foundation; Assistant Professor, Department of Social Policy and Social Work, National Chi Nan University.

understand the vulnerability and resilience of the local livelihood development, then further identify the most effective strategy.

When planning community industries and conducting community resource inventory counts, the SLA model, amended by Yung-Hsing Kao (2015b), can be applied for assessment to recognize the social capital, human capital, property capital, environmental capital, cultural capital, and physical capital of the community. Subsequently, based on this, strategic identification can be carried out, and focus can be placed on local investment. Among the resources of the community, natural capital, physical capital, and financial capital are more likely to be restricted by status quo, while human capital and social capital bear great development potential. Local resources can be strengthened with the help of social investment strategies. Human and social capital can be leveraged and play a pivotal role in the community industry. In particular, community residents are the focus of development, and economic growth is a means rather than a final objective.

Keywords: developmental social work, social investment, community industry, community empowerment, sustainable livelihood orientation

I. Challenges and opportunities of the community industry

Rural communities or tribes are often restricted by inconvenient transportation and insufficient local resources. While it is very difficult to promote the community industry, people also have to resolve the dilemma of the external environment, such as abnormal natural environment, extreme climate, global warming, drought and heavy rains, alongside political and economic uncertainties such as changes in government policies and subsidy strategies.

The situation faced by the community industry is not only a challenge but also a new development opportunity. Under the impact of rapid climate change, prior farming experience is no longer sufficient to meet the demand of the current environment; as a result, adjustments must be made. As for the types of industries and development strategies in communities, if one can have innovative consideration instead of sticking to traditional crops and farming experience, then the community industry can still embrace the opportunity and transform into organic farming, eco-tourism, or develop an under-forest economy.

II. Identify appropriate development strategies

When rural communities and tribes lack local employment opportunities and livelihood resources, people will migrate to other sites and young people will leave their hometowns. The elderly and children are often left behind, which can easily lead to problems such as intergenerational nurture and child negligence. If the community can fully understand local characteristics and identify the appropriate development strategy, then even if it is located in a remote rural area, the community can still have room for development and establish a unique industry. For example, the development experience of the following three sites can be used as a reference and learned from.

i. The development experience of the Bunun Foundation

The Bunun Foundation operates a tribal leisure farm in Yanping Township, Taitung County. In the course of long-term cultivation, they have always attached great importance to the development of human capital, such as inviting tribal elders to share traditional knowledge and becoming teachers of tribal map projects, turning unemployed laborers into farmers or interpreters at organic farms, and turning forest workers into high mountain guides or engineers, as well as transforming housewives into the backbone of the knitting industry. The Bunun Foundation pays a great deal of attention to the cultivation and inheritance of talents, so that tribal people can have job security as well as self-reliance and confidence in their work.

The Bunun Foundation has further used the revenue from the community industry to advance the tutoring work for the tribe's children and youth, and to cultivate aboriginal talents. As of 2020, more than 100 young people in the tribe had attended college. The Bunun Foundation also assists in providing scholarships for children from underprivileged families so that they can receive education and care, in addition to providing a good living environment and learning skills for middle school dropouts.

Even more admirable is the vision and perseverance of Pastor Sheng-kuang Bai, the founder of the Bunun Foundation. For a long time Pastor Bai used the early morning hours to provide English teaching for the tribal students before school, thus cultivating their English competency. There are many young people who can now communicate directly with foreigners.

ii. Seishui Community

Seshui Community is located in Yuchi Township, Nantou County, adjacent to Taomi Community in Puli Township. It is one of the reconstruction community projects which commenced after the earthquake of 21 September. Compared with neighboring communities, Seshui Community lags far behind in the early stage of reconstruction, because in that stage communication and coordination between comunity residents are the first priority to build a consensus. Although this process was very time consuming, the consensus established at that time included the choice of styles and colors in the construction of roads around the village, reconstruction of houses, as well as community beautification and underground wires and cables, etc., with the aim being to build the community into an elegant leisure location. The above-mentioned consensus has boosted the revenues for the community's homestay, black tea, bamboo charcoal and other industries. With the increasing job opportunities and income, young people are more willing to return to their hometowns for development.

iii. Datong and Dali tribes in Xiulin Township, Hualien County

The Datong and Dali tribes (referred to as Tongli tribes) are located in Xiulin Township, Hualien County. They belong to the traditional territory of the Taroko tribe. They are also the only remaining traditional settlements inhabited by the Taroko tribe, currently classified as national parks. Since there are no external roads, the journey to and from the tribe takes approximately 6 hours by foot, and there remains no electricity supply.

Due to the inconvenience of transportation and the fact that the tribe has no electricity, it is a de facto "dark tribe", which seems to limit its development. However, because of its semi-enclosed environment, it has conserved a vast range of rich ecological resources. According to a formal investigation, there are 543 species in 128 families of vegetation in the tribe, including 461 indigenous species. The Tongli tribe enjoys magnificent mountains and rivers. This is exactly the charm of eco-tourism.

The tribe is adjacent to Liwu River and its upstream Shakadang Creek. There are many spectacular valleys and splendid Shakadang trails. It is also the only place where climbers can scale Liwu Mountain, Qianliyan Mountain, and Qingshui Mountain. There are three main hiking routes: Liulongtou Trail, Dekalun Trail, and Shakadang Trail. Among them, only the Deekalun Trail is a stepped trail. The remaining trails are mostly natural mountain trails, with beautiful forests along the way, giving people the chance to observe a wide range of flowers and plants right in front of their eyes.

Tongli tribe currently has ten homestays catering for mountain climbers, with ecological guide services also provided. Tribes often need to support each other when operating homestays. In cases where the number of tourists is large, they often need to share labor and work as a team, which also promotes cohesion and unity among the tribes. Here we can take as an example a particular homestay in the tribe, which received approximately 1,000 guests in a year. Based on a charge of 1,200 NT dollars per visitor, the annual revenue will reach 1.2 million NT dollars—an average of around 100,000 NT dollars per month. After deducting the cost of maintaining and updating food and homestay facilities, more than half of the net profit is left. For the elderly of the tribe, this money is very helpful when it comes to the livelihood of their families.

Based on the development experience of the three aforementioned cases, it can be seen that the industrial development of communities and tribes requires a full understanding of the community's environment and making good use of their own conditions. In particular, this means starting with natural capital, social capital, and human capital, to create a localized characteristic industry with lower capital investment.

III. Community empowerment and industrial development

i. Community empowerment

The concept of assets has often been applied in social development issues. If people in underprivileged communities can be taught how to make good use of their potential assets, they then no longer need to rely too much on external resources. Communities are often embedded with many undetected and not well-utilized resources. Community development workers have the responsibility to highlight these potential community resources and guide people to make good use of them.

Midgley (2010) put forth the belief that community development should have advantages and meanings of empowerment. Therefore, community workers ought to focus on the assets of the community in a positive perspective, rather than what the community lacks, and build community assets by strengthening community capabilities. Li Yijun (2012) opined that community capacity includes two elements: build up competence and skills. However, from the perspective of the possibility and orientation of intervention, skills enhancement is where community workers can put forth effort more in the short term, that is, the need to improve community skills starts from improving the practical ability of community cadres. For example, workshop training, practical guidance and companionship are the most important methods. The improvement of community capability can be regarded as a kind of local social investment. The sustainable development of the community should be based on local residents and focus on local investment. As Midgley (1999, 2010) advocated, development should be people-oriented and recognize local needs.

ii. Industry development

The promotion of the community industry is not only capable of driving the overall development of the community, but can also benefit individual families. Conley (2010) pointed out that typical child protection cases usually emphasize crisis orientation, while adopting coercive measures against the family, or taking children away from the family and the community and placing them in care, but neglecting to provide better alternatives for them. Therefore, many experts in child welfare believe that improvement of only the trivial issues will not help at all. It is necessary to find the source of the problem and emphasize the prevention and strengthening of the family's advantages to be able to truly prescribe the right remedies.

Residents in remote areas (tribes) are often restricted by insufficient local employment opportunities, making it difficult to create a livelihood. When such deficiency becomes a long-term issue, community residents will likely become impoverished people. Families struggle, with no means of livelihood; they may also have to move their families away, or have to let young parents go out to make a living, and entrust the younger children to the older parents to form an intergenerational upbringing, which also places an extra burden on the elderly parents. In this case, it is easy to overlook the normal diet, health and schooling of children. Obviously, the source of the aforementioned situation of children being neglected or even abused is a severe issue of livelihood of the family, but this scenario is often overlooked in reality.

The establishment and development of community industries require many criteria. On the small scale, insufficient resources, products and services need external support, but the community itself does not necessarily have the capability to operate and manage this. In addition to the above, the community industry usually has its localized characteristics or restrictions. However, the operating conditions are more stringent than in ordinary social enterprises. If people rush into it, or copy the methods of others without knowing the position, frustration and financial losses may result.

iii. Sustainable livelihoods approach

The sustainable livelihoods approach (SLA) is often used to construct a livelihood model and development process, so that planners and participants can obtain a deep understanding of the local vulnerability and resilience in livelihood development, so as to further identify the most effective strategy. Since the SLA focuses on the community or a larger area, it will not replace large-scale, cross-regional development plans, nor will it emphasize overall and highly-quantitative economic indicators. The SLA is often used to promote community industries. The SLA's operating model focuses on the participation of local people and encourages local residents as the main body, rather than external helpers.

When planning the community industry and conducting community resource inventory counts, the SLA model revised by Yung-Hsing Kao (2015b) can be applied for evaluation, so as to identify the social capital, human capital, financial capital, natural capital, cultural capital, and physical capital of the community. Based on this, strategic choices are then made, and focus is placed on local investment. Among the resources of the community, natural capital, physical capital, and financial capital are more likely to be restricted by status quo, while human capital and social capital have great development potential. With the support of social investment strategies, localized human and social capitals can be strengthened and leveraged to play a pivotal role in the community industry. In particular, community residents are the focus of development, and economic growth is only a means rather than an ultimate goal.

IV. The strategy of local investment

The most critical feature of developmental social work is the use of "investment strategies" in the process of professional services. Investment may consist of a series of approaches, including the use of human capital and social capital, and promotion of employment, self-employment, and encouragement to accumulate assets. Since developmental social workers are committed to helping clients, communities, and society as a whole to produce positive results, the professional practice field should be incorporated into the concept of social investment as soon as possible. Developmental social work not only emphasizes the advantages of recipients and the importance of empowerment, but also focuses on providing service users with viable social investment to enhance their ability to participate in community life and enjoy economic productivity.

Assisting communities in developing industries with the concept of social investment can be regarded as a kind of local investment. In other words, it is necessary to acquire local materials as much as possible, so as to find the most distinctive elements from the living environment, natural resources, characteristic architectures, historical sites, and traditional culture, with particular emphasis on developing human resources and strengthening the community's social capital.

The community may also need to invest resources in hardware facilities, including the improvement of living environment, roads, and transportation. In addition, communities may be supported by government policies and funding for diversified employment and local creation, but they must also understand that external subsidies have their limitations or are often subject to change. The community should treat such subsidies as a staged resource. It should not be overly dependent, nor should it blindly invest or spend too much of its budget on hardware facilities.

The situation facing the community industry is both a challenge and an opportunity. Given the issues of rapid climate change, such as droughts, heavy rains, and fluctuating heat, prior farming experience has become weak and needs to be adjusted. For example, Taiwan's litchi and longan did not bloom in 2019. In addition to the inability of litchi and longan to bear fruit, the climate change also affected the honey production that year; as a result, fruit farmers and beekeepers suffered considerable losses.

In response to the crisis brought about by the external environment, it is necessary for the community to reposition itself so as to identify the industry, while also pursuing sustainable development. The community industry does not need to be fixed on traditional crops. One can still choose organic farming, eco-tourism, cultural industries, or developing an under-forest economy. Crops should adhere to the principle of being suitable for planting, and the species selected ought to have nutritional value, market potential, and be relatively extensive and easy-to-manage, as much as possible, while it is also important to minimize dependence on pesticides.

V. The application of local investment strategy

The Eden Social Welfare Foundation (ESWF) has long benefited underprivileged ethnic groups and cared for remote communities and tribes. Over the years, it has continued to promote the elephant circle project and extended a number of service programs, such as youth returning to their hometowns, and community mutual assistance. As a cooperative partner of communities and tribes, the ESWF, in addition to providing funding and professional manpower, is more committed to using local investment strategies to assist communities and tribes in developing the community industry, thereby creating more sources of livelihood for communities and families.

i. Dapilas Tribe, Tai'an Township, Miaoli County

The Dapilas Church is committed to nurturing tribal youth, enhancing their understanding and recognition of tribal culture, and promoting tribal industry as well as the surrounding development. The church in Dapilas did not seek resources from the government, and hence the church itself is the main resource system. In other words, the church promotes the tribe's humanity and industry development by linking to the ESWF's mutual assistance and welfare, in addition to other related projects.

The development focus of Dapilas has two goals, namely cultural heritage and industrial development. The cultural heritage includes the cultivation of talents with horns and hooking nets; the cultivation of teachers for mouth springs and bamboo bells; and the making and playing of flute, together with the neighboring primary schools. Lessons involving traditional musical instruments are held continuously, so that adolescents and children can practice on the equipment at the site.

In terms of industry promotion, the church took over the coffee dreams of the elderly tribal couples and planted 500 coffee trees which were ten years old. In order to improve the physique of the coffee trees, via the practice of pesticide-free and organic cultivation, they looked for probiotics in the woods, bamboo forests, and mountain valleys in the proximity of the tribe, and learned how to cultivate them. In order to establish the tribe's coffee characteristics, the tribe actively sought a breakthrough in the processing of coffee beans, trying to adopt honey processing methods. As the honey processing in Taiwan may have the risk of mildew under humid weather conditions, a dryer was purchased to overcome this problem, and each processing stage was recorded one by one for future reference.

By consulting with the staff of the ESWF, the tribe also tried to plant new crops, including Black Sapote (Diospyros digyna Jacq), Inca Inchi (Plukenetia Volubilis Linneo), etc., to assess their development potential. Here we can take the Inca Inchi (Plukenetia Volubilis Linneo), planted by the tribe, as an example. The success rate from seedling cultivation to ground planting has reached 90%. The newly-planted seedlings are expected to become a new opportunity for tribal agriculture in the future.

In 2019, the tribe is committed to connecting tribal youth with the land, enhancing cultural identity and weaving skills. The church pastor leads a team of mutual assistants and mutual beneficiaries which goes deep into the mountains, forests and wild streams, seeking materials needed for weaving and making musical instruments; the team also enters the tree bean garden, coffee garden, and millet garden. The elders who follow the church have experienced the blessing of land. From the process of land preparation, planting, weeding, care, harvesting, coffee and tree peas packaging, all of these have been engaged in by tribal elders, middle-aged people, young people, and children.

ii. Yitun Tribe, Shizi Township, Pingtung County

The Yitun tribe focuses on industrial development while also providing after-school tutoring and attention ministry. In terms of care for the tribal elders, in addition to organizing care bases, vital signs monitoring is provided, including blood pressure, blood glucose, blood oxygen testing, and health promotion activities; resources are also available for sharing meals. During the process of serving and delivering meals, the tribe can notice the changes in the health of the elders and their understanding of medication, while also helping the elders to clean the surrounding environment, so that they can feel more secure. In order to enhance the interaction between children and elders, children are also educated on how to help the elders take their own blood pressure, move tables and chairs, and speak their mother tongue with the elderly.

The Yitun's community industry is particularly good at using local themes. In the production of handicraft woven leather bags, it combines the cultivation of talents with many skills such as weaving, leather processing, and embroidering patterns. A number of products, such as mobile phone sheaths and side backpacks, have been produced, which can be sold through pre-orders and stalls. In addition, there are other locally-produced products, such as Shansu (nest fern), Guoshanxiang (Curved-leaf Wampee), Cassia, and bamboo shoots. These products are derived from local indigenous species, produced by tribal residents, and then developed and marketed to establish tribal characteristic industries. For example, soothing cream and handmade soap are created from the incense of the mountain (Guoshanxiang). The Shansu gift box is based on the marketing appeal of "Shansu with a temperature", and is sold through various channels such as online shops and the cooperative souvenirs service offered by the Hengchun Christian Hospital to create more sources of livelihood for the tribe.

The development of tribes is often affected by subtle interactions between families. For tribes to sustain long-term development, they still need to overcome the barriers between families to establish a mechanism of mutual trust and cooperation. The Yitun tribe actively expands tribal industry and marketing products, implementing a number of attentive ministries with excellent outcomes, while the cohesion and engagement of tribes have been significantly improved. The Yitun's working team believes that the ESWF's long-term companionship, including financial subsidies, especially the linking of resources in product packaging and marketing, as well as the support and encouragement during the hard course of community management, are all critical contributions to the development of the tribe.

iii. Hot Spring Tribe in Taimali Township, Taitung County

The cooperation program between Hot Spring Church and the ESWF is designed to allow young people to work physically in the tribes, to get to know their tribes, and to restore the cultural life of mutual assistance and sharing which was common in the past. It also allows the children to identify their direction and interest by doing and learning. The warm coffee program managed by the church provides young people with opportunities for work-study. The children can truly enter the tribe to care for their elders and understand the tribe's issues from both broad and trivial perspectives. They can also learn the history of the tribe from the tribe's elders, as well as work and study services, and they can establish a more intimate relationship with the tribe.

The students who participate in the internship think that they are very sharp at first, and that working in the tribe should not be difficult for them. However, when they actually engage themselves, they always find that many things are not what they previously thought, such as: coffee-making skills, baking muffins, tempering the ratio of black tea, milk tea and ice cubes, and how to respond to and answer the customer's food catering questions, etc. All of these require training to make customers acknowledge the professional service. In the beginning, the children are inattentive, afraid of being scolded, and frustrated. Later on, however, they are willing to open up, embrace the challenges, be earnest, learn to communicate, express opinions, find solutions, and finally have confidence and be able to enjoy it.

VI. Conclusion and recommendations

When applying the strategy of local investment to assist the community in developing industries, the community must be the domain and take the lead. As a cooperative partner, people must not act too hastily, and must not exceed their duties. To assist the community in developing industries with the concept of social investment, it is necessary to adopt local investment strategies. In other words, it is mandated to use local resources as much as possible, and find the most distinctive elements from the living environment, natural resources, characteristic architecture, historic sites, and traditional culture. People must also focus on the sustainable development of the community and strengthen its human resources and social capital. With regard to the implementation of local investment strategies, the following aims must be achieved:

i. Have an in-depth grasp of local resources. When planning community industries and conducting community resource inventory checks, the revised SLA model can be used for assessment to identify the social capital, human capital, financial capital, natural capital, cultural capital, and physical capital of the community, and then prioritize strategies accordingly, while focusing on implementing local investment.

ii. Select the right investment strategy rather than simply investing blindly. Focus on the accumulation of investment and target long-term benefits. The development progress should be reviewed annually to exam if it has a cumulative effect. Refrain from the activities and programs that are just for one shot. In terms of strategy identification, it is necessary to promote the positive interaction between human capital, social capital, and cultural capital.

iii. In addition to financial support and resource connection, the cooperating unit can also provide know-how, experience exchange, talent training, encouragement and support. It may also require community assistance in marketing the products and improving production facilities.

iv. New types of community industries, whether they are organic agriculture, under-forest economy, or eco-tourism, all may need to rely on experts with related backgrounds, and may also require marketing assistance in product sales, all of which require a cross-disciplinary cooperation team.

References

Chinese

李易駿（2012）。提昇社區能力的輔導：一個短期的行動研究。**台灣社區工作與社區研究學刊**，2（2），第 81-122 頁。

高永興（2017）。社會企業與社會工作。見於王永慈（主編），**家庭經濟安全與社會工作實務手冊**，第 199-223 頁。台北：巨流圖書。

高永興（2015a）。社會企業之制度選擇與價值呈現。南投：**國立暨南國際大學社會政策與社會工作研究所博士論文**。

高永興（2015b）。從社會投資觀點探析社區產業發展。**台灣社區工作與社區研究學刊**，5（2），第 101-140 頁。

English

Alter, Sutia Kim (2006). Social Enterprise Models and Their Mission and Money Relationships. In Alex Nicholls (ed.), *Social Entrepreneurship: New Models of sustainable Social Change* (pp. 205-232). Oxford: Oxford university press.

Cantillon, Bea & Van Lancker, Wim (2013). Three Shortcomings of the Social Investment Perspective. *Social Policy & Society*, 12(4), 553-564.

Conley, A. (2010). Social Development, Social Investment, and Child Welfare. In J. Midgley & A. Conley (eds.), *Social Work and Social development*. New York: Oxford University.

Midgley, James & Sherraden, Michael (2009).The Social Development Perspective in Social Policy. In James Midgley & M. Livermore (eds.), *The Handbook of Social Policy* (pp. 263-278). NY: Sage Publications.

Midgley, J. & Conley, Amy (eds.) (2010). *Social Work and Social development*. New York: Oxford University.

Morel, Nathalie, Palier, Bruno & Palme, Joakim (eds.) (2012). *Towards a Social Investment Welfare State? Ideas, policies and challenges*. Bristol: The Policy Press.

Public-Private Partnerships for the Promotion of Remote Area Regional Innovation: Lishan Long-Term Care Transportation Service[*]

Sheng-Tsun Hou[**]

Abstract

Regions follow different trajectories based on their political, cultural, and economic capacities. In the past, research on regional innovation systems has mostly focused on agglomeration economies, institutional learning, capital, and knowledge flow. In contrast, very few studies have been conducted from the perspective of social value co-creation produced by public-private partnerships. Even fewer have focused on remote areas. To fill in some of these theoretical gaps, the aim of this study is to explore, starting from value co-creation, the establishment of an innovative long-term care system in Heping District of Taichung City, based on transportation services. In this study, the public-private partnership perspective is adopted to investigate how a local university working in collaboration with a local government brought together different stakeholders to implement social value co-creation, successfully transforming an unfriendly environment for transportation services into Taiwan's first remote area, long-term care Uber service. Finally, based on theory elaboration of

[*] Special thanks are owed to former Taichung Deputy Mayor Lin Yi-ying, Le Ge Shi Taxi Company President Yeh Shu-han, and long-term care drivers and social workers providing medical services transportation to the elderly living in Lishan, all of whom were instrumental in the completion of this paper. It is due to their selfless efforts and support of public-private partnerships that the remote area of Lishan has experienced innovation. Much gratitude is also owed to the Ministry of Science & Technology, the Ministry of Education, and Feng Chia University for research funding and administrative support.

[**] Distinguished Professor of the Graduate Institute of Public Affairs and Social Innovation, Feng Chia University.

a case study of remote area innovation in Lishan, in Taichung City's Heping District, principles and practices are proposed.

Keywords: Public-private partnerships, remote area regional innovation, Lishan, long-term care Uber

I. Introduction

Regional innovation systems (RIS) refer to the competitive innovation systems developed by different actors in a region in an effort to establish or change rules to implement resource or knowledge flows and links (Cooke, 1992; Cooke, 2001). In the past, research on RIS has mostly focused on agglomeration economies, institutional learning, flow of talent, and financial capital (e.g. Cooke, 2001). In contrast, relatively few studies have been conducted from the perspective of value co-creation produced by public-private partnerships (PPPs), especially the creation of social value. In addition, there have been numerous empirical studies on RIS in high-tech industries. For example, Cooke (2001) discussed the development of the biotech industry in the Cambridge area of England. However, in recent years, there has been no comprehensive or systematic discussion of RIS in innovation-driven areas, following the rise of creative cities and the creative economy (Hosper, 2003; Cabrita & Cabrita, 2010). To fill in some of these theoretical gaps, this paper includes a case study on the long-term care transportation services in the indigenous Lishan area of Taichung City, Taiwan, with the aim being to explain how a university made appropriate use of PPPs to connect a local government and relevant stakeholders to drive regional area innovation based on new social value, through the implementation of long-term care transportation services.

From the perspective of PPPs (Bryson, Crosby, & Middleton, 2006; Cairns, Harris, & Hutchinson, 2010; Mahoney, McGahan, & Pitelis, 2009; Rangan, Samii, & Wassenhove, 2006; Selsky & Parker, 2005; Swyngedouw, 2005), the aim of this study is to discuss how universities can use PPPs to develop regional innovation, especially unique remote area mobility services. In other words, the main research question is: What are the formation processes, channels, and mechanisms of mobility-driven regional innovation? Moreover, the indigenous Lishan area serves as a case study to carry out qualitative empirical research.

This paper is divided into six sections. Following the Introduction is the second section, the literature review. In this section, we review the literature regarding the theories in two main orienting directions, namely RIS and PPP. Subsequently, the third, or Methods section, is laid out, which explains the research methods and design of the study, as well as data collection tools employed. In the fourth section, Case Study, discussion focuses on how mobility services can be used to build up remote area regional innovation and the channels and mechanisms of PPPs. The fifth section is the Results section, which includes remote area regional innovation theory elaboration on the indigenous Lishan area case study and proposed principles and practices. This paper ends with Section 6, the Conclusion.

II. Literature Review

i. Regional innovation systems and value co-creation

RIS refer to the regional organizational systems constructed by reciprocal division of labor and connections among actors such as enterprises, research institutes, universities, and local governments in a specific geographical location. The purpose of them is to support and promote innovation (Cook, Braczyk, & Heidenreich, 1996). RIS are concerned with how to implement social networking organizations, standards, values, systems, and exchanges, etc., within a certain geographical scope to elevate the overall system's competitiveness (Cooke et al., 1997; Braczyk et al., 1998; Howells, 2005). Cooke (2001) pointed out that, in the broad sense, RIS include suppliers producing innovative products, universities or educational institutions providing innovative talent cultivation, research institutes conducting innovative research and development and knowledge creation, and local governments supporting innovation through financing, policies, regulations, and infrastructure, etc. This differs from how nations use new technologies and new industries to drive economic growth, which is emphasized by the National System of Innovation (NIS) (Freeman, 1995). RIS are focused on the structural design of relationships among different actors and networks in a designated geographical space and proximal areas to promote knowledge flow and mutual learning, with technology and knowledge being the key elements of innovation. Cooke (2001) studied the RIS of the European Union in relation to five aspects: agglomeration economies, institutional learning, associative governance, proximity capital, and interactive innovation. The scholar divided RIS into the following: knowledge application and exploitation sub-system and knowledge generation and diffusion sub-system. The former is mainly driven by businesses, while the latter requires policies and the support of various actors, such as universities, research institutes, and local governments. Therefore, the knowledge, resources, talent flow, and interactions between these two sub-systems enable the establishment of regional social and economic systems and cultural atmosphere, which can lead to the formation of RIS.

In terms of their nature, RIS greatly emphasize the co-creation and evolutionary processes of different types of organizations in regional learning and talent flow. In terms of theory, this corresponds to cross-agency value co-creation in the literature. From observations of organizational type in the value co-creation model of cross-agency interactions and cross-agency collaborations (Austin, 2010), it is clear that this model includes interactions and value co-creation among for-profit organizations; interactions and value co-creation among non-profit organizations and for-profit organizations (Cairns, Harris, & Hutchinson, 2010); interactions and value co-creation among non-profit organizations, for-profit organizations, and government (Bryson, Crosby, & Stone, 2006; Cooper, Bryer, & Meek, 2006); and interactions and value co-creation among clients (Bowman & Ambosini, 2000; Brouthers, Brouthers, & Wilkerson, 1995; Forsstrom, 2005; Lepak, Smith, & Taylor, 2007; Austin & Seitanidi, 2012).

Based on this comprehensive review of the literature on RIS, innovation can be seen as a social process that is cyclical and that involves group learning (Ronde & Hussler, 2005). As such, much of the past research on RIS has been conducted from the viewpoints of learning, systems, and capital to survey the knowledge interactions and relationships among actors. Relatively little research has been carried out from the perspective of value co-creation to think about how to implement PPPs among a system's internal actors. Moreover, universities have rarely been viewed as the focal actor in discussions on the use of public agency capacity and mobility to implement regional innovation structures. Next, PPPs are introduced, as well as how to apply them to RIS.

ii. Public-private partnerships

The purpose of PPPs is to resolve the financial burden problem and the lack of efficiency of government (public agencies). Traditionally, political decision-making and administrative execution have been handled separately and independently. This type of vertical bureaucratic system has the advantage of being divided (Nakumura & Smallwood, 1980). However, from another perspective, an overly-bureaucratic system often leads to poor administrative efficiency and poor communication between agencies. In simple terms, PPPs are based on privatization. On the one hand, they can reduce the financial burden on the government by creating a situation whereby said government does not have to operate various types of agencies. On the other hand, it is hoped that they can elevate the efficiency of policy implementation (Rangan et al., 2006; Mahoney et al., 2009).

From the viewpoint of PPPs, local government creation of RIS that encourage economic vitality and social welfare can be explored. Local governments should consider the design of policy tools such as industrial policies, regulations, and rewards and incentives to enable stakeholders within a region, such as businesses, research institutes, and universities, to develop innovative relationships in which knowledge that is produced is shared and there is flow of resources to promote innovative relationships and innovative results of groups of actors. When RIS are competitive, they balance the possibly conflicting needs of different agencies or stakeholders and local governments are able to properly maintain and administer policies to ensure sustainable development within the region.

In the development of competitive RIS, one of the key issues for local governments in successfully promoting PPPs is whether public agencies, private agencies, and third parties have shared value propositions and concepts (Koschmann et al., 2012; Selsky & Parker, 2005). In general, the formation of shared values is not simply a "top down" authoritative order from local governments. Rather, it is likely to be initiated by the stakeholders in a "bottom up" joint advocacy effort. In reality, if a local government desires to successfully promote RIS, the administrative team must effectively manage PPPs and bring together various stakeholders from different agencies to form a consensus and to standardize value propositions. In other words, before RIS can be promoted, it is necessary to first achieve value co-creation among public and private partners.

iii. Promotion of regional innovation systems based on value co-creating public-private partnerships

After reviewing the literature, it was discovered that, through PPPs, research on RIS could be strengthened. More importantly, in contrast with the "top down approach", in which local governments play the central role in promoting RIS, it is best if there is "bottom up" value co-creation with stakeholders at the center. During this process of regional "bottom up" value co-creation, various stakeholders are motivated by self-interest. At the same time, there is a dramatic decrease in possible negative influences (e.g. external social costs) during the process of economic development. While building up RIS, there is reliance regarding the promotion of the value proposition by the group that is providing leadership (e.g. public agency, government). In addition, acceptance of the value proposition by different stakeholders or social groups is important (Lepak et al., 2007). Moreover, during value co-creation, through complicated multilateral collaborative mechanisms, PPPs provide innovative and appropriate benefits to the residents in a particular region. In a study by Rangan et al. (2006), it was found that the keys to successful PPPs are: (1) resolutions and other external benefits; (2) complementary integration and recombination of resources; and (3) consideration of the benefits of different stakeholders.

Next, in terms of external benefits, PPPs make use of the value co-creation process. In one aspect, they effectively raise the motivation of organizations to work in their own self-interest within a region to promote production factors that efficiently elevate benefits. In another aspect, they reduce the negative effects and arbitrage of market transactions (Lepak et al., 2007). Moreover, private sector resources can effectively be used. Public agency investment and stimulation can activate knowledge flow and cross-disciplinary learning among different actors and collective resources can be well integrated and recombined (March, 1991). Therefore, PPPs value co-creation enables RIS to effectively provide public funding, reducing externalized costs and increasing collective benefits. Finally, value co-creation is a prerequisite for local governments to achieve RIS through PPPs. Especially in remote areas where there is a lack of resources, production factors, and research and development of technologies (e.g. Heping District of Taichung City), there is even more of a need to make use of this type of alternative scenario to effectively link limited resources and stakeholders within a region. This is the formative process, channel, and mechanism from value co-creation to regional innovation, as well as the focus of the present case study.

III. Methods

i. Research methods: action research

From the perspective of a university, this study includes a discussion on how to make use of PPPs, transportation, and mobility to implement RIS structures. No matter if from remote area innovation theoretical development or empirical data, we are in the initial stage and do not yet have much of a theoretical foundation supported by empirical evidence. It is also difficult to understand the actual course and situation from outside to inside. Action research (Stringer,

1996) was the main research method. Records of the author's participation in the Lishan remote area long-term care transportation project were compiled to conduct analyses and provide reflection.

In the field of management, it is generally believed that so-called "academic" research is conducted by "experts and scholars" and that "action" is the responsibility of real-world workers. In terms of research objectives, most have been related to establishing general principles or framework or strengthening/correcting existing theoretical knowledge. Moreover, the results of conventional research have not been able to be directly applied to real-world settings, thus creating an inevitable disparity between theory and practice (Atweh, Kemmis, & Weeks, 1998). In other words, conventional theories are unable to appropriately explain or resolve real problems and phenomena encountered in work settings.

Action research is the combination of "action" and "research" carried out by real-world workers in real-world settings based on the problems that they encounter in order to research and develop channels, methods, and strategies for resolving those problems. Moreover, with practical action, assessment, reflection, feedback, and correction, practical issues are resolved (Denzin & Lincoln, 1998). While action research is focused on practical issues, even more of an emphasis is placed on appraisal, reflection, and thinking to elevate the capacity to act and knowledge of real-life workers and to attempt to establish practice-based theories and theory-based practices to reduce the gap between "practice" and "theory" and the discrepancy between "action" and "research". Action research is well-suited to capturing complicated management phenomena in the real world. At the same time, it is a type of exploratory research that can define unclear constructs (Eisenhardt, 1989; Yin, 1994; Eisenhardt & Graebner, 2007).

In this study, cross-sectional data collection and process analysis were used to investigate the formative process, channels, and mechanisms from "value co-creation" to "regional innovation". During a case survey, due to the collection of new data, there are continuous modifications of the analytical focal point and direction for the next phase of data collection until theoretical saturation

(Eisenhardt, 1989). This is a kind of qualitative research, with "region" as its analytical unit. As the scope of RIS research is broad, stakeholders are numerous, and the level of complexity is high, it is difficult to conduct quantitative tests. In our case study, we used process research methods (Klein & Myers, 1999). Based on the process of a university in the promotion of private-public collaborations, we specifically described regional innovation formation and evolution in the remote area of Lishan to carry out RIS theory elaboration. Our purpose was to explain how to apply PPPs theory to the building of regional innovation, not to validate a relationship.

ii. Data collection

The main source of survey data is a Central Taiwan marginalized group and remote area mobility services support system implemented by the author as part of a university social responsibility project under the authority of the Ministry of Science & Technology (MOST) and the Ministry of Education (MOE). This project began in 2017. More than three years was spent surveying how a university and local government, through PPPs, can integrate various stakeholders and external resources to develop mobility services for mountainous community elderly seeking medical attention in urban areas. This has been a valuable regionally-administered innovation experience. The data collection process is illustrated in the table below:

Table 1: Data Collection Process

Source/Method	No. of interviewees/ participants	No. of times
I. Primary data collection		
i. In-depth interviews		
✓ Interviews with Taichung City local government agencies (including Deputy Mayor, Health Bureau, Social Affairs Bureau, Economic Dev elopement Bureau, Transportation Bureau, and local health station, etc.)	15	8
✓ Interviews with local industries and civic groups (e.g., long-term care organizations, non-profit organizations, churches, transportation operators, and taxi fleets, etc.)	12	7
ii. Participatory observation/Meetings		
✓ Participated in Taichung City Government-organized relevant work meetings		22
✓ Participatory observation of various types of local discussions and gatherings	38	5
iii. Team participation		
✓ Participated in work meetings of different departments and bureaus	48	16
✓ Participated in different stakeholder meetings (e.g., long-term care organizations, private companies, non-profit associations, and churches, etc.) as well as co-creation workshop	52	13
✓ Attended and observed local activities (e.g. cultural health stations, community activities, church cell group meetings)		108
✓ Team internal meetings		53
II. Secondary data collection		
✓ Long-term care and Fu-Kang bus service program data, as well as various health and social welfare-related reports compiled over the years		
✓ Systematic review of relevant research and reports from "The Memory of Taichung" database		

Source: Compiled during the process of research

For this MOST project, we inventoried remote area characteristics and assets, as well as innovative user-friendly technologies. In addition, we explored elderly services design. First, we implemented a large-scale field study on the needs for remote area transportation and of indigenous community residents. At the same time, we visited various Taichung City Government leaders and civic organizations to gain a comprehensive understanding of the complex ecosystem and stakeholders in Taichung's remote areas. In terms of ensuring extensive and representative data, we made every effort to elevate authenticity and reliability. For example, we regularly held discussion meetings with Taichung City Deputy Mayor Lin Yi-ying and various department and bureau heads. Moreover, we conducted interviews and observations at public agencies, private agencies, and third-party agencies on a non-regular basis. We also organized a large-scale workshop during which we invited Taichung City Government leaders and cross-agency representatives to discuss issues related to transportation services for marginalized groups.

Finally, we provide an explanation of the "objectivity" and "subjectivity" of the collected case study data. The case study was part of a large-scale research project. Data collection included objective historical research and subjective case study. In terms of objective data, we collected various types of historical data (both quantitative and qualitative). In terms of subjective data, we conducted in-depth interviews with specific experts (including public and private partners such as government agencies, civic organizations, universities, and non-profit organizations, etc.). In addition, we carried out triangulation and established a chain of evidence. Moreover, we conducted long-term observation and social participation at local venues in Taichung City to understand "the big picture" of remote area RIS. Based on the above-mentioned "objective" and "subjective" historical data and collection of subjective opinions, we implemented theory building exploratory research (Gephart, 2004). This research method, with theory building as the objective, is of importance in the current complex contexts and dynamics, in which it is difficult to make inferences based on a single causal relationship for many social interactions and behaviors.

IV. Case Study

i. Taiwan's remote areas and regional revitalization

1. Declining populations in Taiwan's remote areas

Over the next 20 years, Taiwan's biggest crisis will be its shrinking population. Farming communities which offer few employment opportunities will be hardest hit. Within the next 20 years, rural and remote communities will face a vicious cycle of low birth rates, exodus of people, and declining local industries. Whole communities may even disappear. Based on a research report by the National Development Council (NDC), it is estimated that among the 368 towns and townships in Taiwan, 134, or more than one-third, are in need of urgent intervention. For example, in Zuozhen District of Tainan City, Pingxi District of New Taipei City, Tianliao District of Kaohsiung City, and Jiaxian District of Kaohsiung City, it is expected that populations will decrease by 50% by 2050. For many people this is of great concern, and raises the question of whether their hometowns will continue to exist.

In response, the Executive Yuan designated 2019 the Year of Regional Revitalization. During that year, it promoted regional revitalization policies in an effort to stem the outward flow of people and to balance regional development. It was hoped that, starting from town and township administrative offices and with the assistance of local governments and integration of the opinions of various stakeholders, a consensus could emerge among the private and public sectors for the drafting of comprehensive local development plans. The private sector was invited to provide resources and town and township administrative offices were asked to post proposals on the Executive Yuan's regional revitalization reporting platform. Then, the NDC would implement public agency resource integration and coordinate amendments to the laws and regulations and the investment of funds or provision of resources, while also providing guidance to unearth remote area DNA to find business opportunities, restore local industries, and encourage people to return to their hometowns.

2. Geographical location determines the fate of remote areas

Remote areas are remote due to their geographical location. As they are far from population centers, they are deficient in economic activity. Moreover, since there are no employment opportunities, the youth search for work in other places, leaving the elderly and young children behind. As such, there are no business opportunities. The former minister of the NDC, Chen Mei-Lin, stated that "The core of regional revitalization efforts is people. It is about encouraging people to stay, to hold onto populations. It involves keeping people in their communities and encouraging people from outside to enter those communities".

This brings up a question: How can we encourage people to stay and those from outside to enter? In order to find an answer, it is necessary to look at the difficulties experienced in remote areas. Before revitalizing local industries, it is important to first resolve the barrier to mobility, which is transportation. Only if the issue of mobility has been resolved can we break through other issues. Indeed, the next question then arises: How can we resolve transportation difficulties in remote areas? From the perspective of scientific principles, due to the following three types of failures, the flow of people and goods is obstructed. These failures are market failure, government failure, and service failure.

3. Three major types of failures in remote areas

Below are the definitions of the three major types of failures that explain current difficulties in remote areas.

(1) Market failure: Market failure refers to the inability of private enterprises to efficiently distribute products and services. In a remote setting, the market strength of private organizations cannot satisfy the public welfare demands related to transportation. That is, the market strength is not enough to lead transportation operators into remote areas. The main reason for market failure is that transportation is tied to public funding. As there is a high level of externality, it is difficult to form market mechanisms.

(2) Government failure: Government failure is linked to the government's

efforts to resolve market failure. The government adopts various policy tools and actions to remedy the market failure. However, as public services provided by the government are insufficient and inefficient, the desired objectives are not achieved. Moreover, this leads to government ineffectiveness in promoting policies.

(3) Service failure: This is also referred to as voluntary failure. Voluntary non-government individuals or groups experience various problems in implementing voluntary activities, thus making them unable to operate normally. In one aspect, this is mainly due to the voluntary organization continually carrying out attempts to assist marginalized groups and various sectors of society, providing a certain amount of attention and support. In another aspect, this means that groups in need of help are not effectively receiving it. It may also be that some groups have an excessive amount of help, while other groups do not have enough.

In terms of the division of labor among central government ministries, the main agency tasked with overseeing transportation in remote areas is the Ministry of Transportation & Communications (MOTC). However, mobility services are also under the purview of the Ministry of Health &Welfare (MOHW) and the MOE. That is because access to medical care and education are among the essential rights of a nation's citizens. These both involve transportation services. With regard to the MOTC, its Directorate General of Highways spends much of its annual budget on subsidies for various forms of transportation to remote areas, such as public buses, Xin Fu buses, and Xin Fu taxis. However, due to a lack of understanding when it comes to the transportation needs of residents in remote areas, the government provides excessive resources, which means that many transportation subsidies go to waste. The result is that there are vehicles operating, but with no passengers. Added to this is a lack of flexibility in providing transportation for "the first mile" and "the last mile", thus meaning that residents must find other options for at least part of the way. This is one of the major reasons for government failure.

In terms of the MOHW transportation subsidy policy for those seeking medical attention, the MOHW has, from the long-term care plan 1.0, to today's 2.0 version, provided transportation services for those meeting the eligibility requirements for long-term care, so that they can seek medical attention or undergo physical therapy. The MOHW has adopted the subsidization policy of specific vehicles for particular uses. It has provided remote (indigenous) area long-term care organizations, health and cultural stations, or associations with subsidies for the purchase of vehicles, as well as for driver salaries and operating costs. However, only those individuals meeting long-term care requirements are able to be transported in these vehicles. Therefore, service users are limited. This has led to complaints from residents who do not meet eligibility requirements, as they can "see" these resources but cannot "use" them. In remote areas where there is a serious lack of transportation supply, this creates a situation in which resources are not able to be effectively used or distributed. This is another reason for government failure.

A third aspect is transportation subsidies for children going to and from school in remote areas. The MOE has provided a budget for transportation subsidies aimed at children studying in schools in remote areas. Its subsidization policies differ from those of the MOHW. The MOE provides schools with an annual budget to commission the services of an outside transportation operator or to purchase vehicles and hire drivers. However, school faculty members often have no expertise in the transportation field. Even if they purchase a vehicle, the meager subsidies do not cover operating and management costs. Maintaining a vehicle and supporting a driver require a large sum of money which schools are unable to provide. This is a third reason for government failure.

Transportation in remote areas is part of public transportation policy. Due to the externality of public transportation, it is difficult to use market mechanisms to create stable supply which is sufficient to meet demand. As there are geographical disadvantages, meaning a sparse population spread over a large area, it is difficult to achieve transportation flow on an adequate scale, and enterprises lack incentives to invest in vehicles and drivers. Therefore, the government can only offer subsidies to encourage operators to provide public transportation services in remote areas. Although each trip results in a loss, due to the consideration of "transportation equal rights", the government must provide such services. In addition, as bus routes have fixed stops and times, it is difficult for the transportation needs of residents to be met. This is one of the reasons for transportation industry failure in remote areas.

Although public buses are unable to support local transportation services based on economies of scale, this does not mean that there are no local transportation operators providing services. It is only that they are not operating an enterprise-style transportation service. Local residents serve as drivers to satisfy the needs for transportation in their communities in an informal manner. They drive their own vehicles to transport local residents. These are called unlicensed taxis. (A more accurate description would be unlicensed taxi neighbors.) They operate on their own to support transportation services for local residents and outside tourists. These unlicensed taxi drivers, in addition to serving as guides and providing transportation to tourists, transport community residents to urban areas so that they can seek medical care, while they also assist them in purchasing daily-use items. They become like sons or daughters to the elderly living alone. They may also help them to fill in prescriptions, buy food, send goods, purchase gifts, and bring people to the community. In addition, along the way, they may also help their neighbors to send their produce to urban areas. As drivers and passengers know one another, it is convenient to ask for transportation assistance, and this service is flexible. Residents are happy to pay a little bit more in transportation fees for this assistance. However, such kind of assistance is unregulated and there is no insurance coverage. If there is an accident or dispute, there is no recourse for passengers. This is the main reason for transportation voluntary failure.

Faced with difficulties due to these three failure types, namely government, market, and service failures, a question must be asked: How can mobility issues in remote areas be resolved? In this study, a potential empirical case is provided whereby Feng Chia University collaborated with the Taichung City Government to promote a long-term care transportation services platform.

ii. Transportation challenges for elderly living in Lishan, Taichung

Heping District of Taichung City is the most disadvantaged and remote area of Central Taiwan in terms of geographical location and economic development. Level 1 industries mainly make up the industrial structure. Heping is Taichung City's largest district but possesses the lowest population and lowest population density. It measures 1,037.8192 square kilometers, making it the fourth largest administrative area among Taiwan's townships, towns, county-administered cities, and city-administered districts. There are 4,594 households, with a population of 10,940 (as of May 2019). The Central Cross-Island Highway passes through Heping District, and this was once a main gateway to eastern Taiwan from Taichung. However, since the 921 Earthquake 20 years ago, the section of this highway between Upper Guguan and Deqi, which suffered serious damage, has been open only three times per day (at 07:00, 12:00, and 16:30) to Lishan residents, making life there very inconvenient. For the elderly and the sick, accessing medical services is extremely difficult.

There are four indigenous communities in Lishan (Lishan, Xin Jiayang, Songmao, Huanshan). Taking the Songmao Community as an example, it is an indigenous Atayal community along the border of Taichung City and Yilan County. This is also the home of legendary singer Chang Yu-Sheng. A characteristic of this community is that it is surrounded by thick pine forest. Most of the residents are engaged in agriculture. They grow pears and other economic crops. As planting and harvesting take place along mountain slopes, many farmers have suffered occupational injuries, and have required medical services. However, only the Lishan Health Station is available, which is not a comprehensive medical care facility. If there is a serious injury or illness, it is necessary to seek treatment elsewhere. However, seeing a doctor means a round trip of more than six hours, and a potential cost of approximately NT$6,000 for a private car service. Unlicensed taxis charge NT$600 one way. One seven-person van is often filled with more than 10 elderly people seeking medical care, which is very dangerous.

Of course, residents can choose to take a public bus, which is cheaper. However, there are only three buses per day. Those who miss a bus must wait five or six hours for the next one. Many Lishan residents travel for three days to see a doctor. On the first day, they are transported from the mountains. On the second day, they register at an outpatient clinic to see a doctor (often they visit several outpatient clinics on the same day). Following this, on the third day they are transported home. For remote area elderly, seeking medical attention is a formidable challenge. In addition to the physical fatigue which results from traveling, they also have the expense of staying overnight due to the long period of time needed to see a doctor. No matter if taking a public bus (small number of runs) or a private vehicle (must abide by restrictions) to and from a clinic, transportation is very inconvenient.

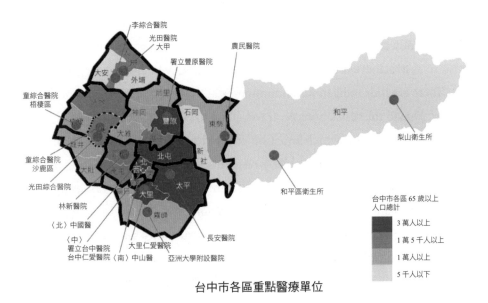

Figure 1: Distribution of medical resources and population density in Taichung City

iii. Remote township long-term care 2.0 transportation service

Based on an announcement by the MOHW, the contents of the 10-Year Long-Term Care Plan 2.0 have been clearly defined. Long-term care refers to the provision of individualized, diverse, and continuous health and social services. These services may be provided by organizations, nursing homes, or communities. Moreover, transportation is the key to the use of various long-term care services, as it enables people to travel between home and the unit(s) providing the services. There have often been complaints that current transportation services are too standardized and inflexible. Moreover, transportation service resources are comparatively lacking in remote areas and subsidies are unable to cover costs. The long-term care 2.0 plan expands the target base. Moreover, services are extended forward to include front-end, preliminary, and preventive services, as well as those with loss of function or dementia. Moreover, emphasis is placed on local elderly, support of families, and home and community-based care. To fulfill the above-mentioned service model, transportation accessibility and convenience are extremely important. To respond to the diversity of public needs, it is necessary to actively promote various innovative services, to strengthen connections to transportation service systems, and to improve resource insufficiencies in remote areas, so as to achieve the goals of local and community integrated care services.

There are four indigenous communities in the mountainous areas of Heping District. Due to the restrictions on travel along the Central Cross-Island Highway and the long distance which must be covered to reach medical care in other parts of Taichung City, many elderly residents have resorted to seeking medical treatment at Camillian Saint Mary's Hospital Luodong and Luodong Bo-ai Hospital in Yilan County, rather than in Taichung City. However, before March 2019, no long-term care plan 2.0 transportation subsidies were provided to the elderly living in Lishan who traveled to Yilan County to seek medical attention or undergo physical therapy. This is because the Health Bureau of the Taichung City Government only subsidized medical care visits within Taichung City. In 2020, due to publicity for the Uber reservation platform for the elderly introduced in this paper, the Health Bureau of the Taichung City Government began providing subsidies to residents of Lishan, so that they could seek medical attention in Yilan County. This reduced the need for elderly residents living in mountainous areas to go to a hospital in Taichung, which could require a drive of more than four hours.

Even if the residents of Lishan were given fare subsidies, this would not be sustainable, as the one-way subsidy is only NT$300, meaning that transportation operators would not make a profit. Based on rational economics, the distance from indigenous communities in Lishan to Camillian Saint Mary's Hospital Luodong in Yilan County is approximately 100 kilometers one way. If this is calculated by taxi meter, the fare is around NT$2,700. Therefore, the Taichung City Government was only subsidizing one-ninth of the private long-term care transportation operator fare, meaning no profit. Therefore, private operators were unwilling to provide transportation services. In Taichung City, there are more than 30 designated long-term care transportation providers, with over 90 long-term care transportation vehicles which provide the public with transportation services. However, no transportation provider was willing to operate at a loss to drive the Central Cross-Island Highway and provide medical care transportation services to indigenous communities in Lishan.

iv. Feng Chia University promotes "mobility as a social service": mobility services support system for marginalized groups and those living in remote areas

1. Center for Service Innovation and Mobility Design (SIMD) of Feng Chia University

Feng Chia University is a comprehensive university, known for its science and technology programs, and is located in Taichung City. The author of this paper heads Feng Chia University's Center for Service Innovation and Mobility Design (SIMD), which is focused on four aspects: service, innovation, mobility, and design. The center blends technology and culture in the integration of cross-disciplinary knowledge of the colleges of business and engineering and science. The author has engaged in research on the taxi sharing economy for over 18 years and has worked with the Taiwan Taxi Co. Ltd. in the transformation of its organizational structure and on taxi industry innovation. With long-term and in-depth research experience, this author has integrated industry-academia collaborative mechanisms, developed theories, and applied for patents based on research results. Taking this a step further, service models have been developed and applied to real situations so as to achieve the goals of commercialization. This center's research experience and results of industry-academia collaborations are shown in Table 2.

Table 2: Research Achievements and Industry-Academia Collaborative Projects of the Center for Service Innovation and Mobility Design

Item No.	Project	Outcomes
1	Successful development of taxi tourism in remote areas	✓ This three-year academic technology transfer project was carried out in partnership with the Yilan County Government and received approval from the Taichung City Government with expected applications to long-term care transportation services in remote areas of Greater Taichung.
2	Diverse taxi plan development for the central government; consultation and advice for the MOTC	✓ For many years, SIMD Director Sheng-tsun Hou has served on taxi industry advisory committees of the MOTC and local governments, suggesting policies and resolutions for the taxi shared economy. Moreover, Commonwealth Magazine launched the independent opinion column entitled "Engaged Academy".
3	Development of seven proprietary mobility service dispatch technologies	✓ Through partnerships with the Industrial Technology Research Institute (ITRI) and civic organizations, taxi dispatch service technologies were developed. Seven patents related to mobile services dispatch have been obtained to date.

Table 2: Research Achievements and Industry-Academia Collaborative Projects of the Center for Service Innovation and Mobility Design (continued)

Item No.	Project	Outcomes
4	Dispatch system for Taitung County taxi companies using satellite allocation. Charter vehicle service to remote areas to facilitate transportation and tourism	✓ In partnership with the Alliance Cultural Foundation, founded by Stanley Yen, taxi tourism in Taitung was promoted. A satellite positioning dispatch platform for Taitung County taxi operators was established by connecting National Science Council research resources, a study of taxi management, and previously developed patented technologies. This platform combines cloud computing technology and service training, making use of an open taxi dispatch system to fulfill the transportation needs of those living in remote areas and of tourists from other areas.
5	Setting up of a cloud platform for ride-sharing services	✓ This center's team possesses over 18 years of taxi industry research and driver community. operations experience. ✓ This is a comprehensive research and development team which has obtained technology patents.
6	Received NT$800,000 grant from the 10th KEEP WALKING project fund	✓ A proposal for the "Taxi Academy of Innovation: Ambassador of Love Dedicated to Remote Areas" aimed to create a cross-fleet training platform and network. Taxi drivers from all over Taiwan joined in this social welfare effort. Providing a taxi service to marginalized groups is a way of promoting the common good.
7	Assisted the Taiwan Taxi Co. Ltd. through its transformation and first IPO	✓ Professor Sheng-tsun Hou, who leads this team, has worked with the Taiwan Taxi Co. since 2003. As a volunteer member of the taxi industry, he helped to organize a company strategy consensus workshop and company leader training camp in 2011. By promoting the "spread the love campaign", he also helped 16,000 Taiwan Taxi Co. Ltd. drivers to become ambassadors of love.

Source: Center for Service Innovation and Mobility Design of Feng Chia University

SIMD has obtained technology patents for mobile dispatch systems and detour route guidance. From 2017 to 2021, this center is responsible for implementing large-scale MOST and MOE projects and university social responsibility practices. The results of its academic research have been applied to the mission of "mobility as a social service" in the remote areas of Lishan. In 2017,

Feng Chia University and the Taichung City Government began collaborating on the promotion of a MOST and MOE "mobility support system for marginalized groups and people living in remote areas". At that time, with the support of Deputy Mayor Lin Yi-ying, Feng Chia University developed an accessible dispatch platform. Public agencies assisted in promoting transportation services to persons with physical disabilities, the elderly, and those living alone in Taichung City. A "people-oriented" approach was designed for this action research to implement innovative service design and integrated mechanisms to provide transportation to marginalized groups, with information based on user, place, and time. In addition to addressing the usage inefficiencies of various types of accessible vehicles, surplus taxis or unlicensed taxis in remote areas have been used for mobility and long-term care services as part of the shared economy.

2. Donkey Move: Mobility as a social service

After spending approximately one year surveying service needs and stakeholders, Feng Chia University and the Health Bureau of the Taichung City Government began formal collaboration in 2018 to develop the Donkey Move long-term care Uber integrated reservation platform. This platform is free for Taichung City's designated long-term care transport operators to use. Following its completion at the end of 2018, it was made available to private long-term care transport operators and car rental companies, also free of charge. However, at a joint meeting of operators, Deputy Mayor Lin Yi-ying, who was in charge of social welfare and health-related policies, asked if any operators would be willing to provide transportation services to remote areas. There was no response.

This unwillingness to provide services to remote areas is reasonable, as to do so would not be profitable, and therefore it is not sustainable. Under the long-term care 2.0 plan of the Taichung City Government's Health Bureau, transportation subsidies are based on trip. Each person can be subsidized for up to eight trips per month. For each trip, the government offers a subsidy of NT$300. Therefore, transportation operators only want to carry out short-distance transportation services within the city center and have declined to offer long-distance transportation services across districts. They have shown no interest in providing transport from Lishan to the Taichung City Center, as just a one-way journey would be 100 kilometers, and only two trips can be completed per day.

To promote the long-term care Uber integrated reservation platform, the researchers visited multiple parties, successfully recruiting three private operators. Three wheelchair-accessible vehicles were purchased to provide the elderly living in remote Lishan with transportation services, so that they can seek medical care. These three operators included the non-profit taxi organization Taiwan Taxi Academy Association, Uber rental car company Le Ge Shi Taxi Company, and Taiwan Christian Good Shepherd Caring Society. The above-mentioned three organizations came together to apply to the Health Bureau of the Taichung City Government as a designated transportation service provider and established a joint dispatch center in the mountainous area of Lishan, working in cooperation with churches in the four indigenous communities. They hired indigenous residents as drivers. With the Feng Chia University-developed Donkey Move long-term care Uber integrated system, joint dispatch services were implemented to provide residents with transportation services, so that they can seek medical attention. It is hoped that innovative technologies can overcome asymmetrical distribution of resources and that through the Internet there can be more ride-sharing opportunities to elevate the service productivity of each trip and make good use of the remaining productivity on return trips. Moreover, consideration was given to other possible service innovations (e.g. reverse logistics, shopping, transportation to and from school, local care, social participation, etc.). This initiated Taiwan's first technology-based dispatch system for promoting long-term care transportation services in remote areas.

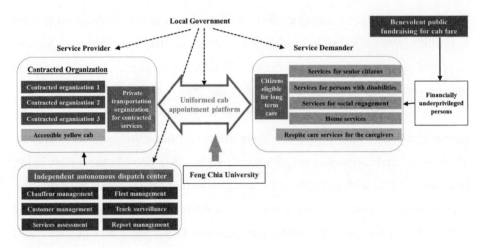

Figure 2: Feng Chia University-developed long-term care Uber: Donkey Move integrated reservation platform

During the process of implementing transportation services in Lishan, we encountered a sustainable operations dilemma. That is, in the long term, finances were insufficient to support transportation demand for marginalized groups in this remote area, especially for economically-disadvantaged residents. As long-term care plan 2.0 subsidies are limited, residents have to pay part of the fare themselves. However, some disadvantaged families are unable to do so. This led to the predicament of having vehicles for long-term care but not being able to put them into service. To bridge the financial gap regarding providing transportation services to economically-disadvantaged residents, the researcher developed corporate social responsibility (CSR) proposals to encourage enterprises to sponsor fares. Feng Chia University successfully raised NT$300,0000 to cover fares in Lishan; the funds were provided by a charity organization that wished to remain anonymous, but which aimed to support residents requiring transportation to seek medical attention. At the same time, 3,481 local Rotary clubs came together to establish the Rotary Circle of Influence Fundraising Platform, through which funds to cover fares were raised. Details regarding the use of these funds are available on the Donkey Move integrated platform. Donors are provided with open and transparent information to encourage long-term support and donations.

V. Results

The Donkey Move remote area long-term care transportation system and services have been in operation for more than one year, with good results. Various stakeholders, including the central government, Taichung City Government, Lishan Health Station, indigenous community churches and cultural health stations, Feng Chia University, Taiwan Taxi Academy, transportation operators, non-profit organizations, long-term care organizations, enterprise foundations, Rotary clubs, and volunteers, have worked together to promote this long-term care transportation reservation platform. Linking up with private fleets which have formally entered Lishan, a remote area long-term care transportation services model has been successfully promoted. As of March 2020, the Donkey Move long-term care Uber transportation services model has expanded to Yilan County, Nantou County, New Taipei City, Taitung County, Hualien County, and Hsinchu County. In 2019, 22,181 trips were completed using this system.

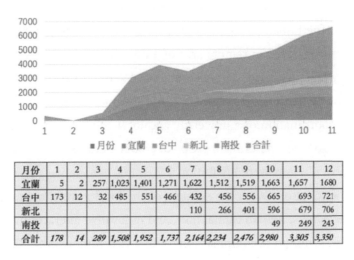

月份	1	2	3	4	5	6	7	8	9	10	11	12
宜蘭	5	2	257	1,023	1,401	1,271	1,622	1,512	1,519	1,663	1,657	1680
台中	173	12	32	485	551	466	432	456	556	665	693	721
新北							110	266	401	596	679	706
南投										49	249	243
合計	178	14	289	1,508	1,952	1,737	2,164	2,234	2,476	2,980	3,305	3,350

Figure 3: Number of trips completed using the Donkey Move integrated reservation platform (2019)

Through the Donkey Move long-term care Uber ride-sharing services, indigenous drivers transport elderly living in the mountains so that they can seek medical care or undergo physical therapy. This provides local residents with long-term care subsidies and job opportunities. The current project is supported by the Department of Humanities and Social Sciences of MOST and MOE. Integrating central government resources, administrative capabilities of local government, research and development capacities of a university, social responsibility of enterprises, volunteer participation of non-profit organizations, and efforts of the Health Bureau and local organizations, an all-new remote area transportation ecosphere has been created. Moreover, the vision of mobility as a social service has been achieved. Below are descriptions of the academic and practical significance of this study.

i. Theoretical contributions

1. Contribution to the literature on regional innovation systems

In the past, RIS studies (Cooke et al., 1997; Granovetter, 1985; Zukin & DiMaggio, 1990; Uzzi, 1996) mostly investigated interactions and learning among actors from the perspectives of resources and systems, and focused on industrial or urban areas. Therefore, there has been a relative lack of studies on RIS in remote areas. The Lishan area of Taichung City, due to its geographical location, has long been considered a remote area of Taiwan that is deficient in resources. This provided an appropriate setting for an in-depth discussion on RIS.

From our experience of regional innovation in the remote Lishan area, through the coordination of a university and local government, the five aspects of regional innovation described by Cooke (2002) were revealed. Among them, the three most obvious were institutional learning, associative governance, and interactive innovation. With the support of the local government driving the PPPs, resource links, human capital flow, and innovative interactions, Feng Chia University was able to accomplish long-advocated remote area RIS based on "mobility as a social service". Relevant services were provided to meet the health and welfare needs of elderly in indigenous communities. It was also possible to implement local innovation and to attract latent resources and stakeholders by incorporating a mobility platform into this remote area's industrial or sightseeing system. This echoes the research conducted by Lepak et al. (2007), in which it was demonstrated that, during the process of value co-creation, it is possible to encourage existing regional social networks and to attract latent regional social networks for broader exchanges and interactions.

Different from previous studies that have focused on technology-driven RIS, the Lishan case emphasized social welfare-based regional innovation and "bottom up" value co-creation. Therefore, the formation of RIS varies due to differences in regional development and settings, as does the connation (Uyarra, 2010). The present case study of the Lishan area of Taichung City emphasizes technology, long-term care, and transportation value propositions. This is better suited to the concepts of shared economy. Based on transportation services for the elderly to seek medical care under the government's long-term care plan 2.0, technology, long-term care, and transportation can be appropriately applied to a remote area's value propositions. In this type of RIS design, from the existing long-term care services, social welfare propositions that emphasize support for marginalized groups can be created. In addition, through the priming of transportation and mobility, a two-way flow of people and goods can be established to attract external funds, talent, and know-how through a non-polluting green industry (tourism). This links latent resources and benefits of stakeholders, attracting even more resources and promoting economic activities, job opportunities, and various derived benefits. These results have been neglected in past research on RIS that has emphasized technology/knowledge-driven developmental channels.

2. Contribution to the literature on public-private partnerships

Research on PPPs (Klein et al., 2013) has mostly attempted to address government and market failures. To achieve legitimacy in the management of public policy issues and policy continuity, it is necessary for public, private, and third-party agencies to coordinate and collaborate. However, this depends on whether PPPs can produce joint value propositions (Koschmann et al., 2012; Selsky & Parker, 2005). In the face of resource deficiencies, it is necessary for different stakeholders to possess similar value systems to promote cross-agency PPPs.

The value co-creation process related to long-term care transportation in the Lishan area of Taichung City provided the opportunity for science-based observation. The results of this case study echoed the views of past theories. Through rewards and other methods, the establishment of knowledge learning and resources integration was encouraged among industry, government, and academia (March, 1991). Although PPPs emphasize co-creation among many agencies, the stability and continuity of the civil service system of public agencies are the key to effective administration and sustainable operations. If there are frequent changes in the administrative team, it is difficult for policy implementation to be stable or continuous, thus leading to difficulties in promoting PPPs. In this case study, following an election, there was a change in administrative team members. The new team stopped promoting this PPP, meaning that the responsibility fell to the university and private partners.

ii. Practical significance

Based on more than three years of empirical research, the importance of PPPs has been revealed. A university can connect with the public power of a local government. Through a bottom up value co-creation process, possible failures of government, markets, and society can be resolved during economic and social development to achieve a dynamic balance of economic growth and sustainable development. The results of this study reveal two points of practical significance.

First, Taichung Deputy Mayor Lin Yi-ying followed the "bottom up" approach to carry out social listening. The purpose was to understand the needs of different stakeholders. At the same time, PPPs (universities, enterprises, civic and social groups), top down and bottom up approaches (vertical implementation and integration of government and public agency policies), reciprocal internal and external factors (external opinion leaders entering decision-making circle, achievement of consensus), and close liaisons (mutual use of scientific research provided by educational and research organizations and government policy implementation) were applied to find the most appropriate innovative and decision-making model for local development. This is not only an important contribution to the research on PPPs, but also an example of regional innovative practices for other city and county governments in Taiwan, as well as for town and township administrations.

In 2010, six cities and counties became municipalities under the jurisdiction of the central government. Many of these local governments had to face development disparities between urban and rural areas, as well as inadequate local funding. Through the public-private collaborative process in Heping District of Taichung City, in the Lishan area, located at an elevation of 2,000 meters, along the Central Cross-Island Highway that has been in disrepair for 20 years, convenient and friendly transportation services for elderly seeking medical care have been provided. Moreover, these services have given rise to high levels of support and satisfaction from local residents. This case is worth studying and should be reflected on by other remote or indigenous areas in terms of how to promote remote area innovation through PPPs.

iii. Limitations of the study and directions for future research

A major limitation of this study was inadequate external validity. From the theoretical perspective, current research on RIS in Asia is insufficient, including a lack of case studies and empirical research. Moreover, under different settings and systems, PPPs possess unique characteristics. Therefore, the scope of application of the results of this study is limited. Hence, the greatest limitation is in terms of theoretical generalization. In addition, as the scope of this research was the Lishan area of Taichung City and action research methods were used, many of the detailed interactions among stakeholders were not discussed or reported. Although three years were spent implementing this survey, during which generalizations regarding the influence of PPPs on regional innovation evolutionary processes and channels could be made, detailed interactions, especially among different stakeholders in the community, were not presented. This is a direction for further study.

VI. Conclusion

The use of social value systems to drive RIS emphasizes value co-creation to link different agencies and stakeholders within the PPPs to achieve economic and social objectives within a regional system. There will be differences in the details of regional systems due to variations in geography, culture, organizations, and environmental conditions. Local governments can bring into play maximum innovative synergy using measures based on local conditions. In this way, suitable administrative directions can be found for economic growth and social development. In this paper, a PPP between a university and local government in the remote area of Lishan was discussed. Due to links with external resources and the integration of different stakeholders, unique remote area long-term care innovative transportation services were developed. The result was a positive cycle that conformed to this region's development value, creating economic growth and social well-being.

The long-term care Uber experience in the Lishan area of Taichung City is a regional innovation story that differs from the stories of high-tech industrial development. Moreover, its ultimate mission is to put into practice the concept of mobility as a social service.

References

Atweh, B., Kemmis, S., & Weeks, P. (1998). *Action Research in Practice—Partnerships for Social Justice in Education*. London: Routledge. Retrieved from http://dx.doi.org/10.4324/9780203268629

Austin, J. E. & Seitanidi, M. M. (2012). Collaborative value creation: A review of partnering between nonprofits and businesses: Part I. Value creation spectrum and collaboration stages. *Nonprofit and Voluntary Sector Quarterly*, 4(6), 929-968.

Bowman, C. & Ambrosini, V. (2000). Value creation versus value capture: towards a coherent definition of value in strategy. *British Journal of Management*, 11(1), 1-15.

Braczyk, H., Cooke, P., & Heinderinch, M. (1998). *Regional innovation systems*. London: University College Press.

Brouthers, K. D., Brouthers, L. E., & Wilkerson, T. (1995). Strategic alliances: Choose your partners. *Long Range Planning*, 28(3), 18-25.

Bryson, J. M., Crosby, L. E., & Middleton, S. M. (2006). The design and implementation of cross-sector collaborations: Propositions from the literature. *Public Administration Review*, 66, 44-55.

Cabrita, M. R. & Cabrita, C. (2010). The Role of Creative Industries in Stimulating Intellectual Capital in Cities and Regions. *Proceedings of the European Conference on Intellectual Capital*, 171-179.

Cairns, B., Harris, M., & Hutchinson, R. (2010). *Collaboration in the voluntary sector: A meta-analysis*. London: Institute for Voluntary Action Research.

Carlsson, B. (2006). Internationalization of innovation systems: A survey of the literature. *Research Policy*, 35(1), 56-67.

Doloreux, D. (2001). What We Should Know about Regional Systems of Innovation. *Technology in Society*, 24(3), 243-263.

Cooke, P. (1992). Regional innovation systems: competitive regulation in the new Europe. *GeoForum*, 23, 365-382.

Cooke, P. (2001). Regional innovation systems, clusters, and the knowledge economy. *Industrial and Corporate Change*, 10(4), 945-974.

Cooke, P., Gomez Uranga, M., & Etxebarria, G. (1997). Regional innovation systems: Institutional and organisational dimensions. *Research policy*, 26(4), 475-491.

Cooper, T. L., Bryer, T. A., & Meek, J. W. (2006). Citizen-centered collaboration public management. *Public Administration Review*, 66, 76-88.

Denzin, N. & Lincoln,Y. (1998). *Strategies of Qualitative Inquiry*. SAGE Publications.

Eisenhardt, K. M. (1989). Building theories from case study research. *Academy of Management Journal*, 14(4), 532-550.

Eisenhardt, K. M. & Graebner, M. E. (2007). Theory building from cases: opportunities and challenges. *Academy of Management Journal*, 50(1), 25-32.

Forsström, B. (2005). *Value co-creation in industrial buyer-seller partnerships-creating and exploiting interdependencies: an empirical case study*. Åbo: Åbo Akademi University Press.

Freeman, C. (1995). The national system of innovation in historical perspective. *Cambridge Journal of Economics*, 19, 5-24.

Hospers, G. J. (2003). Creative cities in Europe: urban competitiveness in the knowledge economy. *Inter-economics: Review of European Economic Policy*, 38(5), 260-269.

Klein, P., Mahoney, J., McGahan, A., & Pitelis, C. (2013). Capabilities and Strategic Entrepreneurship in Public Organizations. *Strategic Entrepreneurship Journal*, 7, 70-91.

Klein, H. K. & Myers, M. D. (1999). A Set of Principles for Conducting and Evaluating Interpretative Field Studies in Information Systems. *MIS Quarterly*, 23(1), 67-94.

Koschmann, M. A., Kuhn, T. R., & Pfarrer, M. D. (2012). A communicative framework of value in cross-sector partnerships. *Academy of Management Review*, 37(3), 332-354.

Lepak, D. P., Smith, K. G., & Taylor, M. S. (2007). Value creation and value capture: a multilevel perspective. *Academy of management review*, 32(1), 180-194.

March, J. G. (1991). Exploration and exploitation in organizational learning. *Organization science*, 2(1), 71-87.

Mahoney, J. T., McGahan, A. M., & Pitelis, C. N. (2009). Perspective-The interdependence of private and public interests. *Organization Science*, 20(6), 1034-1052.

Nakamura, R. & Smallwood, F. (1980). *The politics of policy implementation*. New York: St. Martin's Press.

Rangan, S., Samii, R., & Van Wassenhove, L. N. (2006). Constructive partnerships: when alliances between private firms and public actors can enable creative strategies. *Academy of Management Review*, 31(3), 738-751.

Ronde, P. & Hussler, C. (2005). Innovation in regions: what does really matter? *Research Policy*, 34(8), 1150-1172.

Selsky, J. & Parker, B. (2005). Cross-sector partnerships to address social issues: Challenges to theory and practice. *Journal of Management*, 31(6), 849-873.

Stringer, E. T. (1996). *Action research: A handbook for practitioners*. CA: Sage.

Swyngedouw, E. (2005). Governance innovation and the citizen: the Janus face of governance-beyond-the-state. *Urban studies*, 42(11), 1991-2006.

Yin, R. K. (1994). *Case Study Research: Design and Methods*, 2nd ed. Thousand Oaks, CA: Sage Publications.

Q&A

Q1: During your talk it was mentioned that there was a large space for expansion of the matchmaking platform. For example, this platform can be used to match guests and guesthouses or to market agricultural products. Has this platform been expanded?

A1: Our platform has continued to expand in many areas, such as logistics, reverse logistics system, tourism, and long-term care. As people and goods both need to move, "transportation" is essential to daily life. Therefore, we started to use transportation to connect points, routes, and interfaces to form a smart logistics network (AIoT).

Q2: What is the capital of Donkey Move? How many people does it employ?

A2: We are a start-up that was established a year ago. Our capital is only NT$3.5 million. As we are a university research center, one-third of funding is from research grants. Another one-third is from the long-term care 2.0 program of the Ministry of Health and Welfare. The remaining one-third is from existing capital. Through public-private partnerships we have been able to promote this. Team members are from the university and taxi associations. There are now 20 colleagues. One-third of them are drivers, and one-third of them are engineers.

Q3: Has consideration been given to cultivating Donkey Move clients/service users to enable them to become service providers?

A3: Social enterprises do not only serve persons with physical disabilities. By hiring them, we empower and cultivate them, and enable them to become service providers. For example, in Lishan we hired four local residents, including one who is visually impaired, to serve people in the communities.

Social Design of the Community Life Care Model for the Elderly: The Action Process of the Homie Puli Long-Term Care Innovation Network

Kai-Lin Liang[*]

Abstract

The name "Homie Puli" is based on a transliteration of the Taiwanese (Hokkien) term for "taking care of one another". It is the result of collaboration among National Chi Nan University, the Puli Christian Hospital, and the Quixotic Implement Foundation. Through "social design" and "social economy" theories and channels, long-term care innovative classes, cafes as intermediary organizations, and a self-supporting care system that brings together local social enterprises were established. In the Shuishalian area, which refers to Greater Puli, the Puli Christian Hospital and the Quixotic Implement Foundation's medical care and long-term care systems were applied to the joint construction of a "rural community life care model" for the elderly. This model is based on "manpower for needed services". By connecting community social enterprises, financial resources are obtained for this daily living care system. Moreover, through education and promotion, area residents learn about concepts of an elderly-friendly society. The Homie Puli daily life care system is focused on the needs of elderly care in communities. Based on developmental social work practices, diverse local resources are connected to jointly develop services related to this care system, so as to in turn create a Taiwanese model of community life care. Moreover, information and data regarding these experiences have been compiled and analyzed to provide a valuable reference for government and practitioners.

[*] Assistant Professor of Department of Social Policy and Social Work, National Chi Nan University.

Following the 921 Earthquake in 1999, the major non-profit organizations (NPOs) in Puli providing care services to the elderly were the Puli Christian Hospital, the Quixotic Implement Foundation, the Old Five Old Foundation, the Nantou County Evergreen Association (Bodhi Evergreen Village), and the Life Reconstruction Association of Nantou County. These are local organizations involved in aging and social welfare issues. We also observed various needs related to aging. In 2016, President Tsai Ing-Wen took office and put forth long-term care 2.0 policies and programs. The Puli Christian Hospital, the Quixotic Implement Foundation, and the Old Five Old Foundation were among the first pilot sites. As such, they were given priority in providing long-term care services to local elderly. From 2017 to 2019, they worked with communities on long-term care strategies and services, including the creation of long-term care stations, medical care stations, in-community dementia care stations, and care cafes.

In Nantou County, the population is aging and people are having few children. The above-mentioned professional organizations became aware of the inadequacies of various services. Since 2017, National Chi Nan University (NCNU), located in Puli Town, Nantou County, has focused on long-term care issues. The author has assisted in, or been responsible for, creating connections and promoting resolutions for relevant issues. First, in cooperation with local professional service organizations and community organizations, the needs for long-term care were inventoried and understood. Based on social innovation concepts, such as "social design" and "social economy", an action team was formed from among local groups and organizations to jointly design action plans. The expectation was to build a Shuishalian area (i.e. Greater Puli) sustainable self-supporting elderly care network administrative model. The action team made use of the developmental social work model to inventory long-term care needs, connect local resources, develop local services, and establish three major service models: long-term care innovative classes, long-term care cafes, and social enterprises.

I. Innovative Thinking About Long-Term Care Based on an Inventory of Local Needs

Following the 921 Earthquake of 1999, many NPOs in the Puli area focused on local issues. They commonly applied community building concepts to encourage local identity and consciousness. This led to the formation of dynamic community organizations. Based on the results of a survey of the development directions of Puli area social organizations, they can be divided into the following categories: industry development, ecology and culture, and social welfare. Many communities have also included social welfare aspects in their development strategies (e.g. Wushijia, Zhuzaishan, Lancheng, and Nancun, etc.), such as domestic violence prevention, protection of children and youth, and community care sites. However, there has been hesitation in the establishment of community long-term care stations.

As communities have been concerned about the promotion of long-term care stations, NCNU has begun working with local professional long-term care services organizations the Puli Christian Hospital and the Quixotic Implement Foundation to understand the need for elderly care in communities. During this process (from February to December 2017), they organized four long-term care workshops, 10 regular long-term care meetings, five long-term care salon discussions, and seven co-learning classes. It was expected that these activities would provide an understanding of local communities, residents, and professional service organizations, as well as the difficulties and deficiencies faced during the promotion of long-term care or elderly care services. Combining the above-mentioned activities with a survey of needs and difficulties, the following results were obtained:

i. Due to the rolling style of amendments to long-term care policies, communities and professional organizations are often at a loss as to what to do.

ii. The public and communities do not have sufficient knowledge to implement long-term care and elderly care.

iii. There is a lack of cultivation and joint learning mechanisms for middle-aged and elderly community volunteers, meaning that volunteers cannot be sustainably retained.

iv. Promoting long-term care knowledge is not part of the long-term care 2.0 plan. It is necessary to have sustainable and autonomous financial resources to build community education and promotion models.

v. Being elderly is a lifestyle. Elderly are not simply the subjects of care in a long-term care system. Action plans, not just a model for receiving care, are needed to develop elderly and youth co-learning and co-creation mechanisms.

In addition, the author and professional service organizations partook in further dialogue regarding the promotion of these plans and discovered that, over the past more than 10 years, these professional organizations were unable to satisfy the needs of elderly care through testing or promotion of innovative models due to the restrictions of government programs and subsidies. This led to a reduction in the contributions of professional NPOs in terms of the professional services they could provide. To resolve the above-mentioned difficulties, NCNU, professional service organizations, and local communities, through workshops and co-learning courses, attempted to search for and jointly design action plans suited to local needs and capacities. Through repeated dialogue with local social networks, a "social economy"-based operating model was ultimately developed to promote an innovate long-term care experimental model.

II. From "Empowering the Elderly" to "Homie Puli": Action Design that Expands Local Capacity

In this wave of long-term care action, NCNU quickly achieved consensus among local social groups on directions for promotion. The key factor was the expansion of the experience of the Bodhi Evergreen Village. Following the 921

Earthquake, NCNU and the Nantou County Evergreen Association jointly carried out experimental operation of the Bodhi Evergreen Village. To date, 19 years of operating experience have been accumulated. During this process, the Bodhi Evergreen Village was transformed from a temporary living space for the elderly following the earthquake into a sustainable elderly cooperative community. "Empowering the elderly" refers to the core value of elderly within a community caring for one another. This model is used to reduce the cost of in-community care. Moreover, based on the value concept of "just enough", community industries form the core of a social economy operating model independent of government subsidies. Due to this experimental foundation developed by NCNU and the Nantou County Evergreen Association, when NCNU and local social groups inventoried the needs and difficulties in providing care to local elderly, the operating experience of the Bodhi Evergreen Village was the basis for response.

NCNU, the Puli Christian Hospital, and the Quixotic Implement Foundation quickly developed action plans to build a foundation for the promotion of a long-term care innovative framework for the Shuishalian area. Once values and directions of local action plans were confirmed, expanding them became the focus of the action team. Here a question emerges: How can mutual care concepts be planted in the hearts and minds of residents of this area to encourage a willingness to learn self-care and build capacity to care for others? Moreover, cultivating the capacity of community organizations to promote care for the elderly was an important consideration for this action team.

Faced with a social structure in which there is rapid growth of the aged population, deepening the understanding of self-care concepts and long-term care knowledge and raising awareness of elderly-friendly environments among the public and industries became important targets for the action team in the effective promotion of government long-term care policies. Transforming medical jargon into information and messages that are accessible in ways that are acceptable to the public is one of the major challenges when it comes to promoting an elderly-friendly environment. To overcome this challenge, the author of the present work connected with local youth in Puli to incorporate design into long-term care. Young designers remaining in their communities took action to impart "mutual care" concepts. Through branding they created "Homie Puli" (which is based on a transliteration of the term for mutual care in the Taiwanese or Hokkien dialect), as well as the Hou Xiong (bear) and Xiao Gou (dog) mascots. Moreover, they set the tone for the Shuishalian area long-term care social economy framework, which is based on the objectives and values of mutual care.

In the past, long-term care was considered part of the health administration and social administration fields. In addition to the science and technology fields involved in research and development, no consideration was given to the idea of collaborating with various industries that are closely tied to people's everyday lives in the long-term care industry so as to jointly create an elderly-friendly environment. During this action process, the author of the current work, through design efforts, conveyed the values of the Shuishalian long-term care social economy framework, transforming them into brand concepts that are highly accessible to area residents and industries. This served as a foundation for subsequent educational programs and interdisciplinary collaborations.

Figure1: Homie Puli logo

III. Social Economy Framework Practices and Actions: Mutual Care and Homie Puli

The core concepts of the social economy model are "localized", "small scale", "idiographic", and "diverse". The main strategy is to fulfill social objectives through economic means by integrating industry development within an area. During the process of building this model, it is necessary to take a full inventory of local needs and resources. Through joint participation of local organizations, it is possible to develop a resource network for resolving local problems. This is related to developmental social work.

As mentioned above, the action team made use of developmental social work methods. While implementing actions, methods were developed to respond to local needs and issues. Such methods included innovative long-term care classes, long-term care cafes, and a social enterprise model (Figure 2). In terms of innovative long-term care classes, the action team reworked past curricula on health promotion for the elderly and active aging and learning, expanding them to create classes suited to ages 0 to 99. The action team also discovered that many traditional community courses emphasized crafts making, which could not meet dementia prevention needs. Therefore, based on the professional care knowledge of the Puli Christian Hospital and the Quixotic Implement Foundation, the action team created course modules in four areas: mental stimulation, speech, physical movement, and interpersonal relationships. Taking into consideration the needs for elderly care and prevention of loss of function, through course modules, seed teachers were cultivated. These seed teachers became important elderly care educators in their communities. Focusing on middle-aged and elderly groups, the action team designed salon discussion courses. Every month, an educator from a geriatric-related field is invited to guide informal discussions to provide residents with knowledge and a channel for learning how to care for themselves, while also encouraging them to think about how they live their lives. In addition, the action team believes that the aging society is a phenomenon of the future. Therefore, it is necessary to provide the next generation with knowledge related to elderly issues. The action team developed relevant themed picture books for children and parents to read together. At the same time, they found 12 picture books on the market regarding themes related to the elderly and worked with university students to use these books to design lesson plans and teaching materials for elementary schools and preschools.

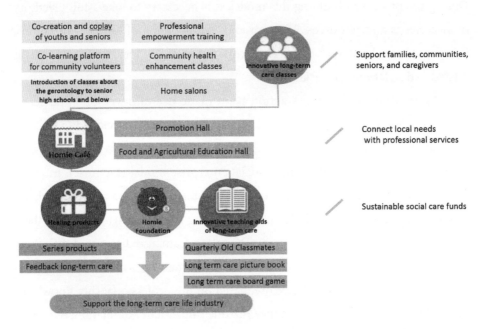

Figure2: Homie Puli care system services

Due to Taiwan's past welfare-based community policies, the main providers of community-based care services have been organizations with a desire to serve. Moreover, relevant policy implementation has mainly been carried out in a top down manner, creating gaps between communities and welfare services. The action team set up care-focused cafes as intermediary organizations to match community needs with professional service organizations. In this way, professional services became demands-oriented, resulting in the building of a resource network. Care cafes provide a welfare services support platform for communities to reduce the gap between needs and professional services.

Finally, the above actions are not government long-term care policy items. Therefore, to enable these services to be sustainable, the action team put in place social economy core concepts, linking local organizations to create a social economy network. The Homie Puli charity brand was set up to develop a social enterprise operating model to obtain financial resources needed for the local care system.

It was necessary for the action team to link up with local service organizations to develop service networks focused on different needs. During the process of action implementation, the participation of local people "traveling the same path" was required. In 2018, Hitoshi Kinoshita's book on regional revitalization was published, which focused on tourism, specialty industries, and branding. He mentioned that "regional revitalization" requires understanding then action. Those who take action become involved in "running a business" or "operating partnerships". The author of this paper discovered that, during the action process, many local young entrepreneurs were facing the problem of care for elderly members of their families and searching for other youth who shared their concerns to collaborate. The aforementioned became this author's first connecting strategy. The next issue was how to satisfy local needs while initiating local industry's willingness to participate. By implementing these two strategies, the action team established a social economy network based on self-health issues of concern for residents and transportation needs of local elderly, as well as issues of concern for the local tourism industry. It also developed products and services based on the Homie Puli brand.

Figure3: Space for parents and children to read long-term care picture books together in a local guesthouse

IV. Starting Operations of a Social Economy System: Setting Standards for Product and Service Development and Operations

To satisfy social objectives through economic means, there must be quality products and services. Setting up operating standards for economic means to satisfy social objectives is an important part of the social economy framework. Homie Puli was established for the purpose of resolving elderly care issues at the local level. In the initial stage, there were actors (e.g. Alley Culturaltainment, 545 Bike, and Feeling 18, etc.) who identified with the above-mentioned objectives, values, and premises. The same was true for subsequent actors (e.g. Papercraft Village, Kids Taomi, and Start Farm, etc.). Therefore, "value identification" concepts became the first and foremost condition for selection of participants in this network. Once the participants had been decided, the Homie Puli framework was used to develop healing products based on the characteristics of participating businesses. Moreover, the participants worked together to establish "operating standards" for this system.

i. Co-creation of healing products across industries and age groups

Making use of social economy value concepts to develop resolutions to local elderly care issues became the priority of the action team. The following local needs and issues were the first to be focused on in the development of the Homie Puli network: lack of knowledge of long-term care among the public; lack of capacity for in-community elderly self-care; transportation issues for elderly in the community; and lack of elderly-friendly environment. Under the Homie Puli network, the following healing products were developed:

1. Grandpa's Memory Treasure Box: Diverse long-term care teaching materials

To deepen the understanding of concepts related to long-term care and self-care among the public, NCNU, the Puli Christian Hospital, and the Quixotic Implement Foundation organize regular lectures at Homie Cafe. In addition, through NCNU courses, long-term care knowledge has been used to create picture books and board games. Moreover, local young designers were invited to assist in creating commercial picture books (Figure 4) and magazines (Figure 5) with Hou Xiong and Xiao Gou as the main characters. The action team expects that through diverse and accessible teaching materials, content can be created for ages 0 to 99, which can serve as an alternative to the traditional classroom lecture and sharing format. In addition, local tourism and long-term care resources served as source materials in the designing of a set of long-term care teaching materials that incorporate local elements and professional knowledge. Long-term care was also combined with local tourism resources to develop experiential learning tours—one of the products of the Homie Puli social economy system. In 2018, NCNU and the Quixotic Implement Foundation began formally providing programs to elementary school students. Picture books are combined with experiential visits to long-term care facilities to develop "social science elderly learning programs". An NCNU student club and the Quixotic Implement Foundation formed a teaching team to provide "elderly-friendly" education.

Figure4: Content pages of a long-term care picture book

Figure5: Old Classmates Quarterly

2. Homie Cafes: Integrated local industry community care and information centers

The key to resolving the lack of long-term care knowledge among the public and lack of capacity in communities for in-community elderly self-care is for professional service organizations to effectively assist residents and community organizations in building relevant knowledge and capacity. Homie Cafe is a community care information center jointly established by NCNU, the Puli Christian Hospital, and the Quixotic Implement Foundation. Differing from general care cafes, which provide long-term care information and referral services, Homie Cafe brings the health administration services of the Puli Christian Hospital and the social administrative services of the Quixotic Implement Foundation into the community to transform the passive model of needing to visit a professional venue to obtain services into one based on "community building". Local volunteers are encouraged to get involved. Through the opening of courses and community building, long-term care services and self-care concepts reach community residents. Next, the public and communities build self-care capacity and an understanding of long-term care professional services.

Based on the need for a deeper understanding of elderly care and self-care concepts in communities and by the public, one Homie Cafe is not enough. This has led to the launching of Homie Cafe No. 2 and Homie Cafe No. 3. Different from Homie Cafe No. 1, which was jointly established by the Quixotic Implement Foundation, the Puli Christian Hospital, and NCNU to operate on a "community building" public welfare model, existing advantages of local businesses were used to develop operating strategies for Homie Cafe No. 2 and Homie Cafe No. 3. Homie Cafe No. 2 is the combination of Homie Cafe and Bo Mi B&B. Its main operating strategy is long-term care education based on picture books and food and agricultural education related to the Mediterranean diet2. Homie Cafe No. 3 is the combination of Homie Cafe and Papercraft Village; it seeks to promote "local paper art"3 experiences and learning. Its major operating strategy is the development of "elderly-friendly experiential and learning tours". Although

Homie Cafe No. 2 and Homie Cafe No. 3 have been combined with industry characteristics to develop different elderly-friendly promotional models, at their core they preserve their role as "community-based care information centers".

To develop community organizations with care capacity, Homie cafes play the important role of intermediary. In terms of community-based elderly care in Taiwan, community organizations most often face difficulties in arranging suitable classes, finding lecturers, and encouraging volunteer manpower. To assist communities in resolving these issues, the action team added the function of "community support center" to the cafes. They provide course modules to assist communities in arranging long-term care classes, train long-term care teachers, and manage a teachers' database. Moreover, the cafes have set up a volunteer cultivation platform. Virtual currency is used to calculate volunteer service hours. Through virtual currency, volunteer services, courses, and products can be exchanged to activate mutual support of local manpower to provide needed services.

Each of the three cafes has different developmental characteristics. However, their core operations involve providing community-based care information and developing products and services to "promote an elderly-friendly society". Homie Cafe No. 1 is mainly operated by a team from the Quixotic Implement Foundation. The other two cafes are commercial operations. Therefore, Homie Cafe No. 1 is focused on health promotion and education. Moreover, the operating costs of Homie Cafe No. 1 are covered by the profits of Homie Cafe No. 2 and Homie Cafe No. 3. The professional care services needed by Homie Cafe No. 2 and Homie Cafe No. 3 are provided by Homie Cafe No. 1 and the Puli Christian Hospital. In this way, each of the three cafes has its own mission and characteristics. However, they provide mutual support to form a Homie Cafe social economy network.

3. Long-term care guides: Satisfying the needs of local elderly for companionship and support

In rural or remote areas, elderly do not have access to public transportation when they need to buy things or seek medical treatment. They must spend a large amount of money on taxi services or a family member must take time off work to drive them. This is a typical problem among the elderly in Puli. In response, NCNU, the Quixotic Implement Foundation, and 545 Bike, a business run by local youth, joined forces, making use of electric tricycles provided by the 18oC Cultural Foundation to offer companionship and transportation support to elderly. The action team has also partnered with a guide association in Nantou County to train association members and NCNU students as long-term care guides. These guides learn emergency first aid, elderly long-term care and communication skills, as well as local specialty industry knowledge. They possess basic service competencies to enable them to provide transportation services to the elderly. The action team took this a step further, making use of these guides and electric tricycles for long-term care experiential tours.

Figure6: Long-term care guides provide companionship and support services

4. Long-term care experiential trips

An elderly-friendly living environment is the key to enabling the elderly to stay in their communities. Indeed, the action team's priorities include how to create an elderly-friendly living environment, encourage communities and businesses to improve spaces, and create atypical employment opportunities for the middle-aged and elderly to bring benefits to communities and businesses. From the results of the needs survey, it is clear that the action team understood that there was great interest among local communities in developing in-depth cultural tours. It was hoped that industry development could provide needed financial resources for communities, so that those communities could offer welfare services. Puli is rich in tourism resources. By combining local community specialty industries, tourism resources, and long-term care resources, "long-term care experiential tours" were developed with "the elderly" as the theme. At the same time, to respond to the senior citizens travel market and long stay accommodation models, the action team brought together local tourism operators and communities.

The action team and local youth jointly planned and designed "Homie tours" based on experiential learning in elderly-friendly environments. The "Grandpa's Memory Treasure Box" picture book served as the starting point for these tours. Tour participants learn about local industries and long-term care resources. Subsequently, Homie Cafe-linked tour itineraries enable in-depth explorations of Puli and the acquisition of elderly-friendly knowledge. Based on the "experiential learning travel" model, linking with local accommodation providers has led to the development of products and services that merge local resources.

Figure7: Homie tour group photo

ii. Social economic system operating standards based on a consensus of action participants

The objective for the development of diverse products and services in the "Homie Puli" system is to enable the economic means to satisfy the social objectives of caring for the elderly in the Shuishallian area. Moreover, transforming economic means into methods for achieving social objectives has tested the confidence and wisdom of the action team and participants in the social economy network. To build a model for social economy network operation, NCNU and the Quixotic Implement Foundation began initiating dialogues with actors in the network. The expectation was a consensus for sustainable development of this system in agreement with the values of each of the actors through equal participation and dialogue. During the more than two-month long process that led to a consensus, operating standards were formulated that are supported by current actors. The six articles and 22 terms related to operating standards include Homie trademark licensing standards, Homie trademark licensing review mechanism, Homie trademark non-profit use standards, Homie trademark for-profit use standards, Homie trademark fund operating methods,

Homie fund collection methods, and Homie fund application and usage methods. Moreover, these standards have been agreed upon and supported by all actors in the network. During discussions, every participant was treated equally, with the right to express opinions and participate in decision-making.

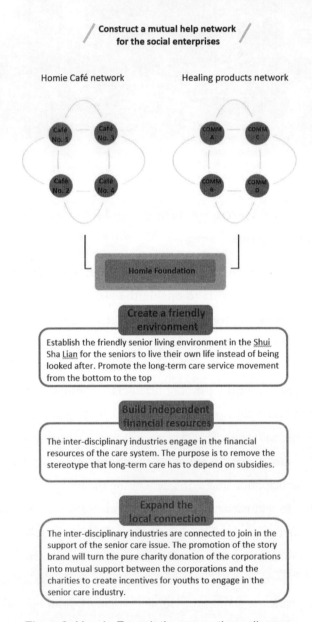

Figure8: Homie Foundation operations diagram

V. Conclusion: A Road Not Yet Complete

Breaking away from capitalist market-based economic thinking to develop an elderly-friendly social economy model is something that NCNU, the Quixotic Implement Foundation, the Puli Christian Hospital and other local groups have pondered. Only in this way can "commercialization" in the name of meeting the needs of elderly in daily life be avoided. If services are calculated in terms of monetary value, this leads to unequal distribution of resources for the elderly living in rural and remote areas. Under this situation, can the elderly enjoy a good quality of life? NCNU and local groups worked together to understand local needs. They inventoried local advantages, resources, and specialty industries. They then connected and crossed industries. Through social design methods, they developed a social economy network operating model to resolve the problems faced by local elderly. Going a step further, by enabling cross-industry understanding of roles in the aging society, they created a consensus on elderly care among different industries to encourage joint development.

It was expected that, through the process of building an innovative social economy system, an ideal environment can be created for the elderly in the aging society. Moreover, it is hoped that the idea of "social welfare", meaning reliance on government funding, can be overturned. From the concepts of "social investment", "elderly" and "care" can drive local industry development and profits. In the future, we expect to implement "community currency – Homie currency" in the Shuishalian area. Through this community currency, the economic benefits driven by the products and services developed under the "Homie" social economy system can remain within the Shuishalian area. In this way, the aforementioned social economy system can truly initiate change at the local level.

Q&A

Q : What is the funding source for Homie Puli?

A : Due to the various business types, there are different funding sources. Business expenses are paid for by funding received from the Quixotic Implement Foundation under the Spread Conscience awards program. In terms of personnel expenses, staff are hired by the Quixotic Implement Foundation. Funding for promotion in schools is sourced from National Chi Nan University's USR project.

Although the programs are currently university-led, it is not possible to support them for long. This organization must become self-supporting. Therefore, we are working toward cultivating organizational talent, so that, in the future, Quixotic Implement Foundation employees can implement projects on their own.

"Running out of Money" and "Moving Forward"?! Employment Challenges and Empowerment of Financially-Disadvantaged Households

Chi-Wen Lin[*], Pei-Chung Wang[**], Yi-Hsuan Lin[***]

Abstract

At present, poverty alleviation programs in Taiwan are mostly focused on passive savings programs, and seldom touch on assisting the economically-disadvantaged population or providing relevant employment service programs from the perspective of developmental social work.

For a long time, the "Enwang Human Resources Service Center" from the Eden Social Welfare Foundation (ESWF) has been implementing the "economically disadvantaged households returning to the labor market" project. It has been found that service subjects are prone to being trapped in the "poverty cycle" between parents and their offspring, due to their prior development experience. In 2016, Enwang tried to introduce the developmental concept of "social investment" into the service system. Through a series of training courses, the sustainable adaptation among service subjects was significantly improved and a support system was established.

This study focuses on interviews with three service subjects who have participated in a series of training courses, supplemented by other service record documents, and explores the possible impact of the establishment of "social

---

[*] Senior Specialist of Office of Director, Taipei District, Eden Social Welfare Foundation.

[**] Director of EnWang Human Resource Service Center of Persons with Disabilities, Eden Social Welfare Foundation.

[***] Section Supervisor of EnWang Human Resource Service Center of Persons with Disabilities, Eden Social Welfare Foundation.

investment" and "social capital" on service subjects. The objective is to understand the transformation and development of the client during said period.

The study found that after taking a series of courses and receiving the companionship of the employment specialists, the clients gradually developed their own social capital: regaining self-confidence, improving interpersonal skills, and increasing economic income.

Keywords: poverty, developmental social work, employment, social capital

I. Research Background

"...There is a "culture of the poor", which produces a unique social and psychological impact on its member...".   (Congqi, 2013, p. 48)

The issue of poverty has been discussed for a long time, and governments in both eastern and western countries regard it as an important governance issue. In the 21st century, the issue of poverty has not been eliminated, with the development of the material economy, while the economic vulnerability caused by poverty has also brought about many social issues.

Since 2014, the EnWang Human Resource Service Center from the ESWF (hereinafter referred to as Enwang) has been undertaking the "Return to the Labor Market for the Disadvantaged Citizens" project created by the Department of Social Welfare of the Taipei City Government. In that time it has accumulated six years of service experience. Enwang has observed the phenomenon of many economically-disadvantaged households in poverty. This phenomenon includes receiving government subsidies for a long period of time, thus resulting in welfare dependence, or parents asking their children not to subscribe to insurance in order to maintain welfare status, an unwillingness to deal with debts, borrowing money from friends, and engaging in labor-intensive work for a long time, which leads to poor health and worsening economic conditions. The reason why these people are unable to break away from the "poverty cycle" can be summed up by the following two factors: 1. personal factors, such as poverty culture and human capital; 2. external environmental impact, such as family structure and labor market, etc. (Li, 2015). Most of the economically-disadvantaged households are trapped in the provision of social welfare resources due to lack of stable jobs, and thus they fail to break out of the "poverty cycle" (Cai, 2008; Lin, 2011), leading to the replication of parents' poverty status among their descendants.

Poverty is not only relevant, but can also be accumulated (Gu & Zhan, 1998). In a society where employment is very challenging, economically-disadvantaged groups with low productivity or insufficient working capacity will find it more difficult to find a job, and may gradually be excluded from the mainstream society and even pass this on to their next generation as the "lower class" (Xiao, 2013). Poverty also affects an individual's health, mind, fertility, employment, economic state, and risk awareness. Seeing that the client was suffering from long-term economic vulnerability, Enwang began to think about how to help the client to break that curse and come up with better ideas and blueprints for their own career planning and future career. Even more important is the issue of how to promote changes in the economic livelihood of the service subject, so that said subject can break away from the poverty cycle.

In the course of implementing the "Project on the Return of the Economically Disadvantaged Citizens Back to the Labor Market", Enwang found that relevant policies in numerous countries and the development of our local policies have begun to move toward the concept of "developmental social work". In addition to the intervention of traditional social work approaches, "the practice of social investment" is another focus. However, during the six years of service, Enwang found that Taiwan's poverty alleviation programs were mostly focused on accumulating wealth and seldom touched on social investment; during this stage, the labor administration service provision and the social administration system lacked connection or an effective collaboration mechanism. As a result, the policy cannot fully support economically-disadvantaged households in eliminating employment obstacles and accumulating capital. Therefore, Enwang tried to incorporate the concept of social investment into the service system, so as to help the economically-disadvantaged people return to the labor market and secure employment.

In summary, this study intends to explore the possibility and impact of social capital investment in relation to poverty alleviation through six years of service experience and the journey of service subjects. Therefore, the objective of this study is to answer the following question: How can the incorporation of the concepts of social capital and investment into the service process enhance the awareness of service subjects and the potential of poverty alleviation among the clients?

II. Literature Research

i. Social investment-oriented welfare policies

From the perspective of the traditional welfare state, welfare is designed to protect the people from being harmed by the market, but the objective of social investment is to promote the integration of the people into the market. Investment-based social expenditures are different from welfare expenditures in the past. The development of social investment policies in European countries emphasizes knowledge-based economic systems, reconciles social and economic goals, uses social expenditures to promote the productivity of the economic system, and emphasizes the cultivation of human capital, while simultaneously highlighting labor market activation policies (Huang & Chen, 2014).

During Blair's tenure as prime minister of the Labor Party, the UK pursued the "third way" concept. In addition to implementing tax reduction and exemption policies for small and medium-sized enterprises, it also vigorously encouraged the unemployed to undertake various kinds of vocational training and urged them back to the job market. Social investment is regarded as a productive factor in such policies, through which social investment can increase labor market engagement and productivity (Lin & Liu, 2017).

Taking Taiwanese society as an example, the "Implementation Measures to Assist Active Independent living and Break Away from Poverty" promulgated by the Ministry of Health and Welfare on 6 June, 2016 emphasized that the methods which are most effective for eradicating poverty include: education investment, employment independence, asset accumulation, community industry, and social participation etc. It can be seen that the focus of domestic social assistance policies has been shifted from passive poverty relief toward encouraging independent living, improving the human capital capabilities of the disadvantaged, and raising awareness of financial education.

ii. Developmental social work and Taiwan's poverty alleviation policy

Implementing "Developmental social work" in poverty alleviation issues is to transform the orientation of traditional social assistance into a social investment strategy. Through social investment, economic policies and public engagement, it is possible to accumulate various assets (human, financial, and social capital, etc.) of the subjects, in order to promote overall economic development (edited by Huang & Zheng, 2014, pp. 3-9). In fact, the strategic orientation of developmental social work is to emphasize the intervention of social investment (Guo, 2017), as well as the following three points: strengthening the investment of human capital, promoting the formation of social capital, and encouraging productive employment and independent living.

Taiwan's current social support policy on poverty alleviation has been re-directed toward the development of educational investment, asset accumulation and active independent living. This trend is similar to the viewpoint of social investment in developmental social work. Take the Taipei City Government's poverty alleviation policy as an example. The first generation of services are mainly for adults with work capacity, such as family development account projects, the Lotto Dream Entrepreneurship Program, housing projects, and temporary work programs to assist with the transition. The second generation of services are targeted at children and juveniles. The poverty alleviation programs for the second generation include child development accounts (children's cooperation), youth financial training and development accounts, workplace internships, youth training and tutoring programs. The second-generation poverty alleviation policy starts with the concept of asset accumulation, plans for the development of accounts for all age groups, and looks forward to various human capital investment plans through education, information equality, vocational skills training, and employment preparation. On the other hand, for the first generation of poverty alleviation policies and economically-disadvantaged households, the service plan mostly favors economic production and housing support, while there are few service programs for human capital investment and financial education. Therefore, this study aims to strengthen the process of social capital of the first generation of economically-disadvantaged households, as the research subject of developmental social work.

iii. Social investment and social capital

Social investment policies emphasize a knowledge-based economic system, reconcile social and economic goals, use social expenditures to promote the productivity of the economic system, highlight human capital cultivation, and accentuate labor market activation policies (Huang & Chen, 2014). Social investment can also be seen as a production factor to sustain the contemporary labor force and promote new labor engagement and human capital (Lin & Liu, 2017).

Social capital is the sum of resources formed by the gradual accumulation of individuals or groups due to relatively stable and institutionalized interactive networks to a certain extent; this means that social capital is referred to as interpersonal relationship. Putnam divided social capital into three types: combined, bridging, and connected. These three types correspond to the connections between close and homogeneous people in social relationships, such as families; the connections formed by those who are more distant but have common interests, such as colleagues; and the relationships between individuals or groups of different social levels, such as the country (Putnam, 1993, p. 22). The social capital defined by the scholar Lin (2001) refers to the investment embedded in the social network. Actors can obtain capital through social networks and then take relevant action, which means that actors in society can obtain and use these resources (Lin, 2006, pp. 19-21).

As mentioned above, Enwang is pursuing a poverty alleviation program focused on accumulation of strengthening social investment and social capital for the clients. Therefore, the application of social investment in poverty alleviation policies can be said to strengthen individuals in the workplace through, for example, vocational training and education. On the other hand, social capital is the sum of the relationships, networks, abilities, etc. possessed by an individual in addition to economic capital, such as relatives and friends, connections, employment skills, etc.

III. Research Methods

i. Continuing training courses for the project "Back to the Labor Market for Economically Disadvantaged Citizens"

In the initial stage of the "Economically Disadvantaged People Back to the Labor Market" project, a single series of courses were taken, which made it difficult for the service subjects to have sustainable benefits in terms of growth and transformation. Apart from the fact that the service subjects are likely to continue to refocus and clarify on similar courses, employment specialists have also spent a lot of effort on leading them from scratch. Therefore, Enwang started to introduce the concepts of "social investment" and "social capital accumulation" in 2016, to integrate the needs and status of the service subjects during the year, and to conduct "continuing training courses". Through continuous courses, Enwang is seeking to increase the willingness of service subjects to enter employment, and establish a support system and network, so that employment specialists can better establish objective relationships with service subjects through this medium. It is hoped that long-term social investment and social capital accumulation will help service subjects to improve their financial status and develop behaviors which will lead to economic productivity.

ii. Screening of research subjects

The continuity training courses for project handling in 2016 not only brought about different opportunities for the service subjects to learn from various courses, but also enabled the service subjects to accumulate social capital, enhance their self-esteem, and create more different potentials. This study intends to explore how the incorporation of the concepts of social capital and investment into the service process affects the perception of service subjects and the possibility of poverty alleviation. Therefore, the selection of research subjects is mainly based on service subjects who have participated in continuous training courses and successfully obtained employment. Enwang contacted the subjects via phone and explained the content of the research. A total of 3 people were willing to participate in the interview. The basic information and service content are shown in Table 1 and Table 2:

Table 1: Basic information of research subjects

Code	Gender	Age	Marital status	Education	Welfare status	Years of service
B	Male	28	Single	College	Mid/Low income	3
G	Female	43	Divorced	Junior high dropped	Low income class 3	2
Z	Female	47	Maried	High school	Mid/Low income	2.5

Source: Enwang, 26 September, 2018

Table 2: The content of the service received by the research subjects

Code	Service content received
B	Continuing training courses: career exploration, interpersonal communication, job hunting skills, financial organization, entrepreneurial costs, product positioning, online marketing, sales practice Services: employment direction discussion, employability assessment, employment matching, workplace adaptation counseling, career counseling, emotional support, resource links, post-employment tracking
G	Continuous training courses: career exploration, interpersonal communication, job hunting skills, financial organization, entrepreneurial costs, product positioning, online marketing, sales practice, computer training, labor rights Services: employment direction discussion, employability assessment, employment matchmaking, interview skills drill, debt negotiation, entrepreneurial consultation, emotional support, resource linking, post-employment tracking

Table 2: The content of the service received by the research subjects (continued)

Code	Service content received
Z	Continuous training courses: career exploration, interpersonal communication, financial groups, entrepreneurial costs, product positioning, online marketing, sales practice, computer vocational training, individualized vocational skills training Services: employment direction discussion, employability assessment, employment matchmaking, interview skills drill, debt negotiation, emotional support, resource linking, post-employment tracking

Source: Enwang, 26 September, 2018

iii. Data collection and compiling

This article is a qualitative research piece. Although it is impossible to analyze big data through qualitative research, it is possible to deeply understand whether the service subjects can successfully absorb and integrate the courses organized by Enwang into their lives, and how their subjective consciousness interacts with external organizations and the physical environment (Ma, 2011, p. 40).

The data was collected during the period spanning September to November in 2018. Alongside in-depth interviews, data was also collected through texts such as worker notes and case service records (data interval from July 2014 to December 2019), in order to understand subjects' transformation and growth during this period. An interview outline was planned prior to the interview, and in-depth discussions were conducted based on the status and response of the interviewees. To ensure the integrity of the information from the interviews, the interviewees were asked if the whole process could be recorded verbatim and transcribed for analysis, and they indeed agreed to this.

IV. Research Discovery

"When the money is exhausted, others only ask me to go out to work, but it is not that I don't want to work; the fact is I can't find a job. If I cannot change my life,

then why do I need to work hard to move forward?"

— The voice of a group of clients

i. Running out of money: the plight of the economically-disadvantaged

With the impact of global economic and technological advancement, as well as the labor market changing with the times, job hunters are facing perpetually-capricious challenges today. Under such a fast-changing society, if service subjects are not aware of the changes in the employment environment and circumstances, and do not have the ability to adapt to the job market, while also lacking competitive advantage, then they are prone to becoming obsolete in the labor market. From practical experience, Enwang has observed that when families cannot fully support the right of education, or due to health factors and improper financial management which leads to debt, they face the following challenges:

ii. The dilemma of the dual roles of care and economy

In a traditional marriage arrangement, women are often given the role of looking after their young children, but they are unable to take frequent leave from the workplace. Therefore, it is a common phenomenon that women are forced to leave professional careers which they have worked on for a long time. In addition, there are many service subjects whose marriage is on the rocks, with one of the couple obligated to take care of the children and family responsibilities alone; as a result, that person must assume the dual role of bread earner and caregiver. Subject G was divorced when her daughter was in primary school due to multiple domestic violence incidents with her ex-husband. As a single mother she has to take care of her daughter and bear the financial burden at the same time, which places more restrictions on her job hunting:

"When the child was young, I first found a place like a restaurant to apply for a dishwashing job.... The child was really too young to adapt to the situation because the catering industry was very busy from morning to midnight. What should the child do? There is no sense of security. I never felt comfortable with it".

(20180930 G Interview: 1)

In terms of when people are forced to make a choice between bread earner and caregiver, although Z has many job opportunities, she prefers to take the role of caregiver and chooses to leave the labor market:

"Because the children were very young at the time, I hoped to be able to grow up with them, so I decided to adapt to their schedules. At that time, there were numerous job opportunities, but since I had set too many restrictions, in the end none of them matched".

(20180930 Z Interview: 6)

Clients are forced to leave the labor market because of care issues; meanwhile, they must return to the labor market because of economic issues. Many economically-disadvantaged job-seekers are prone to being repeatedly dragged between care issues and economic issues, thus limiting their choice when it comes to employment opportunities.

2. A life of debt: falling into a cycle of economic deterioration

In the course of providing its services, Enwang has witnessed that many of its service subjects have suffered from credit debt due to easy access and abused usage of credit cards in the past. Many people use one credit card to pay the expenses of another card. In addition, they may also open dummy accounts for others due to peer pressure or personal loyalty, and even become the guarantor for a loan. They often end up becoming liable for not only their own debt, but also the debt of other persons. However, this huge debt does not prompt the client to work hard in order to pay their creditors. Instead, they often try to avoid dealing with the debt and choose to engage in work without labor insurance. This not only limits their employment options, but also exposes the client to other risks:

"The client expressed concern that his salary might be deducted due to debt issues after he has acquired a full-time job. At the moment he has no idea about his debt status. The clients expect that WR can help them to understand which channels can be applied to confirm their financial status. WR has indicated that further investigation is necessary and will keep the client updated".

(20141023 Z Service Record: 3)

Due to inadequate financial values, service subjects often have debts and engage in long-hour, low-paid, and labor-intensive non-insured work, which not only exhausts their physical endurance prematurely, but also fails to improve their economic situation as they wish. The situation usually further affects future employment competitiveness, leaving them trapped in a vicious economic cycle.

3. Diminished employment options due to health issue

The physical health of service objects is likely to be affected by illness, which will limit their options of job types and working conditions, perhaps even meaning that they cannot go out to work. It is also possible that employers' ignorance toward, or stereotypes of, the disease may leave them concerned about service subjects potentially affecting workplace safety, thereby reducing their willingness to recruit those service subjects. B suffers from epilepsy. During his job hunt, an employer chose not to hire him because of concerns about B's illness and workplace safety issues. B's illness also meant that he had to deal with excessive self-limitation during his job search:

"With my physical condition, do you dare to imagine that a boss would hire someone who might suffer disease onset anytime, anywhere in the kitchen, or while driving on the road? Just imagine if you were the boss".

(20180912 B Interview: 5)

Z chose to quit the job due to the pressure of work and care, which affected his physical and mental health:

"Z used to work as an insurance business assistant for a long time with good performance. However, later on he decided to quit the job due to irregular working hours and excessive caregiving pressure leading to depression and bipolar episodes". (20140805 Z Service Record: 2)

In the process of providing services, Enwang also observed that the client was temporarily separated from the labor market due to health factors, and when he returned to the labor market, he was shocked at the gap which existed as a result of him being away from society for a long period of time; indeed, his original skills no longer met the needs of the labor market, which had a profound impact on his career development:

"I used to have the best knowledge of computers at home, but now I am the weakest. I don't even bother to touch the computer at home. ... I am getting old after graduation, and I no longer know how to use these professional skills and expertise to find a job in this field". (20180930 Z Interview: 7)

4. The stringent challenges in the labor market

(1) The marginalization of working conditions

Social transformation can drive social progress, and has also meant that the current labor market demands more stringent qualifications for job seekers. Under the increasingly-severe challenge of working conditions, when the client is looking for a job, it is easy to feel the frustration of not being hired due to age, education, work experience, license, and any other factors which make them under-qualified. The prolonged frustration makes the client hesitate when looking for a job and even resist employment. Under the pressure of economy and reality, people are always forced to choose a low-level and labor-intensive occupation first:

"When I first moved here, I was working at a breakfast shop.... I have no academic qualifications or licenses. People do not recognize my little

experience.... It's very difficult for me to find a job. My academic record is my

biggest pain point". (20180930 G Interview: 1)

(2) The current situation of the labor market with diverse requirements

In the current labor market, employers no longer expect employees to have only a single profession as they did in the past. Instead, they expect employees to have multiple skills with numerous different job functions. However, in today's labor market, with wide-ranging requirements, clients who do not possess diverse abilities, or cannot adapt to such a workplace culture, are often less favored by employers, or need to find a job frequently on the journey of their career development:

"Even if I find a job at a restaurant, in addition to having to work late, sometimes the boss will ask me to go on the road as a delivery man. So, at that moment, I feel that all bosses are not so honest and it is inexplicable. Why do you want to send an in-house staff member to work on the road? In this case, why don't they ask field staff to work in the office? I will never understand the philosophy of the boss. Forget it, I don't want to talk about it".

(20180912 B Interview: 2)

5. Summary

Enwang realized that service subjects are economically-disadvantaged and marginalized because they are unable to cope with the multiple pressures of the family or social environment, and feel that their lives are hopeless, which in turn affects their self-will to seek employment or change. Therefore, Enwang has introduced developmental social work and social investment-oriented special courses to enhance these people's social capital, empowerment and companionship.

ii. Moving forward: planting the seeds of change

Enwang utilized developmental social work to highlight the intervention via social investment. This approach focuses on education and human capital investment, promoting the formation of social capital, and encouraging productive employment as well as self-employment. The following are the approaches used to support service subjects and allow them to improve their employability and expand social capital through a series of project-style training courses:

1. Repositioning: empowerment to a new start

(1) Career exploration

"Job hunting" seems to be a simple matter, but many people are not clear about their career direction before entering the workplace, or they did not find the answer from school or family education, and so they have to find the answer through work. Z has been out of the labor market for a long time and feels confused about her career development. Through the encouragement of the employment specialist, she participated in career exploration courses to clarify her direction:

> "Z participated in the career exploration course; she and the members began to think, "Is there something that I (we) had dreamed of, but did not find a way to practice it?". Z thought of the time when she took care of her daughters when they were still young; she still remembered the joy of sewing some small bags by hand occasionally, and so she started a series of dream-catching journeys".
>
> (20160930 Z Notes: 1)

Through career exploration, Z realized that her prior life experience could be developed into future work skills, and so the employment specialist guided her via the interaction between lecturers and group members to inspire Z to discover her interests and strengths:

> "There is also career exploration. At first, when the employment specialist told me to join the market fair, I had no idea about how to do it. .... Gradually, with help from the mentor, I have learned how to do it and found my interest in patchwork".
>
> (20180930 Z Interview: 8)

Enwang hopes to intervene in the group momentum model of the workshop, to help clients who are not clear about their personal career development or who want to explore different career directions. The objective is to help them find their own strengths and weaknesses, and raise their awareness of change. Based on the need, Enwang utilizes standardized tests and consultation services at career development centers which are found at public agencies[1]. The goal is to construct a resource network for career exploration, assisting clients in discovering career interests and their potential, as well as understanding the foresight of the industrial market. An additional goal is to clarify the client's career direction by seeking and discussing job opportunities with that client.

(2) Employment skills training

In the process of career exploration, on top of thinking about personal career interests and identifying career directions, some clients also notice that they have insufficient employment skills and begin to learn a second specialty. Z used to work at an office and carry out clerical work, but later left the labor market due to family care issues. With the changes of the times and advances in technology, when Z returned to the labor market, she lacked the employability required for office and clerical work and was forced to choose labor-oriented work or relearn new skills:

> "The first class should be a computer class, entry level computer course, with Word, Excel... The teacher takes a slow pace and there are reviews. In addition, the version is different, and you will learn a lot of different stuff".
>
> (20180930 Z Interview: 7)

G has low-level academic credentials; in terms of facing the new social value, which emphasizes specialization and certification, she firmly believes that having a professional license could help her during the job hunt:

---

[1] Employment service stations and youth career development centers provide services such as career consultation, career fitness tests, workplace visits, career seminars, group courses, resume reviews, mock interviews, and employment assistance.

"I hope that the crisis is a turning point, so I would like to think of a way to start a business. The first thing I could think about is whether there is a chance for me to get a license or something... If I have a license, I can return to the restaurant".

(20180930 G Interview: 29)

When the service subject has a need to advance their skills, the employment specialist will give priority to assisting them in connecting to appropriate vocational training courses. However, when the existing vocational training courses cannot meet the service subject's schedule and care demands, Enwang will provide customized services for people with the same vocational training needs. This is a short-term skill training program designed to improve the social capital of the service subject's work skills.

(3) Entrepreneurship skills training

Some of the service subjects have the dream of starting a business when they come into contact with Enwang, but due to economic criteria they must first have a full-time or part-time job. The problem is that most of the jobs are high-labor, high-substitution, low-skilled positions. On top of this, the rapidly-changing labor market is likely to create a high degree of insecurity among the service subjects, which in turn catalyzes entrepreneurial intention and actions. However, the service subject is also likely to lack the knowledge and ability needed to start a business, while they may also lack sales channels, which leads to the inability to operate and seek self-employment in the long term.

Although G has sold products through physical platforms, he still lacks diversified distribution channels and experience, product positioning, cost control and other capabilities, which makes it difficult for him to market his products:

"The client originally had a Facebook fan group. Through this course, he learned about operating the hit rate, innovative content, interaction with netizens, and live broadcast. It is expected that Facebook will be diversified in the future to let netizens learn more about services and products".

(20170517 G Service Record: 26)

On the course B has acquired relevant knowledge about entrepreneurship and how to develop a marketing platform for himself and establish market contacts:

> *"B's entrepreneurial journey has made a new breakthrough. B, who is shy when*
> *it comes to interpersonal interaction, has actually developed his own store-client*
> *to sell his goods in a coffee shop, and secures cooperation opportunities with*
> *others on a commission basis.... He confidently shares his own entrepreneurship*
> *experience, ideas about developing products, and even actively asks our opinions*
> *on new products".*   (201600520 B Notes: 2)

Enwang has introduced a series of courses on product positioning, product packaging and design, cost calculation, distribution channels, sales skills and product management. The goal of the courses is to teach entrepreneurial skills to service subjects who want to start a business. It also assists clients in connecting with the services of the CTBC Charity Foundation's support project, so that entrepreneurship is no longer just a matter of lip service.

2. Social Waltz-Cultivation of Interactive Skills

(1) Practice social interaction skills

With many years of service experience, employment specialists have found that the service subjects are facing obstacles when it comes to finding employment. In addition to family care and health issues, they are often out of the labor market for too long. They tend to stick to their own opinions in terms of getting along with workplace supervisors and colleagues, which leads to a poor interpersonal relationship, thereby affecting their job stability.

In addition to providing emotional support, the employment specialist will also use demonstrations and exercises to establish appropriate interpersonal interaction skills and emotional relief guidance during the course of accompanying the service subject. A fitting example here is that of G:

> *"...The client indicated that his colleagues were relatively impatient; a senior colleague would deliberately pick up the client's minor problems, and he currently responds in a disregarding manner. WR affirms that the client can respond calmly and intelligently... WR guides the client to think about whether he can train himself not to be affected by people with poor emotional control, and use positive relationships with other colleagues to support himself.......WR said the client can tell the boss what happened and observe how the boss responds to the issue, and at the same time practice presenting events from an objective perspective with the most original version".*
>
> (20180930 G Service Record: 12)

(2) Establishment of interpersonal support network

Through course design and operation, Enwang enables clients to learn interpersonal interaction and appropriate conversation skills in the group process. It also observes that clients often obtain part-time work, social welfare resource information, and emotional support, etc., through informal channels. The connection between people not only creates economic benefits for the service subjects, but also constructs an intangible support network for the service subjects. Z established a people network through skill training courses, which helps himself and others to acquire job opportunities through personal connections:

> *"The student in the patchwork class happened to be the finance committee member of the community who always wanted to replace the previous cleaners in the community, but there were no channels. Once in a chat, I told him that a colleague of mine is a cleaner, and I have worked as his substitute. Yes, I was just checking it out but in the end we went there together".* (20180930 Z Interview: 2)

G is a very open-minded person who is willing to share with others. As a result, after seeking medical help, he has established his personal network, and created a house cleaning career for himself:

"I was very fortunate, because I have high blood pressure! When I went to get the prescription, a doctor asked me about house cleaning, so I started doing it at his home.... Then the doctor introduced me to other customers. He also referred me to this customer as well". (20180930 G Interview: 3)

Networking is a kind of social capital, and is particularly important when it comes to how to expand, operate and maintain a business. Therefore, the practice of interpersonal interaction skills for the empowerment of service subjects can help those subjects to establish good relationships. When they have positive interpersonal interaction experience, the service subjects can successfully create different life resources and establish their own social capital.

3. A good financial manager—building financial knowledge

Most of the service subjects are affected by their primary family, living habits and social environment structure, causing them to create improper consumption behaviors, make bad financial decisions, and then fall into a quagmire of debt. However, Enwang has also discovered that the service subjects are actually not aware of their income status in such a scenario. They are even of the opinion that, if one does not have money, then one can simply ignore it.

(1) Build a financial inventory

In addition to providing individual financial consultations for service subjects, Enwang also conducts financial group courses. Through group motivation and practical exercises, it constructs correct financial knowledge for the service subjects and enhances their awareness of the usage of money and the management of income and expenditure:

"Since I have no idea about money. I think that if I have money today, I will buy what I like. Then if there is no money, I will not consider the value of it.... I can gradually change myself, so now I will look at the relationship between material, value and price to make a judgement". (20180930 Z Interview: 20)

Due to the establishment of correct financial awareness, the service subjects have begun to try to manage their personal consumption behavior, allocate family financial income and expenditure, and even make emergency reserves for individuals or households, so that the family will not immediately fall into an economic crisis when facing future risks in life. Through the learning and implementation of the course, Z began to realize her personal consumption behavior, and then developed better control over her consumption craving:

> "It's how we can differentiate what you want and what you need, what you really want and what you really need.... Especially the finance part is very important. Many people will say they have no money, where did the money go? How is it possible to obtain more resources? How is it possible to reduce expenditure? I didn't know how to increase revenue and I didn't know how to reduce expenditure before.... Now I try to control my craving....".
>
> (20180930 Z Interview: 21)

(2) Increase willingness to handle debt

In the past, clients needed a lot of courage to deal with huge debts and lengthy judicial procedures that had been ignored for a long time. Enwang hopes to explain the impact of debts on individuals, families, and children in response to debt issues and clients. The objective is to assist clients in clarifying their household financial status, linking Legal Aid Foundation consultation and debt negotiation. With the awakening of financial awareness and the companionship and support of the employment specialist, the client's willingness and determination to handle debts will be enhanced:

> "In the early days, Z often had a negative attitude toward managing her debt due to events in her daily life or physical health conditions. The employment specialist needed to remind her constantly. However, after the employment specialist clarified and consolidated with Z during each service, and accompanied her on the journey to the Joint Credit Information Center, Z began

to actively contact the Legal Aid Foundation and proceeded to deal with her

debts".   (20161022 Z Notes: 2)

V. Conclusion: Discussion and suggestions

i. Discussion

In summary, Enwang observed that the reason why clients continue to fall into the poverty circle of economic weakness is mainly due to their lack of economic capital (knowledge, experience and resources) and social capital (education, connections). As a result, they often make incorrect decisions and even give up on their hopes and dreams. After experiencing long-term frustration in their lives and being excluded from the job market, they feel exhausted by such a lifestyle, and are unable to produce hope for the future, which also limits their personal potential. Facing such a diversified employment obstacle, Enwang found that only providing an employment matching service would not mitigate the employment issues faced by service subjects. Therefore, Enwang decided to use the social investment approach to strengthen service subjects' adaptability after entering the job market, in order to help them move forward in life.

Based on literature research, Enwang has produced the following conclusions in terms of how to help service subjects: aim to address the needs of economically-disadvantaged households via assisting the clients in perceiving their own strengths; apply curriculum empowerment and resource linkage to build and improve the social capital of the clients, such as employment skills and networking, which can help the clients to accumulate economic capital. In addition, the employment specialist can guide the clients' self-reflection and strengthen their awareness, so as to inspire their willingness to change and their ability to take action. Of particular note here is the idea of matching service subjects to people with homogenous attributes and needs, cultivating their debt management capabilities, and allowing them to establish better interpersonal interactions with their personal network support system, together with the promotion of risk awareness and other attitudes and abilities that are used to respond to life problems. Indeed, this could actually create an authentic employment competitiveness. From the practical experience of implementing the project, Enwang has compiled the following service flow of the "Social Investment Oriented" approach to assist economically-disadvantaged households, as shown in Figure 1:

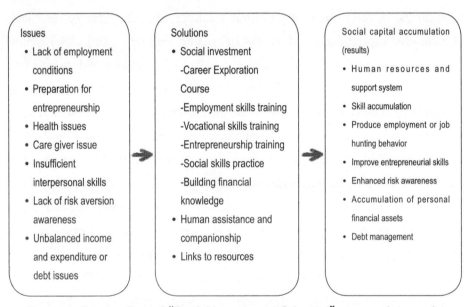

Figure 1: Service flow of "Social Investment Oriented" approach to assist economically disadvantaged households

ii. Recommendation

In the past six years of service, Enwang has found that, in order to help economically-disadvantaged households get rid of poverty, workers must break away from the traditional concept of social welfare and change their mentality. The following are some suggestions:

1. Stable employment is not equivalent to poverty alleviation: companionship and empowerment should go hand in hand

Does sustainable and stable engagement in the job market to obtain remuneration really mean a chance to escape poverty? Assisting clients in stabilizing their employment does not mean getting rid of poverty. Getting out of poverty is a goal that requires internal and external factors to complement each other. Enwang believes that, in addition to providing job opportunities to increase economic capital, it is also necessary to help clients build other social capital, and to rely on companionship to enhance their mental momentum and establish their self-esteem. Moreover, it is vital to support service subjects through the cultivation of financial management and interpersonal courses and the introduction of resources. Only when a service subject's substantive abilities are improved can there be a chance for change, thus creating a new experience in the individual's life, which in turn means that the service subject will gradually move toward a life without poverty.

2. Turning passive assistance into active investment: changing the service philosophy of the employment specialist

When an employment specialist only maintains traditional concepts or practice to serve the client with existing resources, then it is extremely challenging to increase the client's awareness as well as accumulate their assets, since this would likely not be sustainable. The employment specialist should change the mode and value of their practice, apply the concept of developmental social work, pay attention to the strengths of the service subject, enhance the risk assessment ability and judgment awareness of the service subject through education investment, and inspire motivation for change through the accumulation of human capital, raising financial awareness, and engaging in employment to create economic productivity etc. Indeed, this could further encourage the service subject to become independent and cultivate their ability to break away from poverty.

3. The poverty alleviation policy of the first generation of economically-disadvantaged households should be focused on accumulating social capital

Although Taiwan's poverty alleviation policy has been transformed from a passive poverty relief to a positive concept of independent living, it can still be seen, from the policy perspective, that the concept of positive independent living remains mostly focused on empowering the second generation of economically-disadvantaged households with a service based on the concept of asset accumulation. The poverty alleviation policies for the first generation of economically-disadvantaged households tended to favor economic production and housing support, while there was little human capital investment or financial education. Therefore, it is recommended that the government also incorporate the concept of social investment when planning the poverty alleviation policies for the first generation of economically-disadvantaged households, so as to assist the first generation of economically-disadvantaged households in accumulating social capital.

References

Chinese

古允文、詹宜璋（1998）。台灣地區老人經濟安全與年金政策：社會排除觀點初探。**人文及社會科學集刊**，10（2），第 191-225 頁。

李雅萍（2014）。經濟弱勢家戶子女成年後再度落入貧窮循環歷程之質性分析。台北：**東吳大學社工研究研究所學位論文**。

林士傑（2011）。台灣社會排除現象之探索性研究。**台中：亞洲大學社會工作學研究所學位論文**。

林佩璇（2006）。以社會資本理論探討影響社區產業發展因素之研究：以八翁社區為例。高雄：**國立中山大學公共事務管理研究所碩士論文**。

林昭吟、劉宜君（2017）。社會投資觀點之政策理念及運用。**社區發展季刊**，160，第 86-94 頁。

馬淑蓉（2011）。工作貧窮女性單親家庭邁向脫貧之歷程研究：以被社會救助法排除者為例。台中：**靜宜大學社會工作與兒童少年福利學系碩士論文**。

郭登聰（2017）。發展性社會工作在台灣推動的歷程、問題與建議。**社區發展季刊**，160，第 111-124 頁。

黃彥宜、陳昭榮（2014）。埔里菩提長青村的經驗：與社會投資觀點的對話。**臺灣社會福利學刊**，12（1），第 215-252 頁。

黃琢嵩、鄭麗珍主編（2016）。**發展性社會工作：理念與實務的激盪**。臺北：松慧。

蔡貞慧（2008）。社會排除現象的時間趨勢與指標建構。**行政院國家科學委員會補助專題研究計畫成果報告**（計畫編號：NSC96），未出版。

蕭琮琦（2013）。台灣家庭經濟安全探析：生命歷程與貧窮動態觀點的詮釋。南投：**暨南大學社會政策與社會工作學系博士論文**。

English

Lin, N. (2001). *Social Capital: A Theory of Social Structure and Action.* Cambridge, UK: Cambridge University Press.

Putnam, R. D. (1993). *Making Democracy Work: Civic Traditions in Modern Italy.* Princeton,USA: Princeton University Press.

Q&A

Q : Has the ESWF considered incorporating learning processes into its system and making training courses available online?

A : Currently, the ESWF has not made such courses available online, for two reasons. The first is that these courses are not recognized by public agencies as professional skills training courses. The second is that training programs are tailored to service subjects. It is government agencies that provide online professional courses. When service subjects desire to learn a skill, we give them firsthand information by letting them know where they can obtain relevant professional knowledge. Faced with the situation where members of vulnerable households are not able to attend every class, we communicate with the government to hold weekend or half-day classes.

Self-reliance Empowerment and Confidence through Games: Application of developmental social work in community residence for persons with intellectual disabilities

Hui-Min Hsu[*], Chung-Chun Chien[**]

Abstract

The Eden Social Welfare Foundation (hereinafter referred to as ESWF) provides community residential services to persons with intellectual disabilities, as a warm up for independent living in the community. Such empowerment emphasizes the "autonomy" of intellectually-disabled persons. The objective is to help them make choices and decisions for their own lives, while also taking responsibility for those lives.

The perspective of developmental social work emphasizes the importance of the strengths of the recipients, and the empowerment of said recipients. It pays attention to their superior energy, and is consistent with the core values of independent living, such as "self-selection, self-determination, and self-responsibility". This is also the concept and purpose of the community residence service offered by the ESWF, which seeks to support persons with intellectual disabilities as they attempt to achieve independent living in the community.

For the past six years, the ESWF has supported persons with intellectual disabilities in achieving independent living via community residential services. The

[*] Specialist of Office of Director, New Taipei District, Eden Social Welfare Foundation.
[**] Supervisor of Xichih Xiu Feng Community Living Program, Eden Social Welfare Foundation.

organization has taken the empowerment model as a reference, adopting preference analysis to emphasize the strengths of persons with intellectual disabilities. The ESWF has also developed a board game together with persons with intellectual disabilities which allows the latter to experience self-reliance and empowerment. In the early stage of community residential services, the staff need to assist and lead the persons with intellectual disabilities. When the capability of persons with intellectual disabilities is enhanced, as they gradually establish a partnership through participation in discussions, they can take the lead and implement what they have learned in their daily lives.

Keywords: person with intellectual disability, community living, empowerment, independent living

I. The Research Background

"The family you came from isn't as important as the family you are going to have". (D. Herbert Lawrence, British writer)

The image of "home" for the general public is mainly a family composed of a father, mother, and children. However, when this perspective becomes overly obsessed with the members of the family, people may fall into a myth about the "intact family". Nevertheless, a real "home" is not determined by who the members are. Instead, the more important aspect is whether these family members can take care of each other, and provide security as well as emotional support.

In the homestead of the ESWF, some of the service subjects came from families where they were victims of domestic violence, or were even abandoned by their families, while there were also children who left home because their family was unable to perform its functions. When they first stepped into this homestead, we observed that their impressions of their respective past families were mostly nothing but fear, and they were unable to trust others when interacting. The clients receive a period of service where ESWF staff members play the role of family members; they can support and encourage each other to maintain the emotional function of the family, and so these clients can once again experience warmth at home.

In order to allow persons with disabilities to have "autonomy" in life, achieve the goal of independent living, and practice the core values of "self-selection, self-determination, and self-responsibility", community residence services have provided training for independent living. Social workers and educare givers will formulate disabled person-oriented service plans to develop self-reliance in accordance with respective personal needs. This includes organizing activities such as health promotion and management, skills cultivation, and community engagement, so that the disabled persons can develop their potential and learn from each other in the division of labor and cooperation. The objective is to enhance their autonomy and promote the community's understanding and acceptance of persons with disabilities. Moreover, in order to establish their sense of responsibility and financial management awareness, while simultaneously helping them to connect employment channels and teaching them how to manage their wealth, the professional team will assess those with good independent living ability, through the connection of the community and employment resources, so as to help them integrate into the community and have a stable life in the future.

The developmental social work in which this foundation has actively invested over recent years is a new concept which transforms the traditional social relief orientation into a social investment strategy. It is also a new direction for resolving the conflict between "economic development" and "social welfare". Developmental social work pays special attention to the advantageous energy of recipients, while simultaneously highlighting the regional characteristics of the community, and also emphasizes the accumulation of various service objects through the process of social investment, economic policies and public participation, with a positive cycle of productive economic activities assets (manpower, finance, and social capital, etc.). The goal is to make possible, and render opportunities for, self-determination, and even further to generate feedback to drive the growth of regional economic activities and promote overall economic development (Yan, 2015).

Developmental social work emphasizes the power of recipients and the importance of empowerment. It is consistent with the core values of independent living, which are "self-selection, self-determination, and self-responsibility". It is also the concept and purpose of the ESWF to provide community residential services. This research aims to explore the perspective of developmental social work through six years of service experience and courses. In the process of actually implementing the independent living for persons with intellectual disabilities, the ESWF has witnessed the transformation of service subjects and how they can integrate the spirit of independent living and development of social work into the service provider, and fully implement this spirit via the services.

II. Literature Research

From the initiative of "Normalization" in the 1940s to the "Deinstitutionalization" and "Independent Living for Disabled Person" campaigns in the 1960s, all appeals for disabled persons returning to the mainstream and social integration will encourage persons with disabilities to live in society with better dignity and to dominate their daily lives and living style. This process has a profound impact on the development of services for persons with disabilities, since they are no longer required to live in a large-scale shelter home, nor are they excluded from the main society. They have the right to, and indeed should, live in the community like ordinary persons. They ought to be allowed to study at schools in the neighboring community, be employed, make friends and have a life, while also becoming a part of the community and enjoying a good quality of life like anyone else.

To echo the above-mentioned concept of transformation, the "community-oriented" residential service model began to flourish globally in the 1980s. Even persons requiring intensive living support began to move out of shelter homes and return to the community. With such a trend of transformation, various countries have also promulgated relevant policies to support this trend:

1. Sweden closed all sheltered institutions in 1993.
2. It took Norway five years (1990-1995) to achieve total "deinstitutionalization", and all persons with disabilities have returned to the community in the vicinity of their families.
3. Since the 1990s, the UK has started to organize many programs for persons with intellectual disabilities so that those persons can live independently in the community. Moving out of a 20-bed hostel, they can choose preferred roommates, select their favorite community, rent a house in the community, and have staff who will provide them with supportive services. As specified in the 2001 white paper on learning disabilities, in 2004 all persons with

intellectual disabilities should be encouraged to move out of sheltered institutions.

4. The USA has closed sheltered institutions with more than 16 beds, or assisted these institutions in transforming into a residential service mode, with four persons or less.

5. European and American countries now prohibit persons with intellectual disabilities from being placed in sheltered institutions, especially children.

6. Japan has also entered "deinstitutionalization" status. It prohibits the construction of full-time accommodation institutions, while it also rewards the transformation of institutions to provide community residential services.

7. The CRPD (Convention on the Rights of Persons with Disabilities) specifies that persons with disabilities have the right to leave sheltered institutions, move to live in a community, and terminate involuntary institutional services for persons with disabilities.

The United Nations passed the Convention on the Rights of Persons with Disabilities (CRPD) in 2006, whereas our country promulgated the CRPD enforcement law in 2014. Within this law, Article 19 clearly declares that: States parties to the present convention recognize the equal right of all persons with disabilities to live in the community, with choices equal to others, and shall take effective and appropriate measures to facilitate full enjoyment by persons with disabilities of this right and their full inclusion and participation in the community.

i. Independent living of persons with disabilities

Article 19 of the United Nations Convention on the Rights of Persons with Disabilities (CRPD), entitled "Living independently and being included in the community", places emphasis on ensuring that persons with disabilities have the right to fully participate in the community with choices equal to others. Taiwan passed the "Act to Implement the Convention on the Rights of Persons with Disabilities" in 2014. This Act takes the spirit and value of CRPD as the basis for policy norms, so as to protect the equal participation of persons with disabilities in social, political, economic, and cultural opportunities, and to promote their independence and development.

Under the transition of modern society and social development, it is the duty of government to value and protect the rights and interests of the people and the needs of social welfare. It is the concept of humanitarianism to provide assistance to individuals who are in a disadvantaged situation so that they can obtain a quality and satisfactory life (Community Development Quarterly, 2018, p. 164).

Barns, who is a scholar of social models, put forth the belief that the term independent living per se is an apolitical aspect, which makes it acceptable to both the left and the right. Nevertheless, independent living is obviously still political, and it is advocated that necessary environmental and cultural changes allow people with disabilities to enjoy meaningful independent living, which will benefit all people (regardless of their degree of physical impairment or social levels) (Barnes, 2005).

Most of the people who need the independent living service are those who lack support systems and cannot obtain the necessary resources to achieve survival and happiness. Initially, the concept of deinstitutionalization and independent living in the community began to be advocated in the field of disability, and was then gradually extended to different target populations. The service goal of independent living is mainly to "facilitate self-reliance", which is a dual adaptation process of living environment and social roles, including being able to adapt to new social identities, being able to familiarize oneself with corresponding roles, being able to obtain the required resources, and being able to handle and develop intimate relationships. For example, there are the issues of how a person with a disability becomes an "employee", whether they have the corresponding professional skills and occupational social abilities, whether they can make friends, whether there is someone whom they can consult and obtain assistance from when encountering problems, and whether they can handle conflicts and contradictions from an intimate relationship, as well as the development of affection and marriage, etc. (Community Development Quarterly, 2018, p. 164).

Whether it is "facilitating" or "maintaining" self-reliance, the objective of independent living is the same. Even if an individual obtains just a satisfactory quality of social life, this means that the individual feels good self-esteem, has friends, has a sense of control over their life, has a sense of contribution to society, and feels as though they are a useful person and needed by society. Independent living emphasizes that persons with disabilities must have equal rights for "self-choice, self-determination, and self-responsibility". By mastering life and enhancing autonomy, they can also play the role of citizen.

Therefore, when implementing the concept of independent living, we are aware and expect that:

1. Persons with disabilities are able to make choices for their own lives, enjoy autonomy, and actively participate in projects, services and support related to them.
2. Persons with disabilities can learn domestic living skills, assume responsibility at home, and lead a dignified life.
3. Persons with disabilities can have the maximum opportunity to participate in community activities, exhibit self-determination, choose their favorite leisure activities, and be included in the community.
4. Persons with disabilities enjoy the same rights and equal opportunities as ordinary people, and can independently choose lifelong learning courses of interest to meet their learning demands and enhance their personal capabilities.
5. Persons with disabilities receive assistance from experts who understand their own needs best, and support them in expressing those needs, managing their lives independently, and thinking and expressing their inner thoughts like ordinary people.
6. Persons with disabilities enjoy human rights (respect, dignity, equality) and legal rights (citizenship, right to engagement), etc.

7. Persons with disabilities have the right to engage in social activities, enhance interpersonal interaction, and build social friendship networks.

8. Persons with disabilities are aware of relevant health and safety care services and manage their own health conditions.

ii. Empowerment and implementation

In terms of empowerment, the common Chinese translation has numerous similar terms, including "enhancement", "enabling", "bestowing", and "authorization", etc. As for its definition, many scholars have various interpretations. Rappaport (1987) forwarded the belief that empowerment is the mechanism through which people, organizations and communities gain control over their own affairs. Further, Prilleltensky et al. (2001) defined it as the purpose of our endeavors—the state of affairs where people have sufficient power to meet their own needs, as well as working together with others to promote collective goals.

Empowerment refers to the development of professional knowledge through self-identification and self-affirmation, and then innovation (Chen, 2008); empowerment also emphasizes the reconstruction of self-awareness and the awakening of self-consciousness, stressing collective actions and changes after actions (Chen, 2004). Empowerment can also mean the ability to achieve goals, emphasizing that the disadvantaged are not passive in the process, but participants in subjective consciousness and execution capability (You, 2002).

Empowerment is a theory that relates to how people gain collective control of their lives in order to achieve the benefit of the entire group. It is also a method by which social workers can increase the power of people who lack strength (Thomas & Pierson, 1995). The practice of empowerment, as required by the user campaign which it supports, is not only practiced through fighting for power—allowing those who are oppressed to control their own situation—but also through transforming power to promote change (Mullender & Ward, 1991).

According to the definition from the above analysis, the meaning of empowerment can be divided into the following three aspects for further discussion:

1. Grant the power

After examining the publications in the field of management, Conger and Kanungo (1988) indicated that the granting of decision-making authority is the main core of the concept of empowerment; meanwhile, empowerment is the technology used to deal with participatory management. Examples of this include target management, quality circle, and the goal setting method, etc., which are means of power sharing or delegation of authority. Through the granting and sharing of power, members can obtain more decision-making authority and initiatives, be able to assume responsibilities, and provide better customer service. Members can also obtain higher job satisfaction during the authorization process, and thus, to the organization, the identity and goals of the people will also produce a higher sense of commitment (Chen, 2005).

2. Enabling people

Webster's English Dictionary interprets empowerment as "enable", which means to enable people to have the ability through learning and inspiration, from inability to high abilities, to increase the individual's potential, and to be willing to do one's best. When it comes to this aspect, in addition to the process of external empowerment, more emphasis is placed on the development process of one's own internal abilities, rather than just an external inquiry.

3. Promote self-actualization

In this aspect, members have been endowed with external powers while having internal substantive capabilities, and are given the opportunity to fully reveal their knowledge and experience, achieve the realization of their own ideals, and be able to act according to the blueprint they have planned. As a result, they will have more self-confidence and be able to promote higher motivation for engagement.

Based on the above statements, the empowerment training via authorization, capability, and self-realization will enable individuals to gradually demonstrate their abilities and powers, improve the autonomy of the organization, and allow for relevant decisions to be made more smoothly.

For the persons with disabilities, empowerment emphasizes that, from the perspective of social models (Oliver, 1996), people with disabilities are regarded as an ability, not a disability (Harpur, 2012), so that people with disabilities can realize that they are equal to everyone. (Piat & Sabetti, 2012). This also includes the statement from the United Nations Convention on the Rights of Persons with Disabilities (CRPD) that persons with disabilities have equal rights to live in the community, including the ability to live independently and receive personal assistant services.

iii. The perspectives of developmental social work

The knowledge system of social work is constantly undergoing metamorphosis and evolving. In response to the new poverty, migration, social exclusion and other social issues brought about by globalization, social work-related international organizations have advocated cultural diversity, community economy, and social enterprise in recent years. The objective is to mobilize people from the bottom up to improve the common well-being, and at the same time to obtain economic benefits, as well as the benefits of personal empowerment and group cohesion. This trend can be summarized in the publications of developmental social work (Xiuhua, 2012; Guo, 2016).

Traditionally, social work has several different functions, and is generally more inclined toward solving problems. In this process, people will think about how to further prevent problems from occurring. When taking a preventive perspective, there is in fact a tendency for problems to occur. On the other hand, if one looks at things from a fully developmental perception, it will become clear that the mission of social work is to promote general welfare and well-being, and to obtain a proper solution in life to enable people to have the ability to prevent and solve problems (Zhou, 2016).

The key feature of developmental social work lies in the application of investment strategies to the practice of social work professions. It not only emphasizes the power of recipients and the importance of empowerment, but also the requirement for social workers to provide substantial social investment in their service objects. The goal is to improve the recipients' abilities and assist them in independently participating in community life and productive economic activities, while also actively assisting them in seeking broader social goals, such as democratic participation and egalitarian social justice.

There are essentially two approaches for practical implementation: in the field of intervention and strategy, which involves integrating social development and transforming it into a strategy of social investment, thus helping the client develop the ability to become a productive citizen and to fulfill their own life needs; or, at work in terms of goals and methods, which is differentiated from remedial social work.

The former starts from social development, and combines the country, market and society to promote planned social changes so as to in turn promote economic growth and the welfare of citizens. In order to inspire European and American societies to actively respond to emerging social inequality and group conflicts, relevant articles have often mirrored measurements from developing countries, such as literacy education, feminist movement, micro-economy and civilian bank loans (Midgley, 1996). The latter starts from the origin of social work and advocates this part of the professional tradition of developmental social work, which is embedded in the practice of charity associations and good neighborly organizations.

From the perspective of professional social work approaches, these are different from work on cases and groups in the past, which focused on treatment and behavior change. Developmental social work often applies community work, initiatives, social policies, research, social administration, social services, and organizational management. The objective of these macro-vision practices is to promote social development and protect the rights of the disadvantaged, focusing on the functions of prevention and development (Midgley & Conley, 2010).

Developmental social work is committed to advocating that everyone should enjoy an intact social life, and so it opposes institutional placement and care, while emphasizing that support for housing, transportation, education, medical care, and recreation should be provided by the community, and these social services per se also provide opportunities and resources, encourage individuals to participate in the productive economy (employment, entrepreneurship, or participation in the community economy) in the community, accumulate material, social, cultural and other types of assets for individuals, and improve the overall well-being of the community.

Specifically, the intervention of developmental social work has three characteristics:

1. Social investment, based on the community, combined with economic participation mechanisms, to promote the integration of personal life and society.
2. The belief that individuals are capable and willing to change, and utilize personal strengths and community assets.
3. Empowerment orientation, which involves maintaining an equal relationship with participants in dialogue, and promoting their development of the ability to respond to, and even challenge, the social structure (Midgley, 2010).

III. Research Methods

i. Research methods and implementation protocol

One of the characteristics of qualitative research is that it emphasizes the subjectivity of the study subjects. Researchers need to examine and interpret the phenomena in society from their standpoints. In addition to attaching importance to the description and understanding of the context from a holistic perspective, those researchers also need to find solutions to the problems. Moreover, if the study concept or theory is still in the preliminary stage of construction, when researchers want to further explore or define new concepts, this is often the time to apply qualitative study (Wang, 2004; Pan, 2003).

Based on the above understanding of qualitative research, this study explores and clarifies the practice of independent living in a community from a qualitative perspective, and combines relevant theoretical foundations and literature to promote the implementation of such a model. The researchers adopt in-depth interviews and use semi-structured interview outlines to collect and analyze data for persons with disabilities and for staff. The aim is to maintain the privacy of participants, and so the presentation of the information is conducted in an anonymous and non-public manner, while the conclusion is presented only in an overall format.

ii. Background of research subjects

This research mainly intends to present the appearance of persons with intellectual disabilities through the development of independent living in community residential services after being empowered under the concept of developmental social work. Therefore, eight persons with intellectual disabilities and four staff who are currently at the homestead were invited to enroll on this study. Their basic information is displayed in Table 1.

Table 1: Basic data sheet of research participants

Interviewee	Age	Gender	Education	Interviewee	Age	Education	Work experience
C1	44	Female	High school	W1	44	College	19 years
C2	22	Female	High school	W2	49	College	13 years
C3	29	Male	High school	W3	38	High school	3 years
C4	41	Female	Junior high	W4	29	College	1 year 2 months
C5	31	Female	High school				
C6	23	Female	High school				
C7	24	Female	High school				
C8	20	Male	High school				

Note: C-Persons with intellectual disabilities; W-Work staff

iii. Data collection and analysis

Prior to conducting the interview in this study, the researchers designed a semi-structured interview outline by studying relevant literature and thinking about, as well as deliberating, the aspects to be explored; they also employed a recording pen to assist in data collection. Before the end of the interview, the researchers confirmed whether the issues to be clarified and understood had been solved, and then conducted a verbatim transcription immediately after the interview was completed. During the study period, in addition to regular meetings and discussions, issues were discussed from time to time to formulate strategies, and amendments were made in the following interview to acquire more abundant information.

IV. Independent living in community residence format

People learn a variety of skills, knowledge and methods from the process of empowerment, all of which help them and others to enjoy a better quality of life. DuBois and Miley (2005) divided the empowerment process into three stages: dialogue, discovery, and development. The "process of dialogue" includes: 1. establish partnerships, 2. gallantly embrace challenges, and 3. set the direction of empowerment. Moreover, the "exploring process" includes: 1. discover the strengths of service subjects, 2. cultivate the ability to discover resources, and 3. explore ways to solve problems. The "development process" includes: 1. develop active resources, 2. create alliances and opportunities, and 3. acquire sense of accomplishment.

Secondly, in the process of empowerment, the demand of the client should not be regarded as a short-term goal, and the ability of the service subject must be improved in a gradual manner. Arnstein (1969) first proposed the ladder of citizen participation, or the ladder of empowerment model, and applied it to citizens' engagement in public affairs, from the lowest level of "manipulative participation" and "symbolic participation", through "partner participation", to the highest level of "independent participation". Later on, Hart (1992) applied the participation ladder model in the empowerment of young people. At the beginning there was manipulative participation, whereby the adults instructed and assigned tasks to the young people, following which the opinions of the young people were gradually added, and finally the young people and adults made joint decisions (Huang, 2013).

We take this empowerment model as a reference and adopt advantage analysis, emphasizing the strengths rather than shortcomings of the mentally impaired. In the initial stage of the empowerment of the community dwelling, the staff need to assist and lead, but as the ability of the persons with intellectual disabilities increases, they gradually establish a partnership via participating in the discussion, and in the end they will take the lead and apply what they have learned in daily life.

i. Constructing the concept of "home"

Since 1977, the ESWF has been following the trend of community service and has successively undertaken services related to the community of the New Taipei City Government. Since 2013, it has undertaken the "New Taipei City Xizhi Xiufeng Homestead" and in 2014 it undertook the "New Taipei City Yonghe Baofu Homestead", followed by the "Community Residential Services for the persons with disabilities in Wugu District, New Taipei City" in 2018.

Through the concept of "homestead", a living environment in the form of a "home" is provided for adults with intellectual disabilities, rather than stereotyped centralized management. Every person with intellectual disabilities should have the right to live in the community, and no longer be bound by standardized management, but also have the opportunity to dominate their own lives, enter the community, and interact with their neighbors.

Community residence takes the form of a "home", where four or five people with intellectual disabilities live together, while the men and women live separately. All major and minor domestic tasks, such as cooking, laundry, and mopping the floor, must be divided into labor with mutual assistance, and supported by the staff. All clients and staff perform their duties and play the role of family members, supporting and encouraging each other, maintaining the emotional function of the family, and thus allowing the clients to re-recognize the warmth of a home. In addition, a happy home must make residents feel friendly. The internal environment ought to be barrier-free so that the existing residents can live with ease. Moreover, the external environment must also be carefully selected. The most important thing is obtaining the support of the residents in the community.

In addition, to promote community housing and life service programs sustainably, staff members also receive professional training and incorporate the Supports Intensity Scale (SIS), which focuses on support needs, so as to assist and support people with intellectual disabilities to embark on independent living. The SIS consists of six aspects: self-care, community life, lifelong learning, employment activities, health and safety, and social interaction to identify the parts that need support. The objective is to assist the residents in achieving self-protection and in maintaining their rights, while also providing additional services for those with special medical and behavioral needs.

The content which is cultivated in community residence is actually designed to support all the tasks which persons with intellectual disabilities need to tackle in actual community life, such as domestic living, leisure, work, health, social skills, and interpersonal communication, etc. When the person with intellectual disabilities first arrives at the homestead, they may not have the experience of preparing their own meals or cooking, but they might go shopping. As long as they can buy something to eat, this is also a state of independent living. Moreover, their oral expression might be weak, but it may be that they can actively respond, perhaps just nodding as a response to social greetings. We will not regard these conditions as problems, but rather as a basis for accepting the empowerment of independent living.

ii. The concept that residents and staff inspire each other mutually: life is a game

The staff are asking themselves one question from the very beginning: What is the role of the homestead? It should be a "home", but is also a support and training environment. It is neither a school nor a unit of nursing care. Therefore, the relationship between the persons with intellectual disabilities and the staff will not be the same as that of interaction between normal students and teachers. Interaction is rather a service established under the "individual person-centered" concept, allowing persons with intellectual disabilities to build the life experience and living conditions they want to have, which is based on their personal preferences and needs. In response to the spirit of community living, the aim is to strengthen the residents' perception of "I can always do it", to replace dogmatic learning or imagination with personal experience, and to directly improve their abilities.

Therefore, through communication and interaction with the residents, the staff try to find a method that can actually be implemented in this "home". During the brainstorming and unconstrained discussions with the residents, they constructed a fun-filled practice with a clear direction: reality game-live-action Monopoly.

With reference to the famous Monopoly board game, the residents put the items that need to be supported into the design. It was similar to a giant real-world game map, including various empowerment projects, destiny or opportunity, rest, and one more time, etc. The staff assisted them in the completion of the foundation construction, game tour support and companionship. The objective was to support the residents in constructing their own blueprints for life, since residents are the authentic game players.

In terms of the rules of the game, the residents roll points and go to the target grid. The staff will discuss with the residents what needs to be supported in the area marked by the target grid, and then accompany the residents in completing these tasks. For example, after rolling the points, the resident moves to the "community life" grid, following which the staff will discuss with the resident what needs to be supported in this field, e.g. transportation or shopping in a store.

When residents enter the homestead, there will be an observation period of approximately 30 days before they begin to experience real-world games, during which time they will be playing and getting along with other residents and staff, and increasing mutual familiarity through such interaction. The dice is rolled once a month, and it will not interrupt the project that was originally experienced if they enter another empowerment project in the second month.

If the target field of the throw requires a lower level of support for the person with intellectual disabilities, then they can accompany other residents who are also in the same field to implement this empowerment project and thus strengthen the affirmation of one's own ability.

In addition, we have designed certain community service options in the game, such as simple maintenance of the community environment, care for the elders, and assistance in organizing materials, etc. The goal is to invite residents to demonstrate their abilities to provide feedback to the community and become palm-down persons. It is expected that the weak image which the general public have of persons with intellectual disabilities can be reversed.

Finally, when the tasks on the target grid are achieved, the residents can place their own action figure into that target grid, which means that they have fulfilled an empowerment project. This is an endless, cyclical experience game. Persons with intellectual disabilities can constantly find new goals for themselves and continue to move forward to implement independent living.

Considering the fact that most persons with intellectual disabilities are weak when it comes to generalization ability, we therefore integrate the entire empowerment process of independent living into real-world games, and utilize the natural community environment to replace the traditional teaching format. The objective is to use the memory of the body and experience it in the natural environment, which involves applying existing abilities to achieve goals.

The venue of the reality game is the environment of the entire community. The content of the game is actually the content of real life, and it is also the content that the community will support and cultivate. The people, issues, and substance in the community, including community residents and resources, are the elements that make the game more comprehensive, and these elements also directly participate in the entire empowerment process intangibly.

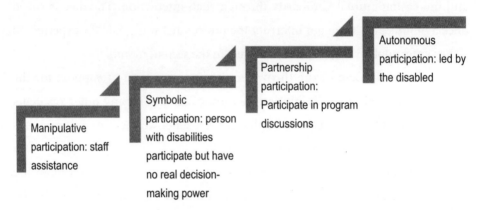

Figure 1: The ladder model of independent living

iii. Blue sky and white clouds are also teaching materials: empowerment has no framework

From the time when the persons with intellectual disabilities first move into their homestead, the staff will conduct interviews from the SIS point of view, analyze the status of the residents in all aspects when they first arrive, and identify the level of challenges in terms of "knowledge", such as:

1. Self-care: being unable to prepare meals by themselves, and not knowing how to clean the environment and storage items; watching TV is all they can do.
2. Community life: do not know how to take a ride, never go out shopping alone, and have no idea about public property.
3. Lifelong learning: lack a sense of color, time and space.
4. Employment activities: poor work quality, and only follow commands step by step.

5. Health and safety: do not know which specialty to look for when experiencing stomach pains; knowing their own medicines.

6. Social interactions: do not know how to introduce themselves, lack social courtesy, and have the same expressions for joy, anger, sorrow, and happiness.

When the residents discuss with each other designing methods that can be implemented in the community, we will try to incorporate those empowerment projects into their independent living naturally, and the staff can also discuss with the residents how to respond to, and deal with, said empowerment projects. In addition, we have embedded various unexpected scenarios in the opportunities and destiny sections, such as: learn to make a phone call, order meals, and pay correctly so you do not have to go out to buy lunch when a typhoon is raging, or if you perform well at work, the company may give you bonuses or raise your wage, or when you have a cold, resulting in an additional burden of medical expenses, and so on. These are a test for the residents, and such an exercise is also a way of verifying the strength of empowerment.

In addition to targeted empowerment programs, we have also designed appropriate and corresponding group activities to support different empowerment programs, so that persons with intellectual disabilities can learn more about what they will encounter in community life through different experience methods. When they reach the targeted grid of the empowerment program, the staff will invite them and ask them if they can spare time to participate in a specific empowerment group during their personal daily life.

It is obvious that there may be more than one project to support the empowerment. For example, the connotation of gender interactive groups at least covers social skills and interpersonal communication, while residential groups include community life, practical subjects and social skills etc.

By rolling dice once a month to determine the empowerment project and matching specific empowerment groups, what the staff see is that persons with intellectual disabilities in this process, through the "arrangement" and "choice" of the game format, can truly experience their own life; they can decide the areas which need to be supported, while also learning and improving their abilities with the assistance of staff and peers. They can share life stories, concerns and expectations for independent living, and support others in moving forward. They can gradually appreciate their own life, and have hope for the future. From the initial perspective of "knowledge", through the process of empowerment, persons with intellectual disabilities begin to progress toward the perspective of "ability" step by step.

We have also observed that, in such a process, we have not only tried to break the framework of the prior life experience of persons with intellectual disabilities, but have also allowed persons with intellectual disabilities to identify their own preferences gradually, which has further strengthened our confidence in the process of empowerment. In actual life, through repeated exercises and practical execution in the process, persons with intellectual disabilities can gradually demonstrate their abilities and approach the independent living as they prefer.

V. Conclusion

Community residence and life services can not only effectively improve the self-determination ability of persons with intellectual disabilities, but can also reduce the pressure of care for their families, improve relationships, and significantly reduce the burden of adaptation to the environment and getting along with others.

However, in terms of reflection on such services, community residences still have certain limitations. We are not an institution at all. In the process of providing services, we still cannot immediately get rid of the format of prior institutional care services. We support the learning of persons with intellectual disabilities through the empowerment of independent living in the community, with the intention of moving closer to the spirit of developmental social work.

However, the impression which persons with intellectual disabilities have of the staff is still that of "teacher".

In the process of empowerment with limited resources, we emphasize the development of the strength of persons with intellectual disabilities. The objective is to create an opportunity for them to learn to express their will, make their own choices and decisions, and be responsible for themselves. But we have also thought about whether there is any milestone for the service of independent living which can be regarded as a reference to complete the project.

We are all human beings. Even if we acquire a lot of "knowledge" and "ability" through learning or practice, we still may not react perfectly when encountering unexpected situations. For example, what should I do if I lose something? How can I deal with typhoons, earthquakes, fires, sexual harassment... etc.? Despite carrying out many drills, we still cannot achieve 100% when we actually encounter the situation. It may be that no one is able to get out of the situation without any blemishes, but we hope that, through continuous experiencing and learning, the response will become an instinct.

We also understand that "independent living" does not necessarily mean that persons with intellectual disabilities no longer require assistance, and the nature of certain empowerment programs does make it difficult for the staff to say: yes, you can live independently. An example in this regard would be how to practice the concept of sex education and make it a reflex action which is deeply embedded in the body's memory. Therefore, there is no set standard to complete the case. When the service subject is ready, we will help the subject return to the community, but there is only a six-month follow-up period. Under current policies and regulations, there is no excess energy for sustainable support. Should the regulations be adjusted to extend the follow-up period, or should we develop a stand-alone follow-up service for "stabilized independent living"?

From the perspective of developmental social work, the ESWF supports independent living for persons with intellectual disabilities through the process of empowerment. It not only provides a shelter to solve the problems which arise, but also encourages persons with intellectual disabilities to learn and gain strength throughout the entire service process. Moreover, the ESWF assists them in being independent and continuing to move forward to seek a better life. Since the beginning of the community residence service undertaken by the ESWF, said service has supported 21 persons with intellectual disabilities as they return to the community. In the future, the ESWF will continue to strive to move forward and support more persons with intellectual disabilities in living independently.

References

Chinese

內政部（2006）。**台灣成年心智障礙者社區居住與生活服務：實務操作手冊**。財法人心路社會福利基金會編印。

王雅各（2004）。質性研究導論。**質性研究**，第 3-55 頁。台北市：心理。

周月清（2005）。發展智能障礙者社區居住與生活：美英兩國探討比較。**社會政策與社會工作學刊**，9（2），第 139-196 頁。

周月清（2006）。現行居住政策檢視——以推動智能障礙者社區居住與生活為例。**東吳社會工作學報**，15，第 155-189 頁。

周月清、尤珮蓉、張淑娟（2016）。比較中老年與非中老年智障服務使用者支持需求與生活品質。**臺大社工學刊**，34，第 85-128 頁。

周月清、李婉萍、張意才（2007）。住民社區居住與生活參與、選擇與自主：以台灣六個團體家庭成年智能障礙者為例。**東吳社會工作學報**，16，第 37-78 頁。

周鎮忠（2016）。**發展性社會工作：理念與實務的激盪**。第 17-26 頁。

社論（2018）。支持、增權與社會融合——推動滿意生活品質的自立服務。**社區發展季刊**，164，第 1-5 頁。

郭登聰（2016）。發展性社會工作在社區產業運用的討論：兼論對於社會企業的思考弱勢族群工作。輔仁大學社會工作學系主辦，「發展性社會工作與金融社會工作推動的檢視與再思考：延續與創新」學術研討會，輔仁大學濟時樓九樓國際會議廳。

陳佩英（2004）。意識與行動——台灣婦女／性別研究建制化歷程之探討。**通識教育季刊**，11（1-2），第 39-72 頁。

陳佩英（2008）。從培力的對話觀點探討教師的專業成長。**高雄師大學報**，24，第 21-48 頁。

游美惠（2002）。增能／增權／培力／彰權益能／權力增長（empowerment）。**性別平等教育季刊**，19，第 98-101 頁。

馮燕（2016）。**發展性社會工作：理念與實務的激盪**。第 3-4 頁。

蔡和蓁、陳武宗、陳政智（2006）。以正常化觀點探討心路基金會社區居住與生活服務方案。**中華民國特殊教育學會年刊**，95 年度，第 39-52 頁。

羅秀華（2012）。將社會發展理念融入社會工作。**社區發展季刊**，138，第 251-262 頁。

English

Barnes, C. (1992). Making Our Own Ohoices: Independent Living, Personal Assistance and Disabled People (Report of the BCODP Seminar on Independent Living and

Personal Assistance Herewood College, Coventry, August, 1992). The British Council of Organisations of Disabled People.

Conger, J. A. & Kanungo, R. N. (1988). *Charismatic leadership*. San Franciso: Jossey-Bass.

Harpur, P. (2012). From disability to ability: changing the phrasing of the debate. *Disability & Society*, 27(3), 325-337.

Midgley, J. (1993). Ideological roots of social development strategies. *Social Development Issues*, 15(1), 1-13.

Midgley, J. (2010). The theory and practice of development social work. In J. Midgley & A. Conley (Eds.), *Social Work and Social Development: Theories and Skill for Development Social Work* (pp. 3-28). New York: Oxford University Press.

Oliver, Michael (1996). *Understanding disability: From theory to practice*. London: Macmillan.

Piat, M. & Sabetti, J. (2012). Recovery in Canada: toward social equality. *International Review of Psychiatry*, 24(1), 19-28.

Prilleltensky, I., Nelson, G., & Peirson, L. (2001). The role of power and control in children's lives: an ecological analysis of pathways toward wellness, resilience and problems. *Journal of Community and Applied Social Psychology*, 11:143-158.

Rappaport, J. (1987). Terms of empowerment/exemplars of prevention: Toward a theory for community psychology. *American Journal of Community Psychology*, 15: 121-143.

Thomas, M. & Pierson, J. (1995). *Dictionary of social work*. London: Collins Educational.

The Sparkling Child

Chan Chun Chung[*]

Abstract

Social impairment is the core deficit of Autism Spectrum Disorder (ASD) (DSM-5, 2013). Systematic and focused intervention addressing this cardinal feature is very limited (Chan et al., 2014). The model of "Cognitive Behavioral Therapy Context-based Social Competence Training for ASD (CBT-CSCA)" has been locally developed by the New Life Psychiatric Rehabilitation Association as a key intervention protocol to address the social training needs of persons with ASD (PWAs), with special reference to the Hong Kong contexts. CBT-CSCA has been adopted for service design to strengthen the social competence of PWAs in order to increase their social inclusivity in different developmental stages throughout the lifespan.

In view of the developmental needs of PWAs from adolescence to adulthood, the iSPARK and employment support services have been tailored for PWAs to build their employability, independence and self-efficacy through the CBT-CSCA training program. Job assessment, pre-vocational training, placement and job matching services are offered to PWAs with ongoing support from the Training and Employment Officers. A total of 256 PWAs have been trained since 2013, 113 of whom have had successful open employment. On the other hand, an iBuddy program has been designed for PWAs to enhance their opportunities for community participation. We have developed a partnership with 12 NGOs and social service groups of academic institutes. Over 100 social activities and voluntary services have been organized for 42 iBuddies (neuro-typical youth) and PWAs to participate and interact with one another. PWAs reported that they not only practiced social

* Center Manager of Jockey Club iREACH Social Competence Development and Employment Support Project of New Life Psychiatric Rehabilitation Association.

competence skills, but also developed friendship with iBuddies. We firmly believe that the strengths and potential of PWAs can be unleashed and enhanced once they have received appropriate training and services, and that opportunities can be created for them to contribute to society, thus meaning that their lives can fully sparkle.

I. Introduction

Social competence deficits are the core characteristics identified in PWAs (Stichter et al., 2010; Chan et al., 2014; Yau et al., 2014). The impairments usually lead to a negative impact in understanding and recognizing feelings, responding and making judgments. Challenges in emotion regulation, executive functioning and cognitive flexibility are also common associated problems. These undesirable attributes usually result in barriers when it comes to developing and maintaining peer relationships (Merrell & Gimpel, 1998; Ozonoff et al., 2000; Bauminger et al., 2003) as well as leaving PWAs unable to perform reciprocal behaviors to sustain social interaction (APA, 2013). Additionally, difficulties in information processing (Central Coherence Theory, Firth 1989), work memory, planning, organizing (Executive Functioning, Ozonoff et al., 1991) and mentalizing (Theory of Mind, Baron-Cohen et al., 1985) are also common features in PWAs.

There is no cure for ASD (Fecteau at al., 2003; de Bruin et al., 2014), but social competence interventions show significant effectiveness in the enhancement of social responsiveness, especially when it comes to the aspects of social skills and executive functions (Stichter et al., 2010; Yau et al., 2014).

According to the Center of Disease and Prevention Control (CDC), approximately 1 in 68 children were identified as having ASD in 2013 in the USA, whereas, in 2002, this statistic was 1 in 150. This figure indicates an alarming increase in the number of PWAs. The rising trend is similar in Hong Kong. According to the Census and Statistics Department of Hong Kong, 10,200 persons were diagnosed with ASD in 2014. When compared with 3,800 people being diagnosed in 2007, this is a growth of almost 270%. However, services and resources in educational, medical and psychosocial aspects had long been clustered mostly for children, leaving adolescent and young adult PWAs lacking sufficient support, especially during their transitional stages. A clear need to expand the intervention to cater for adolescent and young adult PWAs was identified.

Life transitions are critical times for all adolescents and young adults with ASD who are in the stage of identity development and life goal formulation. These transitions are particularly stressful for adolescents and young persons with ASD as well as their families, since inflexibility and difficulty with routines change have always been the landmark characteristics of the autism phenotype.

The establishment of the Jockey Club iREACH Social Competence Development and Employment Support Project for Young Persons with ASD aims at strengthening the social competence of young PWAs in order to increase their social inclusivity in different aspects of their lives. i-R-E-A-C-H stands for Individual, Reconnection, Emotion, Action, Cognition and Happiness, which are the core training domains and service missions of iREACH. The service seeks to support PWAs over the age of 15 who are in the stage of life transition from childhood to adolescence and from adolescence to young adulthood.

The overall design of the service is based on the following theoretical models and evidence-based findings:

i.   A lifespan approach for Autism (Leblanc, Riley, & Goldsmith, 2008);

ii. A recovery orientation;

iii. A systemic approach; and

iv. A self-developed model of "Cognitive Behavioral Therapy Context-based Social Competence Training for ASD (CBT-CSCA)" (Chan et al., 2014).

The below diagram represents an integrative model which serves as a major guide in the designs of iREACH's various services for all adolescents and young adults with ASD:

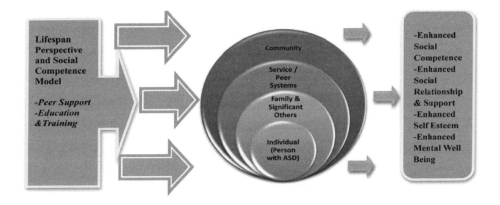

Figure1: An integrative model of iREACH

II. Effectiveness of the CBT-CSCA Training Program

Local research on ASD remains in its early stage of development and greater impetus to realize its growth is imminent. To capture the effectiveness of the CBT-CSCA training program and to develop evidence-based practice to consolidate systemic intervention for PWAs, an evaluation mechanism was built in by iREACH so as to assess the effectiveness of the training program. The professional team, in collaboration with Professor Patrick Leung, Department of Psychology, the Chinese University of Hong Kong, had completed the local validation studies on Autism Spectrum Quotient (AQ-Child, Adolescent & Adult Versions, Baron-Cohen et al., 2001) and Multidimensional Social Competence Scale (MSCS, Yager & Larocci, 2013) and had translated them into Chinese for local adaptation in Hong Kong. The MSCS is employed as the primary measure for its sensitivity in assessing social competence.

Development of the CBT-CSCA is based on the propositions of Cognitive Behavioral Therapy (Craske, 2010), the validated components of social competence for ASD (Yager & Larocci, 2013) and the effectiveness of social skills training for ASD (Reichow & Volkmar, 2010). The CBT-CSCA is locally developed and was empirically tested with both the pre- and post-test design on 94 PWAs in the pioneer initiative, namely iLinks Social Enrichment Project for Teens with ASD, during the period spanning 2011 to 2014. Significant improvement on the Social Responsiveness Scale (SRS) was reported, as the score of PWAs was reduced from 102.54 to 89.17 (p<.001) and remained at 88.14 at the 3-month follow up (Yau et al., 2014). The effectiveness of the CBT-CSCA was further confirmed by the iREACH project in 2015 with a control group study. In the study, PWAs enrolled on the CBT-CSCA training program attended a 2-hour training program within a group of eight members for 15 sessions. Social competence refers to "an organizational construct that reflects the child/ adolescent's capacity to integrate behavioral, cognitive and affective skills to adapt flexibly to diverse social contexts and demands" (Bierman & Welsh, 2010 as cited in Chan et al., 2017). Four training modules were developed, namely the specific social context (social motivation and social knowledge), behavior (verbal conversational and non-verbal sending skills), emotion (emotion regulation skills and demonstrating empathetic concern) and cognition (social inferencing). Concretized behavioral and cognitive skills would be trained through structured didactic teaching, role-play, live and video modeling, prompting, step to step rehearsal, performance feedback, reinforcement, visual cues support, revision and weekly assignments, as well as consistent homework reviews (Chan et al., 2017).

The data collected indicated that there were no significant differences between the experiment (N=33) and control (N=17) groups before training. After completion of training, significant improvement was found in the experimental group for parents' ratings on MSCS-C, a measure of social competence (F=8.15, p=.006), PSS, a measure of parental stress (F=4.88, p=.032) and CBCL, a measure of general psychopathology (F=6.64, p=.013). The PWAs' self-ratings also revealed significant improvement on MSCS-C (F=5.59, p=0.22) but not on YSR, a measure of general psychopathology (F=2.3, p=0.136). The PWAs in the control group (N=17) received the same training after the control period and also reported significant improvement (Chan et al., 2016).

The training results of the CBT-CSCA suggested an improvement in social competence of PWAs and a reduction of symptoms in emotional and behavioral conditions; indeed, these results were maintained 3 months after the training. The quantitative results and qualitative feedback which were translated into English are presented in Appendix 1 and Appendix 2 respectively. Other qualitative feedback can be reviewed on the iREACH website (http://ireach.nlpra.org.hk/board/).

With the locally-adapted translation of the measurement tools, the effectiveness of the CBT-CSCA training program in teaching social competence to adolescent PWAs was further validated in 2017 (Chan et al., 2017). The research paper was firstly published online in October 2017 and print published in February 2018 by the Journal of Autism and Developmental Disorder. Prior to the publication of this research paper, the iREACH professional team also submitted research papers on ASD to the Hong Kong Journal of Mental Health and the Journal of the Hong Kong Society of Child Neurology and Developmental Paediatrics. In conclusion, CBT-CSCA, as an evidence-based practice, is an effective training program for PWAs to enhance their social competence in Hong Kong.

III. The CBT-CSCA Training Program

The training content incorporated the culturally-sensitive and developmentally-appropriate elements after accumulating experiences and collecting feedback from both PWAs and their parents. The common social contexts that the adolescents would encounter, such as dining out with family relatives and visiting shopping arcades with peers, were set as the learning contexts where role-play and rehearsals would be practiced. In response to the growing number of adult PWAs, social contexts in work settings and tertiary education institutes are used to enhance their learning motivation, knowledge integration and practice generalization. The CBT-CSCA training program outline is presented in the following Table 1.

Table 1: A brief outline of the CBT-CSCA training programme

Session	Module	Core Content
1-3	Social context: motivation and knowledge	• Introduce the purpose, structure and rules of the training program; enhance motivation for group participation; • Understand hidden social rules; learn to detect hidden social rules in social contexts which are common to adolescents.
4-7	Behavior: active listening, conversation, and electronic communication	• Learn active listening skills, detect signals of exiting conversations and practice their application; • Learn how to initiate, maintain and end conversations; understand four conversation blockers; • Learn how to join in group conversations and skills in electronic communications.
8-11	Emotion: facial, gesture and tonal recognition and expression; regulation and empathy	• Understand how to recognize emotion through facial expressions; • Understand how to recognize emotions through tonal and gestural expressions; • Learn skills which make it possible to handle criticism and related negative emotions; • Understand what empathy is and how to deliver empathic responses.
12-14	Cognition and integration: social inference and friendship building	• Learn how to make inferences based on others' thoughts; • Understand the interpersonal circle, how to join group activities and how to detect unwelcome signals.
15	Graduation	• Share learning and celebrate for graduation.

IV. Increasing Number of Adult PWAs

The number of PWAs has drastically increased in Hong Kong and globally over recent years. An estimation of at least a 20% increase annually of students with ASD is projected by the Education Bureau of Hong Kong (JCA-Connect, 2015). Given the rapid increase in the number of people diagnosed with ASD since the 1990s, many young people with ASD are now entering adulthood. According to the Census and Statistics Department, in 2014, more than 3,500 age-appropriate PWAs were deemed suitable to enter the workforce. When the projected number of adult PWAs is aligned with the estimation of 20% annually advocated by the Education Bureau of Hong Kong, the estimated number of adult PWAs will probably reach over 6,000 in 2019.

According to the demographic data analysis of the current iREACH service users, 43.4% of them are PWAs aged over 18. They are potential school leavers who will leave the education system and enter the workforce soon. Indeed, there should be provided services which aim to enhance their transition from school to work, from adolescence to adulthood, from dependent to independent living, and from single to building an intimate relationship, as such services would enhance the holistic support for the above-mentioned service users. Hence, with iSPARK (i-S-P-A-R-K stands for individual, Strengths-based, Potential Development, Alliance with Employers, Rewards in Work and Kindling Hope), the employment support services for adult PWAs have been in place since 2013, with the aim of preparing and supporting their employability and sustainability in work environments in response to the rising number of adult PWAs in society. This proposal is designed to meet the developmental needs of adult PWAs and to facilitate their independent functioning as well as inclusion in society.

V. iSPARK—Employment Support Services for Adult PWAs

Entering into the workforce is not at all easy for adult PWAs. Engagement in gainful employment means securing financial rewards, self-respect, a sense of efficacy and social participation, so as to attain social inclusion (Chan et al., 2013). Yet, employment opportunities are always limited and difficult to find for PWAs, because of their unique social competence deficits (Howlin, 2013; Roux et al., 2013; Hendricks, 2010) and the difficulties they experience when attempting to handle life transition challenges (de Bruin, 2007). Taylor and Seltzer (2010) found an unemployment rate of over 82% among young PWAs. For those 18% who were employed, most of them were engaged in low-paid and unskilled jobs and in part-time mode only. Research conducted in Hong Kong revealed a similar phenomenon. Over 87% of employed PWAs (n=33) were hired to carry out manual work with lower social ranks which did not match with their abilities (Poon, 2012). This percentage was much higher than the neuro-typical youth, as only 16.6% of neuro-typical youth would engage in elementary occupations. Services to support PWAs in employment are still scarce and underdeveloped in Hong Kong, although various studies on supported employment services have demonstrated their effectiveness in enhancing employability and job sustainability (Howlin et al., 2005; Herndricks, 2009; Holwerda et al., 2013). The employment support service iSPARK has thus filled the services gap and addressed the needs of the adult PWAs.

Indeed, PWAs have many strengths, talents and skills. For instance, some of them are attentive to details and able to demonstrate excellent adherence to schedules. Most of them are proficient in following instructions and have strong memory abilities. Some demonstrate exceptional mathematics, artistic and musical talents. They are generally valued for their loyalty, honestly, kindness and dedication. These strengths and abilities could be put to good use if the PWAs could be matched to appropriate work trades and work environments. Given the right opportunities, proper support and relevant job matching, PWAs are able to engage effectively in employment and realize their full potential while also becoming useful members of the workforce.

iSPARK has developed two evidence-informed training modules, namely "Social Competence at Work" and "Preparation for Work", both of which are designed to support PWAs in employment. The module Social Competence at Work is based on the model of "Cognitive Behavioral Therapy Context-based Social Competence Training for ASD (CBT-CSCA)". It aims to prepare PWAs to acquire basic social competence in communication, perspective taking, emotional regulation and problem-solving skills in the work context. Pre-vocational assessments of work abilities, job interests, temperament and strengths will be carried out on an individual basis, so as to facilitate matching of placements and open employment for every PWA. The second module of the training is

Preparation for Work, which focuses on teaching PWAs about work concepts, job seeking and interviewing skills, in order to prepare them for placements and open employment. The iSPARK training modules are presented in Table 2 below.

Table 2: The iSPARK training modules

Session	Content
1-6 (2-hr/session)	**Social Competence at Work:** Social competence concepts, emotion regulation, perspective taking, conversation, hidden social rules and problem-solving skills.
7 (3-hr/session)	**Integrated Practice:** Skills practice in a lunch activity at a restaurant and proper dining etiquette training.
8-12 (2-hr/session)	**Preparation for Work:** Training on work concepts, negotiation, organization and reporting skills, job seeking and resume preparation. Interview skills training, individual mock interviews and review sessions are rendered.
13 (3-hr/session)	**Integrated Practice:** Skills practice of negotiation, problem-solving, organization and reporting through planning a party activity held in the community.
120-hour Job Placement	A job placement in an authentic work setting with supportive atmosphere is guaranteed in the Social Enterprises (SE) operated by our Association and its 15 partner companies. User's work and social behavior are assessed by the Becker Work Adjustment Profile-Chinese Version (BWAP-CV) to map out strengths and weaknesses. The identified weaknesses will be remediated during the placement.

It is never too soon to embed positive work habits for adolescent PWAs transitioning to adult PWAs. Career planning and vocational training can start early for school leavers. Assessment of career interest, aptitudes, skills, abilities and sensory characteristics are essential when it comes to enhancing realistic appraisal of interests and strengths. Currently, iSPARK provides three flexible modes to match PWAs' availability and needs: (i) three morning/week group training sessions tailored for PWAs without work engagement, together with 13 training sessions and a 120-hour job placement; (ii) two evening/week group training sessions tailored for working with PWAs to strengthen their social competence at work, in addition to six training sessions on social competence which will be provided alongside an optional job placement; and (iii) individual training provided for PWAs who are unsuitable for group training but motivated to work, including the provision of 11 training sessions (1-6 and 8-12) and a 120-hour job placement.

After completion of the pre-vocational training, a placement trial is included as an integral part of the employment support service to provide a real work setting for PWAs to practice their social competence and strengthen their skills in working. As placements are positively correlated to more successful job hunting (Hendricks, 2009), iSPARK will arrange for PWAs to undertake a 120-hour placement in a real work setting before they pursue open employment. The placement will be arranged in the social enterprises or in the company partners of the Association. PWAs will undergo interviews for the placements, so as better matching can be achieved. The placement will last for 120 hours, and a total of $2,100 ($17.5X120), which accounts for approximately 50% of the Statutory Minimum Wage as stipulated in the Minimum Wage Ordinance (cap 608), will be awarded to the PWAs upon their completion of the placement. The placement subsidy can serve as an incentive to drive the work motivation of PWAs and enhance their sense of achievement.

On-the-job support sessions will be conducted throughout the placement and in the first 6 months of open employment; these will be offered to both the PWAs and the employers. It has been reported that such sessions are essential for monitoring and providing timely intervention to enhance employment sustainability (Howlin, 2005; ASERT, 2013). On-site briefing sessions for employers and work supervisors will be conducted on the PWAs' first duty commencement day, in order to facilitate effective communication and enhance mutual understanding. The Training and Employment Officers will closely monitor the performance of PWAs in work and provide timely intervention through various means, such as on-site visits, phone and WhatsApp consultations. In addition, supportive group and work-related activities, including visits to work places, peer-led work experiences sharing and job expos, will be organized for PWAs, so as to expand their understanding of different work trades and requirements, as well as to consolidate their work attitudes.

VI. The effectiveness of iSPARK

iSPARK has already supported 256 adult PWAs in terms of preparing them for open employment. Among those, 113 successfully gained employment after training. As of the end of 2019, 68.1% (77 out of those 113) of the PWAs are still working and most of them have been sustaining the same job for over 6 months. Compared with the research conducted in the UK, where only 12% of the PWAs were engaged in full-time and 6% in part-time employment (Barnard, 2001), the employment rate of iSPARK is 5.6 times higher.

A total of four assessment tools, including Rosenberg Self-Esteem Scales (RSE), Depression Anxiety Stress Scales (DASS), the State Hope Scale (SHS) and the Multi-dimensional Social Competence Scale (MSCS) were used at the initial intake session, post- and pre-vocational training, post-placement and post-open employment, in order to evaluate the effectiveness and impacts of training after the PWAs entered the job market. The general results suggested that 92.8% of PWAs showed a significant and high level of self-esteem, confidence in working, and improvement in social competencies at the workplace after completing the pre-vocational training, job placement and open employment. Aside from the quantitative feedback, some qualitative feedback was also collected from both the employers and the PWAs; this feedback is presented in Appendix 3.

With the tailored design of the CBT-CSCA pre-vocational training program and the 120-hour placement trial, as well as the 6 months' on-the-job support provided to PWAs and employers, we have been successful in preparing adult PWAs for employment and sustaining work. Besides this, iSPARK has also established close collaborative partnerships with many corporations, such as Delifrance, Chinese Manufacturers' Association, Lane Crawford, PARK n SHOP, Hang Yick Property Management Ltd. and Shatin Recycle Center, to name a few. In the past years, all of these corporations have offered PWAs different work trades, such as administration, catering, logistics and cleansing etc., as well as placement opportunities and employment, and they are ready to continue hiring PWAs in the future. To summarize, the number of successful employment cases has proved the effectiveness of the iSPARK service for PWAs. A higher percentage of service users were able to utilize their strengths and realize their abilities and potential at different workplaces.

VII. Need for Social Inclusion

Life in transition from adolescence to adulthood is not easy for anyone, and adult PWAs are no exception. Moreover, the challenges faced by them are worsened by their deficits in social competence. As a consequence, most adult PWAs tend to become socially excluded after leaving the education system.

Social inclusion means providing opportunities for everyone to participate in key activities in individual, family, communal and societal domains within society (Huxley et al., 2006). Building an inclusive society aims at "lowering economic, social and cultural boundaries, or making boundaries more permeable" for everyone, including PWAs (United Nations, 2008). In recent years, social inclusion has been adopted as the "guiding spirit" to help all individuals enjoy equality and respect in different aspects of life in Hong Kong (The Hong Kong Government, 2012). Taking social inclusion as the service mission, iREACH strives to enhance and empower PWAs to reach fair, if not equal, opportunities to access different domains, such as family, education, employment and cultural life of society (Autism Speaks, 2013).

VIII. iBuddy Program—Community Participation for PWAs

The iBuddy program is designed to expand the social horizons of young persons with ASD and to encourage their development of social relationships. This particular program will recruit a group of neuro-typical youth to become "iBuddies" of individuals with ASD. The iBuddy program contains three levels of services: (i) training to enhance iBuddy's understanding of ASD; (ii) invite the neuro-typical youth to join and support iREACH interest activities as volunteers; and (iii) involve those youth in cooperating with the alumni committee to prepare proposals and activities for other PWAs of iREACH.

i. Training to enhance iBuddy's understanding of ASD

PWAs may experience high levels of discrimination and stigmatization within society in different aspects of life. Negative interactions with others might include direct confrontations such as bullying, or less obvious forms, such as discrimination. These situations can occur at any time during the person's lifetime. Therefore, it is important to educate and provide accurate information to the iBuddies to enhance their understanding and acceptance of people with ASD. In view of this, training not only includes the introduction of ASD, but also role-play practice to provide opportunities for neuro-typical youth to act as PWAs and thus to experience the difficulties and challenges encountered in their daily life. We will also arrange for PWAs to share their personal stories with the iBuddies, which is the most insightful part, as it allows them to reflect on how to get along with the PWAs, as reported by iBuddies themselves.

ii. Invite iBuddies to join and support iREACH interest activities as volunteers

iBuddies will be invited and matched with PWAs to engage in communications, social interactions and relationship-building in various activities, so as to provide a real social environment for them to get along with one another. Communication and reflective listening skills will also be shared with iBuddies in advance, so as to better equip them with the knowledge and skills necessary to interact with PWAs.

iii. Involve iBuddies in cooperating with alumni committee of iREACH to prepare activities for other PWAs and voluntary services for the community partners

An iREACH Alumni Committee, an energetic team of iREACH, was formed under the guidance of professional workers in September 2016. PWAs who have graduated from the CBT-CSCA training program are nominated, selected and trained to be committee members who will contribute to arranging social activities to enhance iREACH members' practices and generalization of social competence skills in different contexts. They will also serve as role models to demonstrate the benefits of having friends, social activities and community integration through joining iREACH. They will have different positions, duties and responsibilities in the committee, which will serve as a platform for them to participate, learn, grow and develop under guidance from professional staff. On the other hand, iBuddies who are passionate and committed to serving PWAs will be invited to join in the alumni committee meetings, which are scheduled on a monthly basis, to discuss and prepare proposal activities for other PWAs and voluntary service for community partners. The committee provides a two-way communicative platform for both PWAs and iBuddies to meet a few times and work together to co-organize voluntary service. This mutual participation is a valuable experience for PWAs, and a chance to get along with neuro-typical youth. At the same time, iBuddies also have more understanding of PWAs. iBuddies shared that they enjoyed doing voluntary work with PWAs, while PWAs expressed positive gain in the socializing experiences with iBuddies. Their confidence to relate to each other was enhanced. 97.6% of iBuddies reported that they had enhanced understanding and acceptance of PWAs. Furthermore, 100.0% and 87.5% of PWAs reported that their emotional regulation (control of emotional expression) and social competence were strengthened.

Besides the above, strengthening partnership ties and collaborating with different community services is one of the major missions of iREACH, through which it hopes to cultivate inclusion and expand the service horizon for PWAs in the community. A series of community education and service campaigns, such as press conferences, mass media interviews or discussion forums etc. are arranged to facilitate experiences sharing and to thus promote the positive image of PWAs while also acknowledging the efforts and contributions from collaborative partners. So far, iREACH has collaborated with 12 community partners, including the social service groups of different universities, non-governmental organizations, and volunteer groups in Hong Kong. Moreover, iREACH has arranged over 100 training sessions and activities for 42 iBuddies and PWAs.

IX. Conclusion

Life transitions are always challenging for people, and especially for PWAs. A diversified range of intervention and continuous supportive services for PWAs is essential in order to address their developmental challenges. The iREACH project team has worked committedly and enthusiastically to serve PWAs and their family caregivers in order to ensure that they can function optimally during life transitional stages. We at iREACH firmly believe that PWAs could contribute to, and integrate into, society after receiving appropriate training, support and opportunities, and hence their lives could fully sparkle.

Appendix 1:

Quantitative Outcome—CBT-CSCA Training Program

Service	Expected Outcome	Assessment Tools	Outcomes
CBT-CSCA Training Program	PWAs who joined the CBT-CSCA Training Program showed an increase in social competence	-Parent-report MSCS-C (*Multidimensional Social Competence Scale-Chinese Version*) -PWA-report MSCS-C	A total of 236 parent-report measures and PWA-report measures were collected. A with-in subject comparison across three time-points, namely pre-condition, post-condition and 3-month follow-up, was conducted. For parent-report MSCS-C, there was a significant difference of mean scores across three time-points, $F(2,106)=12.98$, $p<.001$. The post hoc test revealed that the mean score in pre-condition (M=2.69) was significantly lower than that in post-condition (M=2.93), $p<.001$ while that between post-condition and 3-month follow-up (M=2.93) did not differ significantly, $p=1.000$. For PWA-report MSCS, a trend of improved social competence from pre-condition (M=3.24) to post-condition (M=3.37) and 3-month follow-up (M=3.35) was observed, but did not reach statistical significance $F(2, 84)=2.516$, $p=.087$.
	PWAs who joined the CBT-CSCA Training Program reported an improvement in emotional and behavioral conditions	-Parent-report PSS (*Parent Stress Scale*) -Parent-report CBCL (*Children Behavior Checklist*) -Parent-report AQ (*Autism Quotient*) -PWA-report YSR (*Youth Self Report*) -PWA-report AQ -PWA-report DASS (*Depression Anxiety Stress Scale*)	For parent-report CBCL, there was a significant difference of mean scores across three time-points, $F(2,66)=5.826$, $p=.011$. The post hoc test revealed that mean score in pre-condition (M=55.34) was significantly higher than that in post-condition (M=46.26), $p=.037$, while that between post-condition and 3-month follow-up (M=43.66), did not differ significantly, $p=1.000$. For PWA-report YSR, there was a significant difference in mean scores across three time-points, $F(2,43)=5.946$, $p=.005$. The post hoc test revealed that mean score at pre-condition (M=69.13) was significantly higher than mean score at 3-month follow-up (M=49.40), $p=.003$.

Appendix 2:

Qualitative Feedback on the CBT-CSCA from PWAs and Family Caregivers

PWAs	Family Caregivers
I think this social competence training group is very meaningful. It can integrate the daily life experiences into the content in the classroom. It is beneficial and I meet different friends. I hope more similar groups will be provided in the future! Thanks to our caring instructors!	Very satisfied with the training, allowing both parents and children to learn mutually. Parents can help their children to apply the knowledge acquired in this group. It is very practical. It is the most useful and best training I have ever had.
After fifteen sessions of this social competence training, I deeply felt that the first step of socializing in the adult circle and life in the workplace lies in social thinking. I also need a platform for social adaptation, even if I have other activities in iREACH at the same time.	I appreciated the iREACH social competence training group very much, using simple and down-to-earth examples, so that my child can complete fifteen lessons without pressure. I am also impressed that iREACH focuses on parental education, whereby parents can also practice our skills at home.
I'm so happy that I met a lot of friends, and I finally started to understand what other people are thinking, so that I know that I can join the conversation at the appropriate time.	I am very happy to be able to participate in the social competence training group of iREACH, which provides many tips and teachings, and also improves my relationship with my son. Thank you to all the staff!
Since joining this group I have been very happy, and I have a group of good friends. I felt very sad at the graduation ceremony; I would like to thank everyone.	My son was very happy to join the class and I could see his progress day by day. Now, he has his own social circle. Thanks to all the staff for their teaching, acceptance and care.
Through fifteen sessions of social competence training, I learned a lot about the importance of social skills. It greatly enhanced my communication with classmates, friends and family in my daily life. I enjoyed the snack time and after-class activities with group members most. We will miss each other as the class has come to an end, but thanks to all the members for participating.	Organizations offering social competence training in Hong Kong like iREACH are rare. It is a blessing, and has helped these lonely children. My son found his friends in iREACH, which meant that he also found belonging. He has his own WhatsApp group with his friends now. It is a milestone in his growth. I believe this group of children will excel further in the future.
iREACH made me rich! Not physically rich, but it made us more human and friendly. As a result, it made our lives easier and more enjoyable.	Many thanks to the staff and fellow members. My daughter highly appreciated this training and regarded it as the best social competence training she had ever had!

PWAs	Family Caregivers
I am stepping into society in the future. I can utilize the social skills learnt from the group to get along with colleagues and be welcomed by more people.	Thanks to the iREACH social competence training group for giving my son more opportunities to experience interpersonal relationships. This course also allows me to meet his group members and other parents, with all of us encouraging and supporting each other.
Thank you for holding the social competence training group, which has allowed me to learn a lot of social and dating skills, while I also encountered many new friends. Thank you.	My son became very active after joining the social competence training class. He could utilize the social skills naturally, and he now has more interaction with others. I hope he can become a "superman" in his social life!
I felt very satisfied with this social competence training group, which involved skills such as communicating with friends and fostering effective communication. Miss So and Miss Chan helped us a lot. Thank you!	I wanted to express my gratitude to iREACH for allowing me to realize that my son was indeed eager to seek help. He learnt happily. I have met many parents and learned how to communicate with him better.
I have learned a lot, such as initiating conversation with others; these are very useful skills.	Thanks to iREACH. It is a platform for children and parents to learn together. My son understands the importance of socializing. It also made me better at teaching and understanding him. We have benefited a lot from this course.

Appendix 3:

Qualitative Feedback on iSPARK Services from PWAs and Employers

PWAs' feedback on pre-vocational training, placement and open employment
1. The training materials were very practical; concrete visual aids with cause and effect were included. We could better understand the importance of theories (theory of mind) and practice through multimedia and role-play.
2. The quality of the service was very good and the duration of training was suitable. Through small-class training, trainees could receive sufficient support from employment coaches and be able to build up mutual trust.
3. The mock interview equipped me with the skills needed to perform better in real job interviews.
4. The placement was very practical; it was able to enhance my vocational skills and prepare me for employment.
5. We could contact employment coaches at their work mobile for immediate support.
6. I appreciate that this project existed and helped me socially adapt at the workplace.
Employers' feedback on placement and open employment
1. The PWAs were devoted, hardworking and willing to communicate with others. This experience gave me a new perspective from which to view persons challenged by ASD. I appreciate this service, which allows PWAs to learn and integrate into society. I hope that more PWAs will be able to arrange to take placements in the future.
2. The PWAs treasured the job opportunity. With the employment coach's patience and the regular follow-ups, it was a memorable experience.
3. The PWAs' work attitude was good and the employment coaches provided sufficient support and maintained close communication with the unit; useful suggestions were also provided to guide the trainees at work.

References

ASPECT PRACTICE (2013). Siblings of children with autism spectrum disorder at Autism Spectrum Australia. Retrieved from http://www.autismspectrum.org.au

Auyeung, Bonnie, Baron-Cohen, Simon, Wheelwright, Sally, & Allison, Carrie (2001). The Autism Spectrum Quotient: Children's Version (AQ-Child).

Barnard, J., Harvey, V., & Potter, D. (2001). *Ignored or ineligible? The reality for adults with autism spectrum disorders.* London: The National Autistic Society.

Chan, R. W. S., Lo, T. L., & Tang, C. P. (2014). Social Competence as the Centrality of Intervention for Autism Spectrum Disorder (ASD): Why and How? *Hong Kong Journal of Mental Health*, 40(1), 5-11.

Chan, et al. (2016). The effectiveness of community-based social competence training for high-functioning adolescents with ASD in a Chinese context. Manuscript in preparation.

Chan, Raymond W. S., Leung, Cecilia N. W., Ng, Denise C. Y., & Yau, Sania S. W. (2017). Validating a Culturally-sensitive Social Competence Training Programme for Adolescents with ASD in a Chinese Context: An Initial Investigation. *Journal of Autism and Developmental Disorder*, On-line publication on 16 Oct 2017.

Census and Statistics Department of Hong Kong (2009). *Special Topics Report No. 48*. Hong Kong: Census and Statistics Department.

Census and Statistics Department of Hong Kong (2014). *Special Topics Report No. 62*. Hong Kong: Census and Statistics Department.

de Bruin, E, W., Parker, A. M., & Fischhoff, B. (2007). Individual differences in adult decision-making competence. *Journal of Personality and Social Psychology*, 92(5), 938-956. doi: 10.1037/0022-3514.92.5.938

Hendricks, D. (2010). Employment and Adults with Autism Spectrum Disorders: challenges and strategies for success. *Journal of Vocational Rehabilitation*, 32, 125-134.

Hong Kong Government (2012). Embracing social inclusion. Retrieved from http://www.gov.hk/en/residents/housing/socialservices/youth/SocialInclusion.htm

Holwerda, A., van der Klink, J., de Boer, M., Groothoff, J. W., & Brouwer, S. (2013). Predictors of Sustainable Work Participation of Young Adults with Development Disorders. *Research in Developmental Disabilities*, 34, 2753-2763.

Howlin, P., Alcock, J., & Burkin, C. (2005). An 8 year Follow-up of a Specialist Supported Employment Service for High Ability Adults with Autism or Asperger Syndrome. *The International Journal of Research & Practice*, 9(5): 533-549.

Howlin, P. (2013). Social Disadvantage and Exclusion: Adults with Autism Lag Far Behind in Employment Prospects. *Journal of the American Academy of Child & Adolescent Psychiatry*, 52(9), 897-899.

Huxley, P., Evans, S., Madge, S., Webber, M., Burchardt, T., McDaid, D., & Knapp, M. (2012). Development of a social inclusion index to capture subjective and objective life domains (phase II): Psychometric development study. *Health Technology Assessment*, 16(1), 1-248.

Poon Mak, S. M. (2009). *Adult outcome of children with autism with normal intelligence.* Hong Kong: The Chinese University of Hong Kong.

Yager, J. & Iarocci, G. (2013). The development of the Multidimensional Social Competence Scale: a standardized measure of social competence in autism spectrum disorders. *Autism Research*, 6(6), 631-41. doi: 10.1002/aur.1331. Epub 2013 Sep 23.

Yau, S. S. W., Tang, J. P. S., Li, A.W. H., Hon, C. Y. T., Hung, S. F., Chan, R. S. W., Tang, C. P., & Chan, K. P. (2014). Developing Social Competence among High-functioning Youth with Autism Spectrum Disorders: A Pilot Experience in Hong Kong. *Hong Kong Journal of Mental Health*, 40(1), 12-22.

Q&A

Q : What are the issues that autistic job seekers encounter? What are the reasons they leave the workplace?

A : First, the main issue which autistic job seekers encounter is "interpersonal communication". Because they are unable to understand the expressions and emotions of others, they are unable to respond appropriately. Through training, we prepare them for the workplace. Next, due to poor interpersonal communication skills, they often misunderstand the tasks assigned to them by their supervisor or cannot meet demands, thus making it difficult to maintain a stable job. To resolve these issues, this center provides employment counseling, as well as continuing support during the first 6 months of employment. In this way, we can work with employers and job seekers to resolve difficulties. We can recommend modifications in the nature of the work to employers, while creating a good workplace environment for job seekers.

Socially-inclusive catering outlets: A case illustration from the social enterprise set up by Fu Hong Society

Mak Yun Wan[*], Siu Hing Wa[**]

Abstract

A social enterprise is commonly known as a business bearing a double-bottom line, whereby it must achieve social objectives while also striving to achieve business objectives. The Fu Hong Society (hereinafter referred to as FHS), established in 1977, is one of the leading non-governmental organizations in Hong Kong (HK), and provides comprehensive services to persons with disabilities (PWDs). The society set up a social enterprise, Hong Yung Services Limited (HYSL), in 2003, aiming to enhance social inclusion through providing employment opportunities to PWDs via the operation of sustainable socially-inclusive businesses.

Throughout the years, to achieve actualization of the above-mentioned double objectives, i.e. enhancing social inclusion through providing employment opportunities to PWDs via business operation, HYSL has strategically operated its three disability-inclusive catering outlets at popular cultural venues of HK. These catering outlets are not only able to provide employment opportunities to PWDs (the proportion of employees with disabilities is higher than 50%), but actually served as natural social hubs for employees with disabilities, so as to demonstrate their employability while interacting with up to 150,000 customers from the HK community, as well as different countries worldwide during service operation last year.

For evaluation purposes, HYSL has developed its own matrix to review its

---

[*] Deputy Chief Executive Officer of Fu Hong Society.
[**] Service Director of Fu Hong Society.

business performance in achieving financial as well as social objectives. In addition, O'Brien and Tyne's five-element scale, namely Relationship Building, Community Presence, Respect, Competence and Choices, is adopted to guide the planning and evaluation of fulfillment in social inclusion during business operation. This paper, by application of its own matrix, illustrates how HYSL evaluates the financial as well as social performance of its socially-inclusive catering businesses. Meanwhile, by adopting O'Brien's social inclusion framework, the paper further discusses how the disability-inclusive catering outlets operated by HYSL fulfill the five elements of social inclusion.

Keywords: social inclusive catering outlets, persons with disabilities, employment, social inclusion

I. Introduction

In Hong Kong (HK), engaging and sustaining in gainful employment is a great challenge for persons with disabilities (PWDs). As one of the world's most dynamic economies, HK was home to 1,400,950 registered companies in 2018[1], of which only 0.35% (4,939)[2] offered job opportunities for PWDs. According to the "Hong Kong Poverty Situation Report on Disability 2013"[3] (the Report), the percentage of PWDs being economically active was only 39.1%, which was far worse than the corresponding figure (72.8%) of the general population. The Report further pointed out that the unemployment rates of PWDs was 6.7%, which was almost twice the percentage of the overall unemployment rate of 3.7%. Not surprisingly, the poverty rate of PWDs was 29.5%, far higher than the overall rate, i.e. 14.5%, of the general population. These pessimistic figures demonstrate how great is the challenge for PWDs when it comes to engaging in, and sustaining, gainful employment. Worse still, low economic activity not only leads to a high poverty rate for PWDs, but also undermines their opportunities for social inclusion.

Social enterprises in HK play an important role in enhancing the employment opportunities of PWDs. A social enterprise is commonly known as a business bearing a double-bottom line, whereby it must achieve social objectives while simultaneously striving to achieve business objectives. Fu Hong Society (hereinafter referred to as FHS), established in 1977, is one of the leading

[1] Companies Registry releases statistics for 2018 (6 January 2019). Retrieved from The Government of the Hong Kong Special Administrative Region, Press Releases Web site: https://www.info.gov.hk/gia/general/201901/06/P2019010400706.htm.

[2] LCQ14: Employment of persons with disabilities (23 January 2019). Retrieved from The Hong Kong SAR Government, Press Releases Web site: https://www.info.gov.hk/gia/general/201901/23/P2019012300627.htm.

[3] Hong Kong poverty situation report on disability 2013 (December 2014). Retrieved from The Government of the Hong Kong Special Administrative Region, Web site: http://www.povertyrelief.gov.hk/eng/pdf/Hong_Kong_Poverty_Situation_Report_on_Disability_2013(E).pdf.

non-governmental organizations in HK, and provides comprehensive services to PWDs. The society set up a social enterprise, namely Hong Yung Services Limited, (HYSL) in 2003, aiming to enhance social inclusion through providing employment opportunities to PWDs via the operation of sustainable socially-inclusive businesses.

This paper, by application of its own matrix, illustrates how HYSL evaluates the financial as well as social performance of its socially-inclusive catering businesses. In addition, by adopting O'Brien's social inclusion framework, the paper further discusses how the disability-inclusive catering outlets operated by HYSL achieve the five elements of social inclusion.

II. Background of Fu Hong Society and Hong Yung Service Limited

i. About Fu Hong Society

FHS is a non-profit organization established in HK in 1977. Throughout the years, FHS has dedicated itself to building up an inclusive society for all. At present, FHS is operating over 40 service units, providing rehabilitation services for approximately 3,600 PWDs annually. Among them, there are persons with intellectual disabilities, persons with autism spectrum disorders, persons with psychiatric disabilities, and persons with physical disabilities, etc. Core services provided by FHS include residential services, day training services, community psychiatric services, services for persons with autism spectrum disorders and developmental disabilities, community support services, vocational rehabilitation services and social enterprise. In 2004, FHS was invited by the headquarters of 'Best Buddies International' in the USA and was authorized to be the sole organization charged with setting up the 'Best Buddies Movement' in HK.

Concerning the vocational rehabilitation services, FHS has operated the Sheltered Workshops and Supported Employment Program (SEP), as well as the On-the Job Training Program (OJT) since 1991 and 2000 respectively. Currently,

FHS is receiving government grants to operate two sheltered workshops and one integrated vocational rehabilitation service center (an integrated model combining sheltered workshop and SEP), as well as two teams of SEPs and one team of OJT.

FHS offers a wide range of vocational and social skills training to PWDs according to their abilities and needs. Apart from this, FHS also provides job assessment, job matching, job counseling and relevant vocational support to PWDs, with the goal of enhancing their employability.

ii. About Hong Yung Services Limited

To further enhance the upward mobility of PWDs when it comes to open employment, FHS set up a social enterprise, namely HYSL, in 2003, with the mission being to enhance the employment opportunities for PWDs through its diversified business operations. HYSL offers a wide range of businesses to PWDs, such as retail, catering, cleaning, air sterilization, and pest control. In 2019/20, HYSL provided over 500 hours of vocational training to PWDs. The proportion of employees with disabilities is up to 70% of HYSL's total staffing. HYSL echoes the mission of FHS, and the two organizations work in synergy to provide a one-stop vocational service to PWDs.

The below diagram shows the upward mobility ladder of PWDs in HK's vocational rehabilitation services.

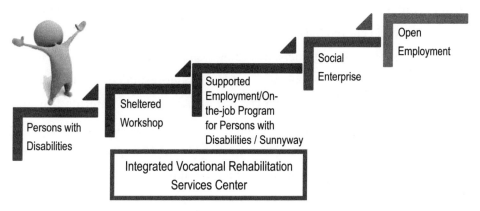

Figure1: The upward mobility ladder of PWDs

III. Disability-inclusive catering outlets operated by HYSL

Throughout the years, to achieve actualization of the above-mentioned double objectives, i.e. enhancing social inclusion through providing employment opportunities to PWDs via business operation, HYSL has strategically operated its three disability-inclusive catering outlets in popular cultural venues of HK.

The three catering outlets are situated among the famous attractions of HK, namely Madam Hong Café at the Hong Kong Museum of Coastal Defense, City Café at the Hong Kong Museum of History, and Madam Hong Restaurant at Ko Shan Theatre. These catering outlets are not only able to provide employment opportunities to PWDs (the proportion of employees with disabilities was higher than 50%), but actually served as natural social hubs for employees with disabilities, allowing said employees to demonstrate their employability while interacting with up to 150,000 customers from the HK community as well as different countries worldwide during service operation in the period spanning 2018 to 2019.

i. The Three Catering Outlets

1. Madam Hong Café—Hong Kong Museum of Coastal Defense

FHS gained the bid to operate a cafeteria at the Museum of Costal Defense with a capacity of 60 seats in November 2013 for 3 years, and won a bid again in 2016 to continue the operation of the cafeteria for 4 more years, in addition to a 2-year renewable contract. The cafeteria serves breakfast, lunch sets, afternoon tea sets and snacks for customers, including visitors of the Museum, staff of the Museum, and students of school tours…etc. This catering outlet not only provides employment opportunities to PWDs, but also serves as a catering training platform for them. It is worth noting that 50% of Cafeteria staff are PWDs. The Museum is currently closed for a major revamp aimed at upgrading the visitor facilities and enriching the permanent exhibition. It is expected to be re-opened at the end of 2020.

2. City Café

Through open bidding, HYSL was awarded, in 2014, the tender to operate the City Café at the Hong Kong Museum of History for a period of 72 months, with a capacity of approximately 130 seats. The theme of the cafeteria is to review the food culture of old HK through the provision of traditional food in an old-styled decorative cafeteria. The cafeteria serves a wide range of customers, including visitors of the Museum from all over the world, staff of nearby offices and commercial buildings, as well as students of local school tours...etc. Since commencing operation, the cafeteria has been receiving good remarks from the customers and has thus far provided 18 employment opportunities to PWDs (equating to 70% of staff).

3. Madam Hong's Restaurant

With a good track record of operating catering businesses, in May 2017 HYSL was awarded, after open bidding, the tender to operate a Chinese restaurant at the Ko Shan Theatre for a period of 36 months. The capacity of the restaurant is 124 seats. Customers of the restaurant are performers and audiences, as well as local customers from the HK community. The restaurant receives good remarks from the customers and has currently recruited, as employees, 11 PWDs or persons from underprivileged groups.

ii. Why HYSL operates Catering Outlets

There are two reasons why HYSL operates catering outlets. The first reason is in response to high market demand, while the second reason is to create natural hubs for cultivation of social inclusion.

With reference to the Census and Statistics Department, the food and beverage services sector was employing approximately 239,200 employees as of September 2019, accounting for 8.4% of total employment in the private sector. Meanwhile, referring to the figure released by the Labour Department concerning the "Employment distribution by industry section", the total population in catering fields ranked in the top five among the 17 industries in HK. The high labor demand of the catering service is obvious. Thus, operating catering outlets so as to provide employment opportunities and catering training to PWDs is on the right track in response to the labor market demand.

In the meantime, by setting up socially-inclusive catering outlets, HYSL is not only able to provide employment opportunities to PWDs, but also create natural hubs to cultivate social inclusion via sustainable business operation. As mentioned earlier, the three socially-inclusive catering outlets located in the popular cultural venue are natural hubs for PWDs to interact with the public and demonstrate their employability in front of customers. These social hubs increase the number of opportunities for PWDs to reach out to customers from all walks of life. The hubs help PWDs to improve their communication skills, boost up confidence through work satisfaction, and facilitate their community presence. To conclude, these socially-inclusive catering outlets are strategically set up in the popular cultural spots and serve as social hubs for cultivation of social inclusion naturally and effectively.

IV. The Performance Review Matrix

For evaluation, HYSL has developed its own matrix to review its business performance in achieving financial as well as social objectives. There are two dimensions in the matrix; the horizontal dimension measures social performance while the vertical dimension reflects the financial performance of the business.

i. Measurement of Social Performance

The social performance measures changes induced by the catering businesses, including the number of employment opportunities created for PWDs, the number of training placements created for PWDs, the number of positive publicities which arose to demonstrate the positive image of PWDs, as well as the number of awards and recognitions received. A marking scale has been developed to mark the positive and negative changes created. For instance, one mark will be added for each award or recognition received, while mark(s) will be deducted when encountering complaints (according to the seriousness) which cause damage to reputation and image. The of social performance is reflected in the horizontal dimension of the matrix, from the left to right hand side. Businesses situated on the left hand side of the matrix reflect negative social performance, while those with positive social performance will be located on the right hand side.

ii. Measurement of Financial Performance

Social enterprise businesses are self-financed; thus, financial performance must be measured regularly. The measurement of financial performance is straightforward, and involves counting the profit or loss of each business. One mark will be added for each business with a HK$50,000 profit, while one mark will be deducted for a HK$50,000 loss. Businesses situated in the upper part of the matrix reflect positive financial performance, while those with negative financial performance will be located in the power part.

In a nutshell, those marked in the top right hand part of the matrix are businesses which achieve positive performance both socially and financially. On the contrary, those marked in the lower left hand part of the matrix are businesses with negative social and financial performance.

V. Performance Review (2018-2019) of the Three Socially-Inclusive Catering Outlets

Based on the above-mentioned performance review system, the below matrix shows the performance review of HYSL's three socially-inclusive catering outlets in the financial year spanning 2018 to 2019. It is worth noting that all three catering outlets are situated in the top right hand part of the matrix, that is to say, the outlets can achieve positive performance both socially and financially. This case illustration soundly demonstrates that setting up socially-inclusive catering outlets is not only able to provide employment opportunities to PWDs, but is also successful in creating natural hubs to cultivate social inclusion via sustainable business operation.

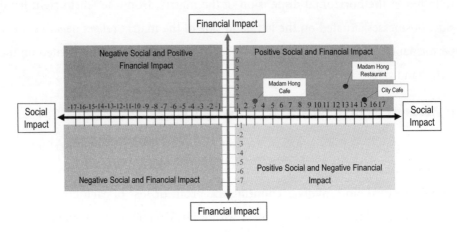

Figure2: The performance review of HYSL'S three socially-inclusive catering outlets

VI. Social Inclusion

Building an inclusive society is the mission of FHS, and the same is true of its social enterprise. HYSL adopts the social inclusion framework developed by O'Brien and Tyne (1981) to guide its planning and evaluation for the facilitation of PWDs' social inclusion. The framework suggests five accomplishments of social inclusion, namely: Community Presence, Relationship Building, Choice, Competence and Respect.

By adopting O'Brien's social inclusion framework, this paper further discusses below how the disability-inclusive catering outlets operated by HYSL fulfill the five elements of social inclusion.

Table 1 below illustrates the fulfillment of the five elements of social inclusion in the catering outlets operated by HYSL.

Table 1: Fulfillment of the five elements of the social inclusion framework

Social Inclusion Element	Fulfillment
Community Presence: Do service users live in the same community as ordinary citizens; for example, do they live in the same neighborhood, work in open employment, and use local shops and local recreational facilities?	The catering outlets of HYSL are situated in the popular cultural venues of HK; PWDs work as normal employees who can interact with customers from all over the world naturally, as everyone does.
Relationships: The right to experience valued relationships with persons without disabilities.	Employees with disabilities are treated the same as those employees without disabilities in the catering outlets. Employees with disabilities are able to experience workmate relationships with colleagues with or without disabilities. All of the employees with disabilities can make friends with their colleagues and even participate in staff social gatherings after work.
Choice: Are PWDs supported in making informed choices that are meaningful to them?	The catering outlets offer different kinds of positions and work patterns for the selection of employees with disabilities according to their ability and interest.
Competence: Are PWDs supported in functioning well with everyday tasks that enable them to be individuals who are able and respected? Are PWDs supported in developing the skills and attributes that reduce dependence on others, such as developing skills in shopping, cooking or a work role?	Employees with disabilities are able to receive on-the-job training in their positions and new skills will be trained up so as to prepare them for further career development.
Respect: Are PWDs encouraged to develop and maintain a positive reputation within their local community by considering the choice of activities, location, dress and use of language that assists PWDs in being perceived as valued citizens?	Just as is the case for employees without disability, employees with disability wear the same type of uniform, without a distinct dress code. Through planned job allocation, employees with disability are able to demonstrate their employability in front of the customers. They earn appreciation and recognition, as does every staff member. All of them are treated as valued staff of the catering outlets.

VII. Case Illustration

The following real case will be used for better illustration of how the disability-inclusive catering outlets operated by HYSL benefit the PWDs and advance their level of social inclusion.

Ah Kwan, a middle-aged man affected by mental challenges, is now working at one of the catering outlets of HYSL as a waiter. Before that, Kwan walked a stormy career path.

Despite having a tertiary-level education, Kwan has been unable to sustain employment over the past 30 years. Since graduation, he has hardly been able to find a job. Even when lucky enough to be recruited, he soon found himself unemployed again whenever obstacles were encountered, no matter how trivial they were. Thus, he relied on government subsidies, and had low self-esteem.

Kwan was then admitted to the sheltered workshop operated by FHS in 2004. In the last 10 years he has not been able to sustain a single employment position for more than 3 months. However, a U-turn occurred in 2014 when the socially-inclusive catering outlet, City Café, opened at the Hong Kong Museum of History, providing on-site training and employment opportunities to PWDs. Kwan was invited to participate in an elementary training program at City Café. Though hesitating, Kwan accepted the placement offered and started his on-site training. After a few months of training, Kwan's performance was well recognized by the café's supervisor, who offered him a part-time post at the café. Again, he was reluctant to become an employee because of his bad career experience and low pressure tolerance level. Upon encouragement, he seized this opportunity and was willing to become an employee again. Since then, Kwan has remained in the post as a waiter and achieved a breakthrough in sustaining employment for 6 years. Kwan has encountered many ups and downs in the past 6 years; he has had thoughts of quitting the job but finally has chosen to carry on because of the flexible policy and all-round support from the supervisor and teammates of the café. At this point, it can be announced, very happily, that Kwan has become one of the café's most experienced staff members.

Based on his real experience, Kwan gave an evaluation of City Café's fulfillment of the five elements of the social inclusion framework, and this is illustrated in Table 2 below:

Table2: An evaluation of city cafe's fulfillment of the five elements

Five Elements of Social Inclusion	Mark (1 is the Lowest and 5 is the Highest)
Community Presence	5
Relationship	4
Choice	5
Competence	4
Respect	4
Average	4.4

i. Community Presence

Kwan works at a very popular cultural venue in HK where he can meet visitors from all walks of life and all over the world. While serving the customers, Kwan can demonstrate his employability and feel that he is a real member of the community. His feeling of community presence is further strengthened when he chit-chats with customers, and hangs out with colleagues, getting to know more about different places...etc.

ii. Relationship

Working at City Café provides an opportunity for Kwan to build relationships, or even friendships, with customers and colleagues. When he was a service user at the sheltered workshop his social network was limited and his self-image was low. Since working at City Café he has started to participate in more social gatherings and has become more optimistic and talkative.

iii. Choice

City Café offers different kinds of positions and work patterns for employees with disabilities, according to their ability and interest. When Kwan came across ups and downs over the past 6 years, he was given the choice to work flexible hours, take a short break, and take no-pay leave, instead of just being given the single option of quitting the job. He is able to exercise his right to choose at work. Kwan has benefited from this flexibility, which allows him to sustain employment even when he is feeling "down".

iv. Competence

Apart from choices and community presence, Kwan has also been given the chance to equip himself with more job-related skills and interpersonal techniques after working at City Café. Last year, Kwan was willing to accept a transfer and started to work at the Chinese restaurant of HYSL. Over the past few years, HYSL has continued to provide chances for Kwan to learn new skills, so as to prepare himself for further career development.

v. Respect

The self-esteem of Kwan has risen since he started work at the inclusive catering outlet. He feels respected as an employee, instead of a person with mental disability. In addition, customers respect him as an ordinary employee, without discriminating against him.

In summary, Kwan concluded that social inclusion is well manifested at City Café. Under this socially-inclusive work environment, Kwan has been able to strengthen his confidence and enhance his quality of life. To sum up, Kwan was glad to work at the disability-inclusive catering outlet, which gave him an important opportunity to re-enter the labor market, thus leading to a better social inclusion status.

VIII. Conclusion

Over the past years, to enhance social inclusion through providing employment opportunities to PWDs via business operation, HYSL has strategically operated its three disability-inclusive catering outlets at popular cultural venues of HK. These catering outlets have not only provided nearly 100 employment opportunities and up to 500 training hours to PWDs in the last year, but have actually become natural social hubs for their employees with disabilities, thus allowing these people to demonstrate their employability while interacting with hundreds of thousands of customers from the HK community as well as different countries worldwide during service operation. It is possible to share, happily, that all employees with disabilities are able to quit or minimize dependence on social security allowance. The positive impacts created by these outlets are remarkable and have induced more than 50 media exposures in the past few years. Despite some good examples, the level of PWDs' social inclusion in HK must still be enhanced, and is far from satisfactory. Last but not the least, we hope that "Every Business can be a Socially-Inclusive Business" and join us on the path to social inclusion.

References

Clifford, J., Markey, K., & Malpani, N. (2013). *Measuring social impact in social enterprise: The state of thought and practice in the UK*. London. E3M.

Companies Registry releases statistics for 2018 (6 January 2019). Retrieved from The Government of the Hong Kong Special Administrative Region, Press Releases Web site: https://www.info.gov.hk/gia/general/201901/06/P2019010400706.htm

Davys, D. & Tickle, E. J. (2008). Social inclusion and valued roles : A supportive framework. Retrieved from http://usir.salford.ac.uk/14089/

Hong Kong poverty situation report on disability 2013 (December 2014). Retrieved from The Government of the Hong Kong Special Administrative Region, Web site: http://www.povertyrelief.gov.hk/eng/pdf/Hong_Kong_Poverty_Situation_Report_on_Disability_2013(E).pdf

LCQ14: Employment of persons with disabilities (23 January 2019). Retrieved from The Hong Kong SAR Government, Press Releases Web site: https://www.info.gov.hk/gia/general/201901/23/P2019012300627.htm

Lysaght, R., Krupa, T., & Bouchard, M. (2018). The role of social enterprise in creating work options for people with intellectual and developmental disabilities. *Journal on Developmental Disabilities*, 23(3), 18-30.

Murray, G. C., McKenzie, K., Kidd, G. R., Lakhani, S., & Sinclair, B. (1998). The five accomplishments: a framework for obtaining customer feedback in a health service community learning disability team. *British Journal of Learning Disabilities*, 26, 94-99.

O'brien, J. & Tyne, A. (1981). *The principle of normalisation: A foundation for effective services*. London: CMH : CMHERA.

Social Food Inc: Creating an effective social enterprise through vertical integration case study (2016). Retrieved from Government of Singapore, Tote Board Web site: https://www.toteboard.gov.sg/docs/default-source/module/case-studies/social-food-inc-creating-an-effective-social-enterprise-through-vertical-integration.pdf

Su, X. Q. (6 July 2017). Unemployment rate for disabled people in Hong Kong eight times higher than official figure, survey finds. *South China Morning Post*.

Table E003: Number of employed persons by industry and occupation (Fourth Quarter 2019). Retrieved from The Government of the Hong Kong Special Administrative Region, Census and Statistics Department Web site: https://www.censtatd.gov.hk/hkstat/sub/sp200.jsp?productCode=D5250003

Wong, M. C. S. & Yap, R. C. Y. (2019). Social impact investing for marginalized communities in Hong Kong: Cases and issues. *Sustainability*, 11, 2831.

Q&A

Q : Has Fu Hong Society considered training service users so that they can become service providers?

A : In our sheltered workshop and supportive employment program, service users are involved in various aspects. They are also given a voice to explain their needs. For example, the government has been implementing a physical therapy program. We established a special working group to enable PWDs to convey their ideas to the government. In this way, PWDs became stakeholders.

Q&A

WISE—Turning Mental Illness into Mental Wellness

Wong So Kuen[*]

Abstract

The New Life Psychiatric Rehabilitation Association ("New Life"), established in 1965, is a social service organization specializing in mental health services in Hong Kong. Since 1994, the Association has pioneered the model of simulated business, later developed into diversified Work Integration Social Enterprises ("WISE"), to address the economic integration and social inclusion of people recovering from mental illness. The Association currently consists of 22 social enterprises under different business categories, including food and beverages, retail, direct sales, eco-tourism, cleansing and property management, employing 77 persons in recovery from mental illness, while these social enterprises are also training over 400 persons every year.

Social enterprise has been evidenced as an effective means to facilitate mental health social work practice. By applying the recovery concepts and developmental approach, New Life has been effectively using social enterprises in building human and social capital to enhance social inclusion and promote well-being. As defined by the World Health Organization (WHO), such an institution is one "in which every individual realizes his or her own potential, can cope with the normal stresses of life, can work productively and fruitfully, and be able to make a contribution to her or his community".

Throughout the years, New Life has developed its distinctive WISE model and continuously adopted innovative strategies to maximize its social impact, including:
1. Development of a unique service model that combines training and employment to

---

[*] General Manager of Social Enterprises, New Life Psychiatric Rehabilitation Association.

maximize number of beneficiaries;

2. Setting up of a vertical supply chain in sheltered workshops to extend social outcomes;

3. Branding for social impact; and

4. Building social capital through partnership programs.

Keywords: social enterprise; mental illness; mental health; well-being; social development

Persons in recovery from mental illness face many challenges related to employment and social inclusion after they are discharged from hospital. Conventional social work practice adopts a rehabilitation model emphasizing institutionalization and professional clinical casework or psychotherapy, but evidence has emerged showing that the social investment approach, which creates opportunities for social inclusion, could be better at improving quality of life and well-being for people in recovery from mental illness (Caplan, 2010). By investing in human and social capital, the social investment approach could "realize important social goals, including supporting workforce participation, building a foundation for later skill development and reducing social inequality" (Conley, 2017, p. 34).

Social enterprise uses a business model to address social issues. It aims to achieve self-sustaining status through generating revenue so that the profits earned can be re-invested in a way which has more social impact. WISE share a social investment orientation. By using a market-driven business model to "break social isolation and exclusion" (Caplan, 2010, p. 80), the major objective of WISE is to help disadvantaged people, who are unemployed and socially excluded, to integrate back into work and society through productive activities (Nyssens, 2006). It "combines the logics of welfare for disadvantaged groups as part of their values and mission with an economic enterprise" (Aiken, 2010, p. 157). Since 1994, New Life, a leading social service organization specializing in mental health services in Hong Kong, has adopted a market-driven business model which focuses on assisting people recovering from mental illness in achieving self-reliance and community integration.

This paper shares how New Life adopted innovative strategies in running WISE to address mental health issues as a case study of the developmental social work approach. The first chapter describes the background of development of social enterprises in New Life as a novel approach to mental health issues including economic integration and social inclusion for people in recovery from mental illness and mental health promotion. The second chapter explains the unique service model of social enterprise employed by New Life, and its characteristics. The third chapter highlights the strategy of developing a vertical supply chain in sheltered workshops to extend social impact. The fourth chapter describes the experience of using branding to promote social inclusion and wellness, while the fifth chapter shares New Life's experience in building social capital through partnership programs in its WISE. The last chapter concludes the social outcomes brought about by the WISE model of New Life.

I. Pioneering the small enterprise model to foster social inclusion for persons in recovery from mental illness in Hong Kong

Established in 1965, New Life is a social service organization specializing in mental health service in Hong Kong. Its vision is to strive to promote mental wellness for people in recovery from mental illness and for their families and the general public, with the ultimate goal of creating equal opportunities, social inclusion, acceptance and full participation for all in the community. For years, New Life has been providing direct social work service in residential, vocational rehabilitation and community support to people in recovery from mental illness. As of 2019, the organization has more than 1,100 staff, while the total number of service users is around 15,000.

In view of the immense challenges faced by people in recovery from mental illness when it comes to employment and community integration after being discharged from hospital, New Life pioneered the model of simulated business in 1994, which was a prototype of WISE in Hong Kong, to address economic integration and social inclusion for people in recovery from mental illness. The simulated business was a small enterprise providing real-work training to assist people in recovery from mental illness move upward to open employment after training. The first enterprise was Kin Sang Market Stall (建生菜檔), which sold vegetables on a public housing estate and provided a "Place & train-place" model: the service users worked on the market stall, where they received on-site retail training from the shop supervisor ("Place & train"). Once having reached a certain level of independence, they would be given a job placement in the open market under the guidance of the Placement Officers ("Place"), who would also conduct case follow-ups. Through training and working in real business settings, service users are able to strengthen their work skills and capabilities, and inspire themselves with hopes and self-confidence, which are important in their recovery journey. The traditional vocational rehabilitation model provides pre-employment training ("Place & train") and time-limited support to people in recovery from mental illness; this "Place & train" model of simulated business has been proven to be more successful when it comes to assisting people in re-entering the labor market and community (National Alliance on Mental Illness [NAMI], 2014). Kin Sang Market Stall was given the "Outstanding Pioneering Service Project Award" by the Hong Kong Council of Social Service and the "1997 Lily Schizophrenia Reintegration Award" for outstanding achievement.

Building on this success, New Life has started other simulated businesses, such as convenience stores and restaurants. Until the early 2000s, the government proactively encouraged voluntary organizations to operate WISE so as to cope with the drastic rise of unemployment and fiscal deficit (Defourny & Kim, 2011) by providing "seed money" through a number of funding programs[1]. The simulated business model was then renamed and evolved into WISE. The source of funding paved ways for the rapid expansion of New Life's social enterprises in the following years (Wong, Ip, & Chan, 2009). As of 2019, there are 22 social enterprises under diversified business categories including retail, food and beverages, cleansing service, direct sales business, eco-tourism and property management services (Appendix 1). The organization employs 77

---

[1] Programs launched to support the (re)integration of marginalized individuals into the labor market through social enterprises in Hong Kong include 'Community Investment and Inclusion Fund' (2001), 'Enhancing the Employment of People with Disabilities through Small Enterprises' by the Social Welfare Department (2001), and 'Enhancing self-reliance through District Partnership' by the Home Affairs Department (2006).

persons in recovery from mental illness, and is also training over 400 every year. All the profits generated are re-invested into the business, so as to achieve social objectives.

There are three social missions to achieve through the running of social enterprises:

i. To improve the workability and employability of people in recovery from mental illness through training and employment;

ii. To enhance social inclusion through providing a platform for the public to interact and understand persons in recovery from mental illness; and

iii. To promote the concepts of healthy living and well-being.

II. A unique social enterprise model that consists of training and Employment

The primary concern of New Life's social enterprises is the work and employment challenges faced by persons in recovery from mental illness, including the absence of work skills and stigmatization. The service users lack work skills relevant to the labor market needs, having lived in hospitals for a long period of time, while many of them drop out easily even if they secure employment, because they cannot get used to the long working hours or the workplace. Besides this, stigmatization is also a major obstacle. Many of the service users have low work motivation, as they feel that their ability has been adversely affected by the mental illness, or they lose their self-confidence in job hunting; they may also be worried about being rejected or fear that their medical history will be discovered by others (Wong, Ip, & Chan, 2009). Apart from the self-stigmatization, social stigma is also challenging. Many employers are not willing to hire them because they do not believe in their ability or mistakenly think that persons in recovery from mental illness may exhibit aggressive behavior. It is believed that this problem can only be improved through changing the stigmatization regarding "mental illness".

In light of this, New Life adopted a strategy focusing on mental wellness, rather than mental illness, so as to change the perception of, and stigmatization regarding, mental illness in relation to both the service users and the public. The WHO defines mental wellness as "a state of well-being in which the individual realizes his or her own potential, can cope with the normal stresses of life, can work productively and fruitfully, and be able to make a contribution to his or her community". Mental wellness is more than an absence of mental illness. New Life has embedded this wellness concept in the service model of social enterprises.

There are several characteristics of the service model of New Life's social enterprise. First, it is based on the belief of "upward mobility" of people in recovery from mental illness: they can move upward to self-reliance through setting goals and hopes for themselves, thus enhancing their work skills and soft skills, and building their self-fulfillment and satisfaction. The role of the social enterprises is to maximize these people's potential, and facilitate them in changing from a passive welfare recipient role to an active productive member of society, making positive contributions to themselves and the community. This also aligns with the recovery-oriented approach, which essentially refers to the idea that people can cope with symptoms of mental illness and lead fulfilling and meaningful lives; it also advocates the core concepts of self-direction, hope, empowerment, nonlinearity, supportive relationships, and meaningful role in society (Caplan, 2010).

Second, the service model focuses on ability, rather than disability. Although the disabling consequences of mental illness can "affect individuals in a multitude of ways, depending on the severity, duration, treatment and the support structure of an individual" (Caplan, 2010, p. 74), the recovery approach emphasizes "strengths" and social development theory mentions "capability" as an asset (Midley, 2010, p. 12). Under the structure dominated by the clinical experts in the rehabilitation field and welfare regime, people in recovery from mental illness are always regarded as a subordinate group by their doctors, social workers, and therapists at rehabilitation organizations. In New Life's social enterprises, the role of clinical experts is kept to the minimum. The enterprises are looked after by shop supervisors, rather than clinical experts, who provide on-site work arrangement. In addition, persons in recovery from mental illness also have equal opportunities to be promoted to shop supervisors. The types of skills available in the social enterprises are all acquirable through training and practice. People may mistakenly think that those in recovery from mental illness are only able to perform the low-skill work such as cleansing. However, New Life recognizes individual's talents, skills and knowledge, and supports them in flourishing. To cite an example, some people felt that the service users could not perform the role of professional barista when New Life started running cafes in 2010, because the skills are too complicated for them. However, over the past 3 years, more than 30 staff members have succeeded in obtaining the international barista accreditation and becoming professional baristas.

Third, individuals' choices are respected. Some people consider "wellness" as "an active process through which people become aware of, and make choices toward a more successful existence" (National Wellness Institute [NWI], 2014); therefore, making choice is also an important element in the recovery journey of people with mental illness. New Life has chosen to open a diverse range of social enterprises to create choices in different work trades that are needed in the mainstream labor market, so that service users can make choices according to their levels of function, preference and goals. They can also request to change their work trades from time to time.

And finally, the social enterprises are community-based, meaning that they can serve as public education platforms to change the social stigma through natural interaction between the customers and service users, as well as through various social inclusion programs conducted on-site. These social enterprises are set up in the community so as to make the workability of the service users visible to the public. So as not to create any labeling effects, everybody in the enterprises wears the same uniform, regardless of their post or whether they are trainees or staff, disabled persons or otherwise. Work engagement in social enterprises has proven effective in alleviating social stigma against people in recovery from mental illness, as they are regarded as workers in the social enterprises, rather than ex-mentally ill persons (Caplan, 2010). Social acceptance and inclusion occurs through their interaction with customers, who cannot distinguish between people in recovery from mental illness and others, and will simply think that 'they are actually the same'. Among the successful stories in recent years is that of the InterContinental Hong Kong employing seven of New Life's service users to work at its hotel since 2012. Indeed, this came about after its management, when visiting New Life's café, found that the service users were actually performing as well as staff without mental illness. It was a great leap for a mainstream service industry to hire people in recovery from mental illness, and served as an example for other mainstream employers in Hong Kong.

In Hong Kong, most of the work integration social enterprises adopt a pure employment model that provides 30-50% of job vacancies for the underprivileged groups—a criterion for applying for government seed capital to run social enterprises. The model adopted by New Life is a unique one that combines training and employment to maximize the number of beneficiaries. Apart from employing 50% of the workforce from disabled groups, the social enterprises also provide 5-10 training placements for the service users in addition to the essential workforce. Service users are admitted as trainees, and receive on-site training at New Life's social enterprises. They can also be promoted to senior trainees. Once they have gained skills and confidence, they are placed on the open market or employed as staff at New Life's social enterprises if vacancies are available.

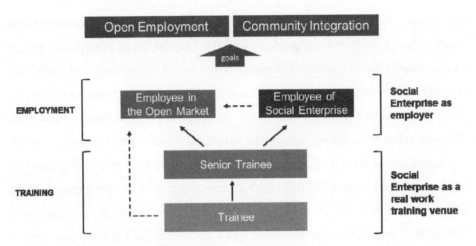

Figure 1: The service model of social enterprises of New Life

There are numerous advantages of this combined model: first, the number of beneficiaries is not bound by the number of job vacancies available in each social enterprise; more service users can be assisted through training and have a chance to secure open employment. Second, the impact could be sustaining and long term, as new service users can be admitted when the trainees are successfully discharged. This model could continuously assist service users in moving from passive welfare recipients to active contributors in society, and finally create an additional workforce in the economy while also reducing reliance on social security. Third, the availability of job vacancies reserved for the disabled has a motivating effect on the service users, as they have a chance to be employed by the social enterprise if vacancies are available. However, there are drawbacks to the business operation: first, there are additional costs linked to the operation of the social enterprises, and particularly the provision of training, such as training allowance expenses, which are not a common expenditure in normal business operation. Second, the shop supervisors must bear an extra workload in the social enterprises, as they need to provide training to the service users.

III. Development of vertical supply chain to extend social outcomes to sheltered workshops

In order to maximize the social impact that could be created under the development of social enterprises, New Life further extended work opportunities to the sheltered workers through developing food production lines at those sheltered workshops. New Life has six sheltered workshops, providing services to over 1,000 persons who are in recovery from mental illness and who have greater limitations in obtaining employment due to their lower level of function. These workshops engage service users in simple work tasks such as letter-shopping, packaging, farming and handicraft making, and the service users are also given a small amount of attendance allowance by the Social Welfare Department when they attend the sheltered workshop, as well as an incentive for receiving job orders. With the provision of stable sales channels by the social enterprises, New Life started to set up new food production lines at these sheltered workshops in 2008. Apart from organic farming at the New Life Farm, there are production lines of baked goods, organic soy products, organic drinks, desserts, Chinese soup, organic pickles, healthy food packaging, and so on. These production lines have produced eight new brands to be sold in the retail stores of New Life and in the market, and for use as ingredients at the F & B outlets. To ensure the quality of production and build customers' confidence in these products, New Life obtained the ISO22000 in these production lines.

This development had multiple benefits in terms of social objectives and business objectives. On the social side, it opened up new work choices and created new income for the sheltered workers so that they could develop their unrecognized capability, and improve their quality of life through receiving additional income from these productions. More income means more opportunities to participate in the community and achieve personal goals while also contributing to others (Conley, 2016). At the same time, through selling these products in the market, New Life can demonstrate its ability to the public, so as to enhance people's understanding of its productive role. On the business side, New Life provides a stable supply of products to the social enterprises. Facing keen competition from the large chain stores in the market, the social enterprises, which are relatively small in scale, have difficulty when it comes to ensuring that there is a stable supply of healthy food products. Many vendors choose to fulfill the big orders from the supermarket prior to supplying the social enterprises. With New Life's own-production lines, the social enterprises have a guaranteed supply of unique organic and healthy food products that help sustain the business.

IV. Re-branding strategy for maximizing social impact to address mental health issues

In promoting mental well-being, the WHO (2013) suggested the concept of "primordial prevention" to stop the occurrence of risk factors in the population. New Life believes that social enterprises could also serve as a public education platform to promote mental well-being which is beneficial to the service users, consumers, the community and the economy. New Life rebranded its social enterprises with the concept of wellness in 2010, by collaborating with a team of local designers serving a similar vision to that of New Life. The newly-created brand, "330" (signifying "health of body, mind and spirit" in its Cantonese pronunciation) replaced the brand name "New Life", which is a representation of "rehabilitation" and has a strong sense of "philanthropy". Rather than appealing to customers to make a "sympathetic purchase", the new brand connected people with its focus on "wellness", which is a concern for most customers. Moreover, the concept of wellness was incorporated into the business model of New Life's social enterprises, e.g. disseminating health tips on the feature walls of the shops, designing a menu with "food that makes you happy", promoting mindfulness practice in cafes, and so on. The new brands of "cafe330", "farmfresh330", and "ecotour330" immediately drew a great deal of media coverage and caught the public's attention, especially the young people, health-conscious customers and middle-class families, who became the new customer segments. The new brand got rid of any labeling toward people with disabilities. Customers return because the products and services are fulfilling their healthy living needs, with the added value of supporting the disadvantaged. The campaign was regarded as a success, since it built up New Life's reputation instantly and helped the organization to gain more catering contracts from different universities and more corporate partnership opportunities.

New Life also revamped the branding and improved the packaging of products made by the sheltered workshops. Each own-brand product line was given a new brand name to replace the original name of "New Life". The products obtained ISO 22000 certification and are being sold in certain large chain stores. At first glance customers may not know that these are products from social enterprises, because the packaging is professionally-designed, much like that found in the commercial market. They will soon discover, however, that these products are made by people in recovery from mental illness, which becomes, in the eyes of the customer, an added value. Indeed, the packaging features a "Bright Buy" message[2] and a remark made by a cartoon illustration of a person with mental illness. The products are welcomed by customers because of their healthiness, quality and organic nature, but not philanthropy.

As shown by a survey conducted before and after the rebranding campaign, more people gave positive feedback on the newly-branded shops and products; most importantly, more people found that the new brands could communicate New Life's social missions in a better way and enhance their support for the social enterprises. There was an immediate positive impact on New Life's business outcomes. Taking farmfresh330 as an example, the shop's sales increased by 30% immediately after the launch of the new brand farmfresh330. Another example is the sales of organic soy milk, which grew by 18% after the new brand was launched. The positive response in the market enhanced New Life's service users'

---

[2] The content of the Bright Buy Message: "Purchasing Bright Buy products not only brings you good health, but also helps bring new life to persons in recovery from mental illness".

self-confidence, as they can adopt their own identity as producers/providers of economically-viable goods or services; through this, they can in turn gain a greater sense of dignity and self-esteem.

V. Building social capital through partnership programs

By adopting the wellness concept in the branding and operation of the social enterprises, New Life has been able to connect with different sectors to build social capital through partnership programs over the past decade. Social capital, an important element of the social investment approach, is "the building of a cohesive relationship between people for mutual benefit" (Caplan, 2010, p. 80). The following are three examples:

The first example is a cross-over brand partnership with a renowned local artist named Anothermountainman (又一山人); this artist is charged with designing products made by New Life's service users at sheltered workshops that promote positive thinking. The designer is famous in the design, art, photography and advertising fields. He started using a very localized fabric called red-white-blue in creating art pieces and installations that have been collected and exhibited in museums. This is a material which is very familiar to Hong Kong people, and became a collective memory since it was widely used in the 60s and 70s. Indeed, New Life's sheltered workshop started making small souvenirs with red-white-blue fabric in 2005. Owing to the same mission of promoting the wellness concept to boost the morale of Hong Kong people, New Life and Anothermountainman decided to create a cross-over brand, known as rwb330 (紅白藍 330), in 2012. Anothermountainman designed products with red-white-blue fabric, each of which carries a positive message in the hope of cheering up the Hong Kong people. The service users of the sheltered workshop handled the production, so as to give multiple values to the products and create more income for sheltered workers. The products have been made trendy because of the use of traditional material and have become popular among young people, middle-age people and tourists. They are sold online, in pop-up stores, and in other retail outlets such as Design Gallery, Hong Kong Tourism Board, etc. These products have had a number of positive impacts: first, the sewing skills and techniques of service users have been enhanced. Second, sheltered workers have received more job orders and their income from sewing has increased by 68%. Third, because of the fame of Anothermountainman and the multiple values of this partnership, there has been a great deal of media coverage, thus meaning that the ability of persons in recovery from mental illness is showcased to the public.

The second example is the partnership with InterContinental Hong Kong (ICHK). New Life and ICHK have been working on multi-facet initiatives since 2009. The senior management of ICHK was impressed by the mission of New Life's social enterprises and started by sharing their expertise on customer service and recipes development so as to enhance the competitiveness of New Life's social enterprises in the commercial market. Besides this, ICHK also conducted volunteer programs, promoted New Life's products to its customers, and ran annual fundraising programs for New Life. In addition, ICHK is also a company that cares for the mental wellness of its staff. The organization invited New Life to arrange health talks, well-being workshops, and seminars conducted by clinical psychologists and psychiatrists. In 2012, the hotel launched an employment program for service users being trained at New Life's social enterprises. Indeed, there are now seven service users working at the housekeeping and the F & B outlets in the hotel. To help New Life's service users better adjust to the workplace, the hotel offered flexible working hours and assigned a mentor to each service user employed. All of these initiatives aim to support the business operation of the social enterprises, while simultaneously enhancing social inclusion through exchanging knowledge and providing genuine employment opportunities for people in recovery from mental illness.

The last case is New Life's partnership with the universities and youth center to conduct the "Inclusive Barista Program". cafe330 has collaborated with the University of Hong Kong since 2014 to organize this program to promote social inclusion on the campus. Every year, 40 students are recruited to attend the barista certificate training course, which is sponsored by the university. Indeed, this barista certificate course is the first of its kind in Hong Kong, incorporating knowledge on mental health into a coffee workshop; each student then commits to 10-20 hours of volunteer work at the café after the training. Through working together with the café staff, the students will develop a better understanding of people with mental illness. At the end of the program, students can initiate further social inclusion events; for instance, some students organized the "Music Friday" program to play live music together with the cafe330 staff every week. This "Inclusive Barista Program" was further extended to the Chinese University of Hong Kong and a youth center called Warehouse in the following years, and it has been completed by over 300 university students or youth.

The above three examples of partnership initiatives have illustrated the synergy and mutual benefits generated. Making use of the expertise of different partners helps create additional resources for both parties. Indeed, the knowledge and skills exchanges are mutually beneficial. These partnerships help social enterprises sustain their business through improving business know-how, expanding their customer network and enhancing the brand image. More importantly, such partnerships have brought about more opportunities for New Life's service users in terms of new employment opportunities, additional job orders, and social inclusion opportunities. The partnering parties have thus become valuable social capital in terms of improving the well-being of society.

VI. Conclusion

WISE manage "to displace thousands of disadvantaged persons from the conventional welfare structures in which they were simple objects of assistance, to re-integrate them fully in society by transforming them into producers and generators of value for themselves and for others" (WISE, 2009, p. 6). The social enterprises run by New Life are training over 400 service users every year, around 20% of whom could secure open employment in the market. These social enterprises have also created approximately 77 job opportunities for the service users. In addition, over 150 service users at sheltered workshops are engaged in the production of New Life's own-brand products, through which they could earn an additional income. The monetary benefit created for people in recovery from mental illness is around US$2M annually in terms of salary and training allowances. Apart from these effects, the social enterprises also bring about positive impacts on people in recovery from mental illness, including improved sense of competence, enhanced self-esteem, and, most importantly, reduced stigmatization through the natural interaction between customers and New Life's service users in the social enterprises, as well as through the vast amount of positive media coverage and the awards that recognize the ability of people in recovery. WISE, with a market-driven business model and a unique focus on promoting social and economic integration for persons in recovery, have proven to be an effective way and innovative means to address mental health issues such as poverty, social exclusion, and stigma, as evidenced by the experience of New Life. By integrating social objectives and economic objectives, WISE could "produce returns and promote future social well-being, making a positive contribution to social and economic development" (Midgley, 2017, p. 14).

Appendix 1:

Type and list of the social enterprises run by New Life Psychiatric Rehabilitation Association (as of 2019)

	Business Type	Project / Brand name (Location)	No. of projects
1	Food and Beverages Business	cafe330 (The Chinese University of Hong Kong)	10
		cafe330 (The University of Hong Kong)	
		cafe330 (The Prince of Wales Hospital)	
		cafe330 (The Caritas Medical Centre)	
		Sun Garden Café (The Kadoorie Farm)	
		T. CAFE (The T. PARK)	
		Onecafe (The Castle Peak Hospital)	
		Delight Kitchen (Tsuen Wan)	
		Drinks330 (Tsuen Wan)	
		Party food and outside catering service	
2	Retail Business	farmfresh330 (Tai Wai)	6
		farmfresh330 (Tuen Mun)	
		farmfresh330 (Admiralty)	
		New Life Gourmet (Shek Pai Wan)	
		New Life Convenience Store (West Wing, The Kowloon Hospital)	
		New Life Convenience Store (Rehabilitation Building, The Kowloon Hospital)	
3	Direct Sales Business	Fruit wholesale business	3
		eshop330 (Online Store)	
		rwb330 (Online Store)	
4	Tourism	Ecotour330 (New Life Farm at Tuen Mun)	1
5	Cleansing Service	Cleansing contract for all government recreational sites in Kwai Tsing District	1
6	Property Management Service	Property Management Service contract for Mindset Place in Fanling	1
	Total number of social enterprises:		22

References

Aiken, M. (2010). Social enterprises: Challenges from the field. In D. Billis (ed.), *Hybrid Organizations and the Third Sector: Challenges for Practice, Theory and Policy* (pp. 153-174). New York. USA: Palgrave Macmillan.

Caplan, M. A. (2010). Social Investment and Mental Health: The Role of Social Enterprise. In J. Midgley & A. Conley (eds.), *Social Work and Social Development: Theories and Skills for Developmental Social Work* (pp. 71-86). New York. USA: Oxford University Press.

Conley, A. (2016). Social Work and Social Development from the Global Perspective. In Z. S. Huang & L. Z. Zheng (eds.), *Developmental Social Work Theory and Practice* (pp. 27-37). Taipei. Taiwan: Song Hui.

Conley A. (2017). Social Investment in early childhood in Australia. In J. Midgley, E. Dahl, & A. Conley (eds.), *Social Investment and Social Welfare International and Critical Perspectives* (pp. 33-51). Cheltenham. UK: Edward Elgar.

Defourny, J. & Kim, S. (2011). Emerging Models of Social Enterprise in Eastern Asia: A Cross-country Analysis. *Social Enterprise Journal, 7*(1), 86-111.

Midgley, J. (2010). The Theory and Practice of Development Social Work. In J. Midgley & A. Conley (eds.), *Social Work and Social Development: Theories and Skills for Developmental Social Work* (pp. 3-30). New York. USA: Oxford University Press.

Midgley, J. (2017). Social investment: concepts, uses and theoretical perspectives. In J. Migley, E. Dahl, & A.W. Conley (eds.), *Social Investment and Social Welfare International and Critical Perspectives* (pp. 13-32). Cheltenham. UK: Edward Elgar.

National Alliance on Mental Illness. (2014). Road to Recovery: Employment and Mental Illness. Retrieved from https://www.nami.org/About-NAMI/Publications-Reports/Public-Policy-Reports/RoadtoRecovery.pdf

WISE. (2009). Work Integration Social Enterprises as a Tool for Promoting Inclusion: A Wise Way of Working Work Integration Social Enterprises and their Roles in European Policies National Cross Cutting Reports. Retrieved from http://www.isede-net.com/sites/default/files/social_economy/WISE%20report.pdf

Wong, G., Ip, S., & Chan, P. (2009). *New Life: Scaling Up Social Enterprise Start-ups.* Asia Case Research Centre Ref. No. 809-045-1. The University of Hong Kong.

World Health Organization. (2013). Promotion of Mental Health: Pursuit of Happiness. Retrieved from https://apps.searo.who.int/pds_docs/B5012.pdf

World Health Organization. (2013). Mental Health Action Plan 2013-2020. Retrieved from https://www.who.int/mental_health/publications/action_plan/en/

Q&A

Q : Has Fu Hong Society considered training service users to become service providers?

A : We have hired some service users who have undergone training, providing them with the same level of benefits and opportunities. Sometimes, those who have been trained by us become senior aides or store managers and have more opportunities to actively participate in providing services.

Part III:
Dialogue

Panel Discussion

Date: 29 November, 2019

Topic: Competency Cultivation and Building—Knowledge, Skills, Tools and Resources for Interdisciplinary Collaboration

Moderator: Julian Chow/School of Social Welfare, UC Berkeley

Panelists: Manohar Pawar/International Consortium for Social Development; Charles Sturt University, Australia

Marie Lisa M. Dacanay/Institute for Social Entrepreneurship in Asia

Jer-San Hu/Taiwan Social Enterprise Innovation and Entrepreneurship Society

Ping-Der Huang/Eden Social Welfare Foundation

Pei-Shan Yang/Department of Social Work, National Taiwan University

Sheng-Tsun Hou/ Graduate Institute of Public Affairs and Social Innovation, Feng Chia University

Over the past day and a half, we have discussed many issues. Moreover, during this conference, we have discovered that developmental social work emphasizes interdisciplinary and technological collaborations. We have invited six experts and scholars from different fields and backgrounds to provide their thoughts on social enterprise and social innovation. It is hoped that this panel discussion achieves the objectives of exchange and dialogue.

Q1: Based on your professional and educational backgrounds, what do you feel is currently the largest challenge to social innovation?

A1_Manohar Pawar:

First, I received my social work training at the Tata Institute of Social Sciences, one of the best social science schools in Bombay, India. As part of the curriculum, a question that was often asked was: The professors in this school were mostly educated in the USA. Therefore, the concepts that students learn in this school are those of the USA. Are these concepts suited to India?

Since 1950, professional educators at the United Nations have jointly proposed social development-related theories and formed the International Consortium for Social Development (ICSD). In 1970, the first school of social development was established. Some 50 years later, there are over 2,000 schools of social work listed in the ISW directory. From this, we can see that although the concepts of developmental social work have been around for years, they are only discussed in lectures or research. I believe that, in the future, developmental social work concepts need to make use of social innovation methods, so that they can be transformed into "training" and "practical action" and be applied to local societies.

A2_Marie Lisa M. Dacanay:

As a researcher and social entrepreneurship educator, I believe that the largest challenge to social innovation is in determining a "direction" for social innovation. When we talk about social innovation, we need to first ask ourselves what we are doing. Only in this way can we fulfill set goals. For example, when we serve persons with disabilities, social inclusion is our goal or endpoint. If we only use social enterprise or social innovation to create transformation and enable persons with disabilities to be brought into mainstream society, we do not change mainstream society's thinking about, or meet the needs of, persons with disabilities. In this case, the term social innovation is just empty words.

I believe that social innovation must result in social "reform" or "transformation". It is not just about social inclusion for persons with disabilities. Rather, there must be changes in the thinking of mainstream society, social measures, and lifestyles to enable sustainable development of social innovation.

A3_ Jer-San Hu:

I agree wholeheartedly with what Dr. Dacanay has said. I believe that social innovation is an independently-single activity. Everyone may have a different idea about a social issue, but we must consider creative action as we attempt to resolve a social issue. Moreover, from the viewpoint of enterprise, social entrepreneurship is first based on survival. In light of this, there must be some social enterprise skills, such as business administration (MBA) and science in education (MSE). These also become part of the creative action loop.

Returning to the question, I believe that in Taiwan there are three relatively large challenges to social innovation. The first is that social innovation has become popular, thus leading to the involvement of many young people who may not be experienced or possess sufficient social resources. This may in turn lead to immature action. The second challenge is that funding from private sources is often "competition-based". In addition, it may be that promotional subsidy activities are used to invest in a newly-created team. Although this provides a certain level of support, the public easily loses focus. Finally, as government leaders believe that social enterprises can care for neglected or overlooked vulnerable groups, they have become very involved. This has led to unfair competition for resources. I believe that the government should keep a proper distance from social enterprise activities, with its role limited to creating policies for allocating resources to social enterprises.

A4_ Ping-Der Huang:

In terms of social innovation, the largest challenge that I have observed to date is "inadequate scope and scale of involvement". First, due to inadequate scope and scale of involvement, there are insufficient resources, thus making it impossible to effectively resolve issues of concern. Second, this creates "one-person shows" in social entrepreneurship circles, rather than opportunities for collaboration. This in turn means that social innovation is a temporary movement. It becomes just a fad.

A5_ Pei-Shan Yang:

I believe that social innovation is currently facing two challenges. The first is that the social work and business worlds have not found a common language, which makes it difficult to work together. For example, there are many restrictive government regulations. National university professors cannot be chief operating officers or the heads of private companies. This makes it difficult for social innovation derived from social work education to be turned into social "enterprises". I believe that if social work is to actively embrace social enterprises and social innovation, the process must start with the transformation of ourselves.

The second challenge is that, in education, the level of practical training provided is inadequate. When graduates of social work programs enter the social work field, they must cross a very large gap. In Taiwan, social work internships tend to emphasize direct services, and assignments are mostly related to psycho-social topics. However, social innovation should be about person-centered social work, including aspects of daily life experiences such as economics, culture, and society, so that persons are able to rapidly enter community work, mobilize community resources, make connections, and develop sustainably. From a global viewpoint, social development should be brought into social work training.

A6_ Sheng-Tsun Hou:

I believe that the main challenge to social innovation is "collaboration".

First, the world is undergoing a major transformation. Old models are collapsing, while new models have not yet been established. Thus, we are now in the turbulent process of shifting models. Collaboration becomes a ticking time bomb of possible loss and self-interest.

Next, observations of the process of extending innovation reveal that there are early innovators and early adopters who have been willing to attempt to implement innovations. This then spreads from people in the earlier stages to others in the later stages. Finally, those unwilling to attempt innovative methods are perceived as falling behind. Viewing this in terms of the current situation, we are still in the very early innovator phase. Moreover, the issue of who will become earlier adopters depends on collaboration among government, large enterprises, small and medium enterprises, and micro enterprises. Currently, government systems are too rigid, which is leading to large enterprises holding onto resources with no intention of investing in innovation. Niche social innovators are unable to change the structural aspects, resulting in barriers to social innovation progress. I believe that governments can reduce the rigidity of systems to enable large enterprises that possess resources to be willing to guide the youth in implementing social innovation practices. Through collaboration, we can achieve co-creation among the young and the old.

Overall, I feel that collaboration is most difficult. After all, most people and organizations talk about benefits from their own point of view. Therefore, the issue which should be considered is how to cross fields and carry out thinking from different points of view so as to implement collaboration and see oneself as a little bit smaller and society as a little bit larger.

Q2: Based on your knowledge or expertise, what tools or techniques can be used to resolve the above-mentioned challenges?

A1_ Sheng-Tsun Hou:

Just as I mentioned, currently the biggest challenge to social innovation is, in the process of shifting models, insufficient dynamic energy among new start-ups. As the founder of Donkeymove and a scholar, I feel that, in this aspect, the resources the government can provide are very limited. To achieve the goals set by the government, we must connect the strengths of relevant organizations and seek strong alliances to put social innovation into practice. Then, we can create collaborations among large non-profit organizations, government, and central government agencies. However, to a certain extent, we return to depending on ourselves. In the end, we can indeed only rely on ourselves. Through continuous attempts and moving forward, we walk a broad path. It does not matter if other people see this, as long as God sees it.

A2_Pei-Shan Yang:

Internationally, we can observe social work from a broader perspective. However, in Taiwan, there is a limited perspective. So, in 1997, after finishing my graduate studies in the USA and working for eight years, I came back to Taiwan. I hope that I can broaden the view of social work in Taiwan.

When we talk about social innovation and social transformation, I feel that maintaining partnerships with intermediary roles is very important. Therefore, I recommend that, in terms of education, schools provide a broader curriculum. For example, in the Department of Social Work at National Taiwan University I started a community resource management course to make use of systematic theoretical concepts in the practice of social work, with the hope that social work can contribute to society.

A3_ Ping-Der Huang:

I believe that, in Taiwan, there is no shortage of creative thinking. However, there is a major deficiency in methods for transforming creativity into specific actions. To resolve this issue, it is necessary to expand the "scale and scope" of social enterprises in terms of funding, human resources, organization, skills, professional knowledge, and self-determination.

To achieve the above-mentioned scale and scope, relying solely on non-profit organizations is not sufficient, as current policies have not endowed these organizations with the conditions they need to succeed. Under this situation, collaboration between non-profit organizations and enterprises is one method of resolution. Although Taiwan has not yet developed legislation focused on social enterprises, the government has started to place importance on social enterprise responsibility. This has led to the availability of more resources for enterprises with social innovation, resulting in much greater influence. If we can build independent consciousness and civic consciousness based on self-reflection, we can change this society. I believe that non-profit organizations, through collaborations with enterprises, and even connections with international capital markets, can step onto the international stage, enabling the expansion of the scale and scope of social innovation and social enterprises and driving their development.

A4_ Jer-San Hu:

Continuing on from my previous point, I feel that social innovation and entrepreneurship are flourishing in Taiwan. However, there are three hidden concerns.

The first is that people with professional skills are scattered among various organizations, meaning that the strength of each organization is limited. The society that I founded hopes to resolve this issue by providing education and training. Our society transforms the experiences and stories of different organizations into textbooks so that there is sharing of knowledge among organizations. At the same time, there is learning and growth.

Next, social enterprises often run into roadblocks when trying to obtain resources, especially when government resources are insufficient. To solve this problem, our society turns to "enterprises", especially overseas enterprises. For example, SGS provided US$50,000 as a start-up fund to develop social innovation programs.

Finally, when we talk about social innovation and social enterprises, much of the focus is on "agriculture". I feel that there are already many social enterprises and organizations that have been working in the agricultural field for a long time. If a new organization wishes to develop a social enterprise, there is no harm in doing so in the agricultural field. By connecting talent and resources and designing appropriate organizational channels, action can be taken to create breakthroughs in agriculture.

A5_Marie Lisa M. Dacanay:

As I mentioned, the major challenge to social innovation lies in innovative directions and vision. I believe that there are three methods of resolution. First, we must cultivate young people to serve as leaders who can stimulate and drive transformation of organizations. Second, social enterprises need to build knowledge systems that focus on professional knowledge related to society, the economy, and management to arrange training programs to cultivate management and leadership competencies. Third, organizations need to carry out experience sharing, to learn from one another and to promote growth.

A6_Manohar Pawar:

I heartily agree with what the other panelists have said, especially in terms of social worker training. Therefore, I believe that the role of instructor or expert is very important. I have discovered that textbooks and regulations are often disconnected from real society. As an educator, I need to reduce the degree of disconnectedness in theory and practice. The knowledge learned from books should reflect reality to prevent gaps between the academic world and the professional world.

In addition, I feel that a social worker must leave behind old concepts and gain new knowledge across disciplines. Through professional collaboration across disciplines and the integration of microscopic and macroscopic views, the challenges and difficulties faced by society can be resolved.

Furthermore, social work must continue to break through old concepts and to apply innovative and creative perspectives to handle difficulties related to individual cases. Especially for repetitive problems, we need to search for innovative methods that focus on the root cause.

Q3: Based on your expertise, if you could choose one thing to do to promote social innovation, what would that be?

A1_Manohar Pawar:

If I could only do one thing to promote social innovation I would follow the concept of Mahatma Gandhi, the father of India, which is to start from yourself, and to continuously work hard to improve yourself. To be able to change yourself, it is necessary to elevate your sense of identity with social work and social innovation. I tell my new students every semester that social work is like a bar of soap. When you shower with it, the more you use, the cleaner you become. This is a slowly-evolving action. So, for change to happen, the most important step is to elevate your sense of identity. Then, you can influence the sense of identity of others. In addition, you need to consider if there is any deviation in your ideals, attitudes, and perspectives. Over a period of self-reflection, you elevate your consciousness and then influence society and the public to promote social consensus.

A2_ Marie Lisa M. Dacanay:

As social enterprises in Asia are regional organizations, I think there is one thing that we can do for social innovation, specifically building a platform for exchanges among social enterprises to enable them to learn from one another and grow.

A3_ Jer-San Hu:

One aspect on which I have been continuously working is the organization of "social innovation/creativity workshops". As current classroom education and theories are insufficient for managing complexities and resource deficiencies in entrepreneurial activities, it is necessary to bring students to places where social work is practiced to observe the real issues faced by people living in a community and to understand the lack of resources. This will in turn enable students to think up creative ideas and to guide community groups in developing business models, which will thus mean that case-centered social innovation can survive over the long term.

A4_ Ping-Der Huang:

The United Nations has drawn up a set of sustainable development goals (SDGs). It is hoped that enterprises fulfilling their corporate social responsibilities will develop sustainable developmental goals for themselves. I also feel that non-profit organizations need to search for enterprises with similar missions to theirs and collaborate on supply chains to access needed funding, scale, skills, and markets to strengthen themselves.

A5_ Pei-Shan Yang:

As societies in Asia are rapidly aging, if we continue to apply past policies or strategies, we will be unable to respond to the aging crisis. Therefore, what I want to do most is to ask everyone to set a goal together every year to do something they are not doing now. Assuming that resources and competencies are sufficient, we can attempt to formulate more objectives and together become the start of social development and social innovation.

A6_ Sheng-Tsun Hou:

I believe that although resources and social capacity are limited, Taiwan has an opportunity to change society through social enterprises. I have long had a dream which can only come true if everyone works together. Taiwan currently has 134 remote townships. To provide outstanding services to the elderly and vulnerable groups in those 134 remote townships, I hope that we can find 134 enterprises. Each enterprise can raise one million. At an annual interest rate of 3%, the principal can be returned in 5 years. In this way, every rural township and area can have Donkeymove vehicles. Indeed, this is my biggest goal.

I have long felt that it is not that Taiwan does not have the opportunity to achieve the above; it is only that current resources and capacities are insufficient. Just as Ping-Der Huang mentioned, since the government is unwilling to provide such services, as is Uber, focus must be placed on the Eden Social Welfare Foundation, which possesses Taiwan's largest Rehabus fleet and would thus have the ability to achieve such a vision.

Q4: It seems that social work professionals and management professionals use different terminologies. The former tend to make use of traditional social work terms, such as "competency cultivation", "accompaniment", "growth", "needs", "grassroots", "participation", "resources", "mutually beneficial", and "co-creation". The latter emphasizes "management", "industry", "technology", "innovation", "business models", "investment", and "platforms". What are some ways to cross academic disciplines and fields to transform the terminology and build a bridge between social work and business?

A1_Manohar Pawar:

I believe that social problems are integrative. Therefore, it is necessary to break through the boundaries of academic disciplines and fields and to avoid taking blind action or everyone acting on their own. I feel that experts from different academic disciplines and fields should be brought together from time to time to carry out discussions. This will enable the flow of different thoughts and viewpoints. Moreover, dialogue can be implemented to build all-new concepts and resolve current social issues. This is a marginal effect, similar to when two rivers converge and flow into the sea. Fishermen gather there for the opportunity to obtain large catches of fish. This place of convergence is the marginal effect. So, when various professionals gather, such as businesspeople, social entrepreneurs, economists, political scientists, sociologists, and social workers, and jointly think about how to respond to social issues, good methods and channels for resolution will be created.

Furthermore, to achieve sustainable development of social enterprises, in addition to involving experts in social work, we need to enable the participation of vulnerable groups or communities to implement co-creation and participatory development. This is person-centered development or, as the World Bank calls it, community-led development. Through collaborations between experts and community members, which is one of the avenues for co-creation, we can face and deal with community issues and provide suitable solutions.

A2_ Marie Lisa M. Dacanay:

I believe that social enterprises need a dominant leader with business administration and social development competencies who can gather together talent from across disciplines and fields and understand the importance of collaboration. In addition, such a person can construct bridges of communication, smoothly make use of talents, and achieve success. Therefore, in terms of education, leadership courses should be designed to develop students' leadership abilities so that they can guide society and the business world.

A3_ Jer-San Hu:

Talking about education, in the past not much importance was placed on the interaction between social science and business programs. However, building a bridge between social work and business administration should be part of the university curriculum. As such, university education will certainly change, no matter in terms of learning tools or areas of learning. Therefore, I feel that it is necessary for social innovation experiences to be incorporated into educational programs. Through learning about social services and professions via practice, the gaps in conventional education can be filled. For example, I developed an "international social participation" graduate program. In this program, students actively participate in an area or organization for two years. During that time, they study problem-solving methods and techniques. They also bring innovation and entrepreneurship to an area. Students learn new knowledge and cultural creativity in a specific area.

A4_ Ping-Der Huang:

I think that if non-profit organizations want to be leaders in a field or area, they must possess the abilities to make judgements and decisions and to raise public awareness of important social issues. I will use a metaphor to explain this. A non-profit organization is like a pastry chef who decorates their pastries to attract consumers (i.e. focuses public attention on social issues). This pastry chef uses their experience to create good results (i.e. brings together resources).

A5_ Pei-Shan Yang:

In terms of my past collaborative experiences, I have often been the only person on the team with a social science background. There are many interdisciplinary challenges to be faced. From such experiences, I believe that social workers must invest in themselves. I also recommend that non-profit organizations invest in their staff members to elevate their own and staff competencies. In this way, such organizations can have the ability to participate in interdisciplinary matters. It is hoped that one day Taiwan can organize an international workshop in the World Trade Building to enable social workers to share their experiences and to present their achievements of investing in themselves.

A6_ Sheng-Tsun Hou:

Based on my own experience, I believe that interdisciplinary collaboration involves the "power of one". This means that something is done to its best and deepest, with the highest possible proficiency. For 17 years I first researched taxis, and then came across Uber, which I also studied. My research area has now evolved into long-term care, and so I study long-term care. Only by defining a field and continuing to move deeper within that field can we broaden and deepen our thinking.

Just as Ping-Der Huang stated, in this world there must be the crossing of disciplines. But who does the crossing? Perhaps you become the core and other individuals or organizations take the initiative to link up with you. Alternatively, it may be that someone else becomes the core and you attempt to link up with that person. No matter which, if everyone does their work well, they provide something that others have not imagined. Once these steps integrated, the world becomes better.

For example, we have encouraged the instructors at Feng Chia University's B Academy to become three-in-one, meaning they carry out service, teaching, and research. First, service is proposed to resolve a social issue and that service field is included in the curriculum design. This enables students to deepen their learning in said field, producing research results related to it. When knowledge production is systematized and connections with social resources are formed, cross-disciplinary collaborations become effective.

Q5: Finally, please provide a metaphor for social innovation and then describe or explain it in one sentence.

A1_ Sheng-Tsun Hou:

I feel that social innovation can be compared to a donkey. It must be able to carry a heavy burden and to move at a steady pace. It cannot be hurried or show off as it slowly completes its mission. In other words, one person can walk quickly, but a group of people can walk for a long time.

A2_ Pei-Shan Yang:

I feel that social innovation is like a blade of grass. It is fragile, but also tender and green. When blades of grass cluster together, they create a wonderful scene.

A3_ Ping-Der Huang:

I believe that social innovation is a dessert. It is delicious but never enough.

A4_Jer-San Hu:

I will respond with a short poem: "The snow of winter has ended, and the budding and blooming of spring has begun. On the wounded earth, flowers, plants and forests appear. Take care of it. Defend it. Anticipate it. Then, it will be better able to report the joys of life".

A5_ Marie Lisa M. Dacanay:

I believe that social innovation is hope. Although this world is filled with all sorts of problems, if there is social innovation, there is hope.

A6_ Manohar Pawar:

I believe that social innovation is a better, happier, higher quality, and more blissful life.

A7_Julian Chow:

For me, social innovation means "transformation". I hope that everyone who is involved in social work will make use of unlimited imagination and transform all that they see and hear into concern for vulnerable groups. In this way, we can strive for a better life and environment.